STARDUST

STARDUST

Cinematic Archives at the End of the World

HANNAH GOODWIN

 University of Minnesota Press
Minneapolis
London

The University of Minnesota Press gratefully acknowledges the financial assistance provided for the publication of this book by Mount Holyoke College.

Portions of chapter 1 were previously published in "From Diagrams to Deities: Evoking the Cosmological Sublime," in *Contemporary Visual Culture and the Sublime*, ed. Temenuga Trifonova, 153–66 (New York: Routledge, 2017); reprinted by permission of Taylor and Francis Group, LLC, a division of Informa plc. Portions of chapter 3 were previously published in "Atomic Tests: Experimental Filmmaking in the Nuclear Era," *Journal of Film and Video* 73, no. 2 (2021): 11–25; courtesy of the University of Illinois Press. Portions of the Epilogue were previously published in "Los archivos cósmicos del cine y Nostalgia de la luz," in *El cine documental histórico de Patricio Guzmán*, 109–24 (Brussels: Peter Lang Press, 2022); courtesy of Peter Lang Press.

Copyright 2024 by the Regents of the University of Minnesota

All rights reserved. No part of this publication may be reproduced, stored in a retrieval system, or transmitted, in any form or by any means, electronic, mechanical, photocopying, recording, or otherwise, without the prior written permission of the publisher.

Published by the University of Minnesota Press
111 Third Avenue South, Suite 290
Minneapolis, MN 55401-2520
http://www.upress.umn.edu

ISBN 978-1-5179-1649-7 (hc)
ISBN 978-1-5179-1650-3 (pb)

Library of Congress record available at https://lccn.loc.gov/2023048968

The University of Minnesota is an equal-opportunity educator and employer.

CONTENTS

Introduction: Filming a Precarious Universe   1

1 Lights All Askew: Relativity and New Astronomy on Film   29
2 New Constellations: Aerial Cinema in the Second World War   65
3 Destroyer of Worlds: Cinema of Atomic Experimentation   93

Epilogue: Witnessing after the End   123

Acknowledgments   143
Notes   147
Index   175

INTRODUCTION

Filming a Precarious Universe

WHAT ARCHIVES OF HUMANITY will exist after the end of the world? The question is a cosmic one, for when we are gone, the universe is what remains to hold our traces. But it is also cinematic: when we envision a meaningful archive of human life beyond its material artifacts, it is cast in light and set in motion. This is evident at the level of an individual life, as home movies summon the presences of loved ones who have passed and actors of bygone eras seem to live again as we rewatch their filmography. The idea that the cinema might similarly promise a form of immortality for our species has long permeated film theory and filmmaking, and it hinges on cinema's intrinsic connections to the cosmos more largely. This chapter begins by tracing those connections before returning to the central question of how cosmic and cinematic archives are imagined as preserving some aspect of human existence in the face of catastrophe.

Cinema as a Cosmic Medium

That cinema can be framed as a cosmic medium is at once taken for granted and, like anything so naturalized, not obvious. Perhaps without realizing it, audiences around the globe and across the history of cinema have accepted the linkage between the cosmos and the cinema, which is reinforced over and over at the opening of so many films. When we enter a theater and the lights dim, plunging us into an artificial night, often some of the first images we see are cosmic. A spinning globe, its halo of city lights beaming outward toward the twinkling stars that surround it (see Figure 1). A star shooting across the sky, arcing over a fairytale castle. A radio tower, its outsize dimensions dwarfing the planet beneath it and piercing through the clouds to send its signal through the enveloping darkness. A boy, cradled by a crescent moon, fishing for a star. Searchlights connecting the dots between the electric lights of a city and the starry sky above. A trail of stars streaming down from the sky to circle around a snow-crested mountain. These are the images—representing Universal, Disney, RKO, DreamWorks, 20th Century Fox, and Paramount—that so frequently mark the beginning of a Hollywood feature film, signaling our transition to another realm. The moment one of these cosmic logos appears on the screen, the cinematic journey begins.[1] And this phenomenon is by no means limited to current Hollywood cinema. From Gaumont's rotating globe surrounded by a halo of rays, which marked its films from 1953–1970, to Indian producer Ramu Films' searchlight-studded remix of the 20th Century Fox sequence in the early 2000s, to the current Shanghai Studios logo with its glowing globe and whirling galaxies, cosmic images invite audiences into the cinema. There is something genuinely universal in the familiar iconography of Universal. In the context of these logos, the resonance between the cosmos and the cinema gives expression to a desire to harness the wonders and anxieties of the cosmos on behalf of a commercial enterprise. But as this book will explore, we can also trace correspondences between the histories and iconographies of cinema and those of the cosmos through films that lie outside of mainstream cinema. The mysteries of the universe and entanglements of cinematic and cosmic space and time are the province of diverse forms of filmmaking.

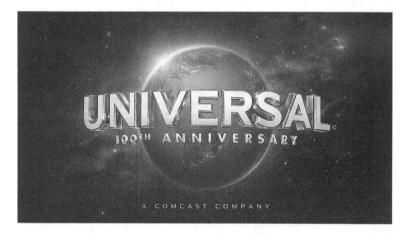

Figure 1. Universal Studios logo, 2012. Screen capture courtesy of Logopedia. CC-BY-SA.

Strong affinities between the cosmos and the cinema explain the consistency with which the cosmos has been a cinematic subject in commercial and independent filmmaking alike. To begin with, the stark contrast of light and darkness that we see when we look up at night is also a fundamental aspect of the cinema's ontology; the projector light pierces the dark surroundings of the theater much as a star punctuates the night sky, and the interplay of light and dark that cosmic representations demand is essential to film images. Moreover, the stars and the cinema share a place in our imagination, promising experiences beyond the everyday, allowing us to escape our ordinary lives, inviting dreams of other worlds and times, and reflecting on our own place in the universe from a perspective that moves beyond our planet and beyond the timeline of human existence. Scott Curtis argues that cinema and science share "philosophical affinities" based on their engagement with temporal manipulations and their ability to turn an objective gaze on natural phenomena.[2] This is especially evident in the case of astronomy and astrophysics. In astronomy, the lenses of a telescope allow for a deeper glimpse into the universe and the revelation of light that emanates from events further back in time, preserved across space due to the limitations of the speed of light. In the cinema, the lens of a camera captures and indexes the movement of light at one particular moment, and the lens of a projector casts light through a filmstrip, revealing a preserved version of the past. Cosmic cinema invites us to take a position of remote witness to moments saved from oblivion by the presence of a camera. When cinema draws on cosmic images, it foregrounds its own ability to carry viewers on a voyage through space and time. Universal's logo, for instance, takes an extraterrestrial perspective that frames whatever visions follow as cinematic emanations for our otherworldly eyes—a perspective that can lend itself equally to a sense of unmooring and a sense of omnipotent viewing.

The cover of a 1923 issue of *American Cinematographer* suggests the allure of this cosmic positionality for filmmakers. Adopting a gaze akin to that of Universal's implied camera, it depicts a cameraman standing on a cloud, his camera pointed back at the earth, which is surrounded by a spattering of stars and a cosmic haze (see Figure 2). "Give us a place to stand and we will film the universe," the caption reads. The idea of "filming the universe" draws on the possibilities of cinematic exploration; filmmakers, given the proper tools and the creative space to do their jobs, are able to access other worlds and give us new perspectives on the world in which we live. Of course, the vision afforded the cameraman in this image, at a distance from the earth that allows him to see the planet in its entirety, was not yet physically possible at the time of its drawing. That impossibility, too, has been a consistent part of the appeal of cosmic subject matter to filmmakers. Cinematic visions of the cosmos—of the dim light of stars, the slow revolutions of planetary motion, the faraway galaxies whose shapes cannot be seen without extreme magnification, and the totality of the planet to whose surface we were until recently bound—are stubbornly resistant to straightforward filming. The cosmos demands visualization and artistic representation, and cinema has had a special place in the ongoing process of providing this representation. Cosmic visions in the cinema are emblems of the latest technological innovations and creative renderings that permit celestial encounters with varying degrees of realism.

The cosmic, in this book, is more than just the astral. I use the words *cosmos, cosmology,* and *cosmic* to describe a consistent impulse in filmmaking and film theory. While astronomy is concerned with charting and explaining celestial motions, cosmology is more philosophically expansive, theoretically rich, and culturally embedded. Since Isaac Newton's time, cosmology has been considered "the science or theory of the universe as an ordered whole," but it is also defined as "that branch of metaphysics which deals with the idea of the world as a totality of all phenomena in space and time," or even simply, as Thomas Blount defined it in his 1656 *Glossographia,* "a speaking of the world."[3] Crucially, as geographer Denis Cosgrove discusses, cosmology is intimately connected with terrestrial geographies.[4] Scientific cosmology involves taking into account large scales of both space and time in order to understand the origins and future trajectory of the universe.[5] Thus, representations of the cosmic often carry us far into the future (or past) and expose us to worlds both unfathomably large and unfathomably small. Zachary Horton writes of the power of such scalar alterity, the human drive to "assimilat[e] and coloniz[e]" scalar differences, and how various media address these tensions.[6] Some representations seek to bring order to these worlds at various scales, creating a sense of totality and cohesion. But this is not always the case; reckoning with scales of space and time that defy comprehension can also lead to art—and cinema in particular—that expresses the disturbance and alienation of encountering such alterity.

Film theorists of the early twentieth century wrote with enthusiasm about the cosmic attributes of cinema. In his 1923 essay "The Art of Cineplastics," Élie Faure writes that the ability of cinema to communicate

Figure 2. Cover of *American Cinematographer* promising to "film the universe," January 1923. Courtesy of Media History Digital Library.

both vastness and variation of scale without any sense of discord may allow us to access the "profound universe of the . . . telescopic infinite, the undreamed-of dance of atoms and stars, the shadows under the sea as they begin to be shot with light."[7] He goes on to envision "the majestic unity of masses in movement that all this accentuates without insistence" that the medium is uniquely able to represent. Film is poised to capture the interplay of shadows and light and trace movements both grand and minute. In moving between these scales—including, importantly, the human one—moving pictures can express "divine intoxication," "the spiritual life of the world," and the joy of feeling "eternity imposed by ourselves upon nothingness."[8] Jean Epstein, in 1921, similarly imagines film's ability to represent and unite an array of scales from the microscopic to the cosmic, potentially displaying the "majesty of the planets" alongside "anemones full of rhythm and personality."[9] The famed French science-fiction writer Camille Flammarion was equally excited about the potentials of cinema to channel the cosmos, writing, "With the cinematograph, in contrast [to mere lantern slides], the earthly globe can be photographed turning on its own, seemingly isolated in the depths of the dark, starry sky, tilted on its axis, and seen from every angle, from the equator to the pole. Now, we can have before our eyes an image of the Earth just as we might see it from the moon, for example, and watch our planet turning slowly and majestically on its own, its movement calm and steady."[10] One can sense that this excitement lies in the cinematic mechanism's technical ability to animate and thus bring to life the movement of cosmic bodies, as well as in the sensations afforded by the mechanism's otherworldly gaze—there is something splendid in this alienated perspective.

In addition to philosophical and aesthetic affinities, film and other moving-image technologies also share historical convergences with astronomy and astrophysics. In the late nineteenth and early twentieth centuries, as the visual practices of film and photography were rapidly developing, astronomy was also undergoing dramatic changes that brought it increasingly into popular discourse. In Europe and the United States, observatories opened their doors to the public, amateur astronomy clubs blossomed, and popular accounts of astronomical discoveries piqued the interest of broad publics.[11] Edwin Hubble's 1924 discovery of the boggling expanse of the universe received abundant and enraptured press coverage. Albert Einstein, whose theories of relativity stumped even some of the most seasoned scientific minds, wrote a more accessible account of these theories for a general audience, and in 1921 set out on a lecture circuit that reached enormous, enthusiastic audiences of scientists and laypeople alike in the United States, Europe, Palestine, Ceylon, Singapore, and Japan.[12] As astronomy gained traction in popular culture across the globe, photography and film became tools in scientific practice, as well as means of disseminating discoveries and parsing complex scientific ideas for mass audiences. At its best, film could both expose natural phenomena to further the scientific endeavor and do away with the abstraction that made science seem inaccessible. As Siegfried Kracauer bemoans, "Most sciences do not deal with the objects of ordinary experience but abstract from them certain elements which they then process in various ways. Thus the objects are stripped of the qualities that give them 'all their poignancy and preciousness.'"[13] Film, Kracauer writes, has the ability to present nature in an unabstracted form that can restore these qualities.

Cameras were turned upward almost from the moment of their development, and they played a crucial role in changing practices of scientific observation, as well as the popularization of abstract theories.[14] The very origins of cinema as a photographic medium can be traced to the animation of photographs in astronomy. As early as the 1874 transit of Venus, during which French astronomer Pierre Janssen used a telescopic camera to photograph the planet moving across the sun at regular intervals, chronophotography traced and documented astronomical events and conveyed changing notions of the cosmos and its temporal and spatial structure to the public.[15] Science historian Jimena Canales outlines a few of the ways in which astrophysicists used film to test, visualize, and popularize their theories and observations, and the first chapter of this book foregrounds how film and photography—as a medium that must be considered alongside film, because it also was and is used to trace, measure, and reconstitute astronomic motion—shaped astrophysics and its popularized forms in the early twentieth century.[16] Film historians Oliver Gaycken and Curtis also write about the circulation of scientific ideas through film. Curtis looks at how moving-image technologies in the silent era were adapted into the "expert viewing" practices of scientific fields.[17] Gaycken considers the popularization of scientific footage in early cinema, positing that the lines between entertainment and science were thoroughly blurred in science movies.[18] As I hope to demonstrate, the fluidity of these boundaries has never been more apparent than in the context of astronomical images, which could tip as easily toward fantasy as toward disciplined, objective observation.

As vehicles of fiction, moreover, film and photography were able to access the imaginative horizons of outer space—places still beyond the reach of scientists, or places whose enchanting and terrifying mysteries science could not adequately explain. From the early years of cinema's history, filmmakers have represented cosmic subject matter in fantastical ways.[19] This is evidenced not least by the films of Georges Méliès, whose cosmic images in films such as *The Astronomer's Dream* (*La Lune à un mètre*, literally "The moon at one meter," France, 1898) and *A Trip to the Moon* (*Le voyage dans la lune*, France, 1902) have become an indelible part of the iconography of early silent cinema. The work of Émile Cohl, who combined animated forms with live-action filmmaking, also expresses a sustained interest in the cosmos and in the ways film can both draw on and enliven scientific visual practices. These films, including most notably *Spanish Clair de Lune* (*Clair de lune espagnole*, 1909), are experimental, working with the temporal and spatial dimensions of the medium. Even before astrophysical theories of relativity warped concepts of cosmic space and time, filmmakers like Méliès and Cohl were doing the same, with their lighthearted tricks that depart from continuity and cohesion and play with the laws that govern rational space and time. In *The Astronomer's Dream*, for example, cosmic characters from an ethereal realm enter the astronomer's laboratory and disappear suddenly into thin air; the astronomer draws measured charts of celestial globes, which then take on a life of their own; and objects flicker in and out of the set and turn into other objects. But the most spectacular trick is the abrupt entrance of the moon, which has until now been visible only through the window as a distant, static, luminous body, and which suddenly joins the astronomer in the observatory as he looks through the lens of the telescope. This moment humorously dramatizes the effect of looking through the telescope—a process that takes the observer on a visual journey through space, effectively compressing space to attain a closer look at an astronomical body. The scene continues to unfold incoherently: the astronomer strikes the moon with a broom, and just as suddenly as it entered the window, the moon lurches back into the sky in one jolt, not moving through space but hopping from one place to the next, eliding time. Méliès toys with expectations of cinematic movement, defying the rational idea that to go from one place to another requires movement through space and time. This universe does not operate according to such laws. His cinematic cosmos is a platform for fantasies of irrationality, including illogical relationships across temporal and spatial registers.

Drawing on the intersecting trajectories between technoscience and filmic representation both technical and fanciful, this book traces the development of cosmic imaginaries within film history and film theory from the late nineteenth century to the present. Film has not only documented, represented, and narrated shifting conceptions of astronomical space and time; at the level of the medium, it has also provided a model for their theories and principles. New astrophysics illustrated ideas about the movement of light through space and time by using analogies to film, and several film theorists conceived of film's relationship to the dimensions, and particularly to the malleability, of time by referring to astronomical models. While the examples of Méliès's and Cohl's filmmaking capture some of the stylistic playfulness around this relationship, representing cosmic dimensions has often entailed a confrontation with a sense of the unknown: of precariousness and even apocalyptic threat. In the remainder of this book, I focus on moments of enormous global upheaval, as Western imperialism reached its peak and began to crumble, and world wars reverberated across much of the globe. These upheavals changed perceptions of the world at a planetary scale, raised the possibility and eventually probability of apocalypse, and prompted the reformulation of persistent cosmological questions.

In the beginning of the period covered in this book, film figured in a historical shift in the cosmic imagination: from a romanticized period of preindustrialization, with what is retroactively imagined to be a more contemplative engagement of the cosmos, to a fast-paced, globalized modern era, in which the cosmos becomes entangled with the illumination of new technologies, from city lights to movies to bombs.[20] This shift is whimsically articulated in "Modern Astronomy," a short poem published in *Film Fun* in 1918, in which filmgoing is articulated as a new commercial substitute for old-fashioned pastimes like stargazing. "When wife and I were sweethearts / It really was amazing / How many blissful hours we spent / In innocent 'star-gazing.' / But now the modern couple / Such old time courting bars; / They hie them to the movies, / And there they gaze at 'stars'!"[21] While the poem's premise hinges on a humorous link between film stars and celestial ones, it also emphasizes the break between modernity, with its implied urbanity and superficiality, and a leisurely, nature-oriented temporality that is nostalgically attributed to the past. The fragmentation and refiguring of time and space that new theories brought to astronomy, and that the world wars intensified for a global imaginary, were also constantly being negotiated through film, itself a medium of new temporal and spatial registers.

As historian Stephen Kern traces, during the period of cinema's emergence at the turn of the twentieth century, "a series of sweeping changes in technology and culture created distinctive new modes of thinking about and experiencing time and space."[22] Many film historians and theorists —including Benjamin Singer, Tom Gunning, Mary Ann Doane, Philip Rosen, Leo Charney, Vanessa R. Schwartz, Miriam Bratu Hansen, Murray Pomerance, and Lynne Kirby—situate the emergence of cinema within a particular moment of "modernity" characterized in part by changing conceptions of time and space.[23] These scholars contextualize cinema's invention within an intensive period of modernization characterized by urbanization, industrialization, and globalization. This period witnessed the development of transportation infrastructures like railways, streetcars, airplanes, and communication networks like the telegraph and telephone, which connected rural and urban areas, as well as the territories of sprawling empires, to an unprecedented degree. The proliferation of the pocket watch, meanwhile, heightened individuals' awareness of time and forged a sense of simultaneity and order. Rosen notes that cinema contributed to a rethinking of time, because it was a time-based medium that also, on an industrial level, relied on "labor, production, and marketing schedules," as well as leisure time.[24] New scientific principles, including thermodynamics and evolution, as Doane argues, added to a sense that time was moving irrevocably forward.[25] Accompanying these shifts, as well as the development and intensification of global-scale conflicts, came new waves of apocalypticism, particularly in the United States, where Seventh-day Adventism and Mormonism began to spread in the nineteenth century.[26] Time may have been more regulated than ever, but it was stubbornly, threateningly unknowable—and perhaps its unflinching race forward made its end feel all the more inevitable.

Cinema and the Time of Apocalypse

Thinkers and critics in the early twentieth century wrote about cinema in the context of the changing experiences of time that resulted from new technologies and theories, in ways that suggest that those experiences were marked by disorientation and discontinuity despite the increased regulation of time. For example, French German poet and intellectual Yvan Goll wrote of cinema and modern temporalities in 1920:

> For years, a new speed has been making our world spin three times or even ten times faster on its axis. The planet has received a shock. We have entered

a new age: an age of motion. All of this has occurred thanks to technology. For its sake, the countenance of the entire globe has changed. . . . The calculation of time, the calendar, the twelve-hour clock have all been turned upside down. Night chases day with ever increasing speed; the hour becomes a day, the minutes too. Everywhere, we see motion, only motion. . . . Static laws have crumbled. Space and time have been caught by surprise.[27]

In answer to this accelerated temporality, Goll wrote, "We now have film." He went on to remark that only film could adequately capture the pace of human experience in the modern world: "Cinema will be the basis of all new art. No one can create art any longer without this new movement, for we are all spinning at a different speed than before." Berlin-based film critic Erich Burger, writing in 1929, expressed a similar sense that time was accelerating at a planetary scale, noting that "suddenly, the world turns more quickly; each second becomes more precious." For Burger, not only did cinema participate in the acceleration of time, it also provoked it. "In the end, the picture's hellish tempo is the reason why we convince ourselves that we must always hurry and can no longer walk slowly," he lamented.[28] Cinema seemed to reflect the whir of modern time even as it provided a metaphor for understanding the imaginative tug of cosmic transport through inconceivable scales of time.

There is something dark in the evocation of this "hellish tempo." For if time since the era of early cinema has been marching at an irreversibly accelerating pace, it seems to be marching toward some precipice, some radical end to all that is known. And just as cinema has, according to these film theorists, matched and evoked such modern temporalities, it has boldly taken on apocalyptic ones. Cinema's obsession with the cosmos is accompanied by an obsession with what happens when the world ends and in probing the question of the ongoing meaning of human life and archives in the context of such obliteration. Film, because it derives so much of its power from its twinned investment in the past and the future—its status as a medium that preserves the past *for* the future, and thus depends on that future to carry on its meaning—is, like astronomy, poised to explore questions of deep pasts and futures in cosmic contexts, including confrontations with the primordial and the postapocalyptic. Vladimir Nabokov's *Speak, Memory* famously begins by recounting the anxiety of confronting the time before one was born, which in its very existence without oneself threatens with the inevitability of a future time in which one will also not exist. Nabokov writes, "The cradle rocks above an abyss, and common sense tells us that our existence is but a brief crack of light between two eternities of darkness."[29] He goes on to recount the story of a "young chronophobiac" whose panic about the future is ignited as he watches home movies of the time shortly before he was born: "What particularly frightened him was the sight of a brand-new baby carriage standing there on the porch, with the smug, encroaching air of a coffin; even that was empty, as if, in the reverse course of events, his very bones had disintegrated." It is not a coincidence that a movie is what brings about this sense of impending doom. In presenting us with a past that predates us, cinema warns of a future in which we are gone. Astronomy, as it probes the prehuman, pre-Earth origins of the universe, also suggests the symmetrical finitude of human and earthly futures. A universe without human beings existed, and so it will exist again, the night sky tells us. And the "brief crack of light" that is cinema, in its continuous fascination with cosmic images and themes, plays with these anxieties and explores its own role in revealing, documenting, and preserving our lives for temporalities beyond the ordinary.

Cinema thus serves as a "revelation"—a word used interchangeably with *apocalypse* in biblical study. Importantly, the temporality of apocalypse is one of both ending and opening up to something new and is not devoid of hope.[30] *Apocalypse* as it is commonly used is associated with cataclysmic destruction, the extinction of humanity, and the end of the world. Yet the Greek word itself means "disclosure" or "vision" and is associated in the Judeo-Christian tradition with the possibility of salvation or transformation.[31] When I discuss film as apocalyptic, I am interested in these multiple valences—how cinema addresses the end of time, but also how, through such visions, it introduces possibilities for transformation of both the future and renderings of the past. In his book *Apocalypse-Cinema*, Peter Szendy writes of cinema as predisposed to the apocalyptic. The end of a film, he writes, is necessarily apocalyptic, ending the world the film has created.[32] A cinematic perspective, moreover, with its inhuman ability to move outside of any human point of view, alludes to a perspective that keeps seeing even if no human being can.[33] No matter what happens within the film, the camera remains, "after the end of the world." This apocalyptic positionality is also a cosmic one: returning to the cover of *American Cinematographer*, we see a manifestation of what I term a *cosmocinematic gaze* from the outside. This cosmocinematic gaze is the reciprocal side of a highly embodied form of looking up and viewing the heavens from the earth. It encompasses the promise (or threat) of a revelatory celestial view from above that may be imagined as disembodied but that takes various embodied forms across the films and photographic media I discuss. The cosmocinematic gaze is at the heart of cinema's potential to expose the universe, in all its sublimity and dynamism and terror, and to turn a lens back on our world, too, capturing, animating, resurrecting, and at times annihilating its sublime and spectral presences.

In the image from *American Cinematographer*, such a gaze is situated in the White, male body we are accustomed to associating with the classic liberal humanist subject, who is imbued with the reassuring power of human subjectivity. But this cinematographer's gaze, which we as viewers are invited to adopt, too, also makes clear that the globe is delimited. The text on the cover expresses a sense of the infinite possibility of "film[ing] the universe," yet the image, like any that takes a planetary perspective on the earth, can also be read as unsettling. The globe's reflective sheen—one can see the squares of an invisible windowpane reflecting off it—makes it look like a shiny toy, a marble that could roll away. The apprehension of the planet as a whole is accompanied by a recognition of its precariousness.[34] The cosmocinematic gaze, while linked to the potentials of cinematic world-building, is apocalyptic in that it suggests cinema's ability to display the earth from such a distance that its use and meaning to human beings are transcended by its status as a planet that has existed and will exist without us.[35] Jennifer Fay, in *Inhospitable World*, demonstrates how this capacity of cinema links it to climate change in the Anthropocene, with both phenomena lending a sense of "disorientation" that makes "the familiar world strange"—unhoming us from our ordinary experience of the world.[36] This sensation invites us to take on an apocalyptic viewpoint that imagines the disappearance of humanity altogether. With such a gaze, we confront the ends of the earth, and in doing so we recognize another kind of end, a temporal one and not just a spatial one. The increasing association between an aerial gaze and a military one, which I explore in chapter 2, has only strengthened the link between apprehending the planet at a distance and the perception of a world-ending threat.

Indeed, cosmic and apocalyptic thinking are profoundly connected. When apocalypse looms, we look to the heavens. To apprehend the cosmos is to confront both a sense of infinitude and an apocalyptic recognition of the precariousness and transience of earthly existence. As Fay points out, the very word *disaster* speaks of this profound connection between the stars and apocalyptic endings; from the Italian *dis astro*, disaster is what happens when the stars descend.[37] Saint John's apocalyptic Book of

Revelation is full of such disasters: at the opening of the sixth seal, for example, there is a "great earthquake; and the sun became black as sackcloth of hair, and the whole moon became as blood; and the stars of the heaven fell unto the earth."[38] When things are truly falling apart, the universe lets loose its signals. Thus the cosmos is both a respite and a threat: our planet has always been unstable and vulnerable in the vast sea of unknown time and space, but there is a certain solace in this knowledge that the end has always been inevitable and part of something greater. The persistence of apocalyptic and cosmic themes in science-fiction cinema evinces this connection. Sean Redmond and Leon Marvell, in their volume *Endangering Science Fiction Film*, write of science fiction as a genre of doomsday scenarios and looming apocalypse. Outer space, in such films, is an "Othering environment" that threatens "the established order of things."[39] Marvell writes of how the universe's extent in science fiction creates both awe and terror, and Redmond explores how science fiction uses images of outer space to evoke a sublimity that threatens in its totalizing incomprehensibility.[40] While science fiction dominates discourses concerning film and cosmology, my hope is to uncover the richness of cosmic discourses beyond this genre. The films I write about in this book fit into an expansive category I term *cosmic cinema*—expansive because films across multiple genres and practices engage with cosmic imagery and themes and because, as I have already suggested, cinema as a whole is already in some sense cosmic. Cosmic cinema overlaps with, but is not reducible to, science fiction. Rather than dismissing science fiction, I wish to demonstrate how expansive the cinematic cosmic imaginary has been and what diverse forms it has taken as it confronts the apocalypse with which outer space threatens us.

Appeals to cosmic imaginaries have resurged in the cinema at times of crisis in two ways that are both intertwined and at odds. Survivalist responses to this looming sense of planetary demise tend to stage explorations and colonizations of the universe beyond Earth's atmosphere or confront a cosmic threat and save the planet at the last moment. One might think of Elon Musk or Newt Gingrich or of science fiction's obsession with narratives of new planets. Indeed, most mainstream science-fiction cinema takes survivalist approaches to existential cosmic threats. These narratives do not always explicitly refer to Earth's unsustainability, though some do; rather, they all take on the task of imagining alternative atmospheres. *The Martian* (dir. Ridley Scott, 2015), for example, envisions what it would look like to create a habitable, fertile space on a planet otherwise hostile to human life as astronaut Mark Watney (Matt Damon) gets stranded on Mars and farms potatoes in his own excrement to survive until he can be rescued. While Watney's return to Earth at the film's conclusion is cause for celebration, the film devotes the bulk of its two-and-a-half-hour run time to imagining what it would take to make a barren planet hospitable. This impulse precedes the current moment and is eminently cinematic: as I have noted, since Méliès, filmmakers have relished the challenge of depicting other worlds convincingly. The tenor of these films has varied depending on the direness of our planet's state—the perceived immanence of its demise—but ultimately the fantasy of space travel and colonization transcends historical epochs even as the specificities of its execution and impetus evolve.

It is the other realm of cosmic storytelling that interests me most here. This realm engages with finitude, the end of human and even planetary existence. Instead of asking how human life can find new homes, it confronts an abyss and asks instead about the ongoing meaning of the present in the face of obliteration. The visions of the films I write about often raise questions about the filmic medium itself as an ephemeral archive that has also been used to violent and apocalyptic ends. Responding to recent scholarship that turns to "useful cinema," I consider a wide range of films, from science-education films of the 1920s that seek to elucidate Einstein's theories of relativity, to wartime propaganda films that take an aerial perspective, to avant-garde films from the 1950s and 1960s that address the profound scalar upheavals of the atomic bomb, to popular cinema and independent documentary that take on more recent apocalyptic concerns. Collectively, these films explore questions of illumination and invisibility, archives and futures, universalism and fragmentation, science and spirituality, and enchantment and entropy in the entangled domains of the cosmos and the cinema. Through close analysis of films and theoretical writings on cinematic time, I demonstrate that conceptions of time in film and astronomy since the late nineteenth century evince a widespread desire to preserve the past for the future, to bear witness to disaster, and to imagine a mobile temporality that might disrupt a linear history that is accelerating toward the end.

It is worth mentioning that cosmic archives other than those linked to a cosmocinematic gaze also exist as testament to human life. Traces of humanity in the cosmos can be quite material, even infrastructural, and linked to an array of media forms other than cinema. The Voyager mission represents one such attempt to document human life for the posthuman future and the nonhuman expanse of outer space. Sending a Golden Record with audio of various earthly sounds and etched with two images of human forms (one male, one female) deep into interstellar space in 1977, the Voyager mission embodies the hope of marking a literal permanent record of our presence beyond our temporary place on Earth's surface. In Jimmy Carter's words, the record was a "present from a small, distant world, a token of our sounds, our science, our images, our music, our thoughts and our feelings. We are attempting to survive our time so we may live into yours."[41] It is easy to critique an effort to present a collective vision of our species to some hypothetical future civilization, and unsurprisingly, the record, while it attempts inclusivity, is largely biased toward a White, Western, masculine version of humanity. Like most archives, its curation reflects the priorities of a small group of privileged people. But there is something poignant about the effort—as I listen to the snippets of audio included on it, I cannot help but feel not a hope that this will reach some alien ears but a profound sadness about the loss such a hope acknowledges. To try to encapsulate our species, to salvage something about us for some unknown time and place, is to admit that it needs salvaging, that we will not be around forever to preserve its meaning for ourselves. The attempt to distill everything into one small record hints, despite Carter's language of entering a "community of galactic civilizations," that everything we have imbued with meaning, everything we have created and valued and loved, everything that has made us feel anything, that has connected us to our past and to each other and to our souls, is ephemeral.[42] The tangible record for posthumous extraterrestrial analysis is but a crumb.

Debris from satellites circling in orbit will also outlast our species, leaving a small mark on our cosmos beyond the surface of our planet. A less immaculately thought-out rendering of our humanity than the Voyager disc, the debris of our media infrastructure circling the circumterrarium nevertheless stands for something about yearnings, both idealistic and militarized, to extend our visions and our reach across the globe and into space. Alice Gorman, an archaeologist whose work focuses on human traces in outer space, writes of such physical traces of human life in space as "monuments to preserve memory and ensure continuity beyond the grave. They're tangible reminders of who was there: an object standing for an individual, a nation, or an ideology."[43] These projectiles not only stake claims to the sky and to physical presence beyond mortal life; as artifacts of human existence, they also obscure the cultures of those whose cosmologies have not depended on technologization of the sky. These archives, too, tell a highly selective story of human existence—one that has been picked up with some fascination by various recent films concerned with archives and endings, including *WALL-E* (dir. Andrew Stanton, United States, 2008), *Gravity* (dir. Alfonso Cuarón, United States, 2013), and *Don't Look Up* (dir. Adam McKay, United States, 2021), as I explore in my final chapter.

The film *Contact* (dir. Robert Zemeckis, United States, 1997) presents another alternative to the Voyager's carefully curated accounting of our existence, one that leaks out from terrestrial broadcasts, moving through and beyond our atmosphere via the same kinds of ethereal waves our own devices harness to show us the mundane visions of daily media. As Dr. Ellie Arroway (Jodie Foster), a scientist researching extraterrestrial life, deciphers a set of repeating radio signals emanating from a distant star system, she realizes they include a video broadcast of Adolf Hitler making a speech at the 1936 Berlin Olympics. Here, the version of earthly culture that gets preserved in space is beyond curatorial control; instead, the worst of humanity is permanently casting itself outward. The most revealing archives are not those that are strategically selected by those who have some arbitrarily assigned power to designate what is important and universal. They include what is ugly, what we wish had not happened but did. When I write about cinema's cosmic preservation, then, I write about partial glimpses of history, glimpses that obscure and misrepresent but that also, unconsciously, reveal what some might wish they did not. Cinema can provide such an archive, if only for a time.

Cinematic Archives and the Cosmocinematic Gaze

In the face of mortality at any scale, we rely on memory and preservation to provide a sense of continuity with the past, and so we turn to archival media. But we know these are always just temporary. The end to human history that is posed by the apocalypse in various forms raises questions about what archives will persist beyond these ephemeral media and what their meaning will be. Despite the ephemerality of cinema's physical substrate—whether film, VHS, hard drives, for example—cinema navigates such questions from an advantageous position. It aligns with a cosmic imaginary in its ability to manifest and move through the past, carrying it into the future, but it is also undeniably precarious itself. Cinema thus embodies the urge to preserve and to document precarity; even as it summons the past it makes clear the fragility of its presence. It always speaks of death, of endings, of what is gone, even at its most animated.[44] This ghostliness is not just a reminder of what is gone; as James Leo Cahill writes, "Aging photographic media . . . mark the unsettling experience of knowing that we too will be swallowed whole, unredeemed, by and in the black hole of time's passage."[45] And at a larger scale, cosmic cinema's omniscient view of space and time is apocalyptic in its reference to a world whose presence is but a ghost. Cosmic cinema in particular has a privileged role in archiving at the end of the world. As we collectively face questions of where repositories of human life will be found after we are gone, cinema—in its metaphorical and transcendent similarities to the cosmos—holds promise of preserving something other than just the scars and detritus of our time here that are etched on the surface of the earth and that orbit above it. As a cosmic medium that recasts ghostly light, cinema provides some hope of showing us in motion, mummifying us as change, dynamizing us, perhaps allowing us a shadowy kind of afterlife characterized not just by absence but by a *present* absence, or absent presence.

Indeed, the cosmocinematic as a way of imagining earthly archives also transcends any specific archival medium, suggesting the possibility of a record that exists for all time even if all manmade media are subject to decay. Both popular astronomy writers and film theorists have written about the night sky as a cinematic space where archives of light await the exploration of some extraterrestrial time traveler, imagining a cosmocinematic gaze whose ability to move through the past is both cinematic and cosmic, unbounded from any single medium or temporal thrust and providing a way of imagining archives as responding to, and moving beyond, any apocalyptic end of human life. Felix Eberty, in his 1846 popular science book about the cosmos, *The Stars and World History*, describes the universe as a space in which the speed of light's limitation preserves all of history in a moving archive that emanates away from Earth.[46] He begins by stating that our perception of everything we see operates on a delay because of light's finite speed; while we do not notice this in our daily interactions, cosmic scales of space exacerbate the delay such that, for example, we see the moon as it was just over a second ago, because that is how long it takes the light to travel the 239,000 miles to our eyes. It is in the returned gaze of the universe, though, that he finds reason for excitement. For just as we see the sun as it was eight minutes ago, the nearest star as it was three years ago, and other stars further and further back in time depending on their physical distance from Earth, hypothetical observers on these astronomical bodies would witness our earthly past at various intervals, as if it were unfolding in the present. By this reasoning, the whole of the universe is like a set of ever-larger concentric spheres storing world history in perfect regularity through a homogeneous space, with each larger sphere capturing a slightly older moment in the historical narrative.

Writing before Einstein's discovery that the speed of light is insurmountable, Eberty imagines that a faster-than-light trip back to Earth from any distance would enable a visual engagement with events of the past. In a passage that to a current reader may evoke a time-lapse film, he writes:

> Let us imagine an observer with infinitely strong vision on a star four thousand light-years away, from which he would—at this very moment—be seeing the earth as it was in the time of Abraham. Let us imagine this observer propelled toward our earth at such a speed that in just a short time, let's say an hour, he reaches a distance of 20 million miles from our earth, where he would be as near to us as the Sun is, and where the Earth would at this moment appear to him as it was just 8 minutes ago.... This would undoubtedly mean the following: that before the eyes of this beholder, the whole history of the world, from the time of Abraham to this very day, would have rolled past in the span of an hour.[47]

While we could add to Eberty's itinerary movements back and forth through time, or around a single sphere to see different parts of the world at the same moment, Eberty sticks with one continuous, progressive thrust, focusing on major moments in biblical and Western history. He writes that we would see Abraham wandering through Egypt, Jesus performing miracles, and Martin Luther at the Diet of Worms. Importantly, for Eberty, this preservation of time in space is also a form of temporal flattening: because the images of history's entirety coexist in the present—albeit dissipated in space—he argues that we can truly understand a godly omnipresence. An ordinary observer must travel through space to view a film of history, but God's "spatial overlook of all of outer space" allows him to see all time and space spread out before him at once.[48] "Omnipresence" thus entails a flattened, spatialized present that Eberty imagines as God's experience of time and that forestalls any dread that might come with acknowledging an actual end. By this logic, anything that seems to be over is in fact just spatially displaced in the sky's infinite light archive. Lives and civilizations and species gone are still, somehow, reassuringly present.

Given the debunking of Eberty's scientific premise by early twentieth-century astrophysics—the speed of light, it turns out, is constant and insurmountable—his fantastical voyage through time is more useful as a point of departure for film theory than as an explanation of genuine possibilities of travel through space-time. Of course, when Eberty offered these speculations, film as such did not yet exist. But his ideas and ones similar to them permeated European popular consciousness in the period leading up to cinema's emergence and, on more than one occasion, were taken up by film theorists as a way to convey how cinema provides access to and navigates the past. Eberty's vision points to the celestial sphere, and to natural physical processes of light within it, as a cinematic mechanism of its own, in that it visually preserves events of the past in a spatial form, "embalming time" in the space of the universe.[49] Thus, while he may not properly be a theorist of film, he is nevertheless a theorist of the cinematic.[50] Cinematic concepts were explored long before technologies allowed for its material manifestation, and Eberty's work is evidence of a cinematic imagination that preceded film as a distinct apparatus or a recognized cultural practice. This cosmocinematic gaze also allows us to understand the future of the cinematic as independent of a particular material substrate. If the cinematic existed before cinema, its gaze may continue beyond any technology or any human witness. Indeed, even as I focus on "movies," throughout this book I write about the cosmocinematic gaze in relation to media from still photography to satellite imaging; the "cinematic," as a concept that involves an animated and archival relationship to time, can be channeled by various visual media that allow us access to the temporal horizons of the cosmos. Most notably, I write about photography as a medium that preceded film as an indexical medium that was frequently used sequentially to document and reconstitute motion, especially in the field of astronomy.

Eberty, an amateur astronomer and science writer, was widely read in Europe, and his book was translated into both French and English the same year it was published in Germany. Art historian Karl Clausberg traces Eberty's broad influence on philosophical discourses in the mid to late nineteenth century, finding references to his work in writings by various figures in German intellectual history, including Albert Einstein and Walter Benjamin.[51] One can also see his influence in two passages of film theory that reveal a persistent interest in cinema's similarity to the dark expanses of the universe in archiving light from the past. The first of these is a passage from Élie Faure's "The Art of Cineplastics," and the second appears in Siegfried Kracauer's *Theory of Film*. Taken together with Walter

Benjamin's writings with their frequent turn to cosmic metaphors, these passages reveal a persistent fascination with the cosmocinematic gaze and how it allows for temporal preservation and a dynamization of history even after human civilization is gone.

For Faure, the ability of film to preserve the ephemeral is integral to its magnificence and wonder: cinema is, as a result of this function, capable of substituting for our lost faith in eternity beyond life. Faure writes of the film actor with a sense of envy, for he, "alone among living things, has the privilege of knowing that though his destiny is without hope, he is yet the only being to live and think as if he had the power to take himself to eternity."[52] He goes on to extol how cinema's record of time in space allows for the preservation of a moment—here, simply the swirl of dust that a horse's galloping hoof kicks up, an ephemeral moment to which our eyes might ordinarily devote little attention—thousands of years into the future, extending duration beyond the fleeting instant and, what is more, beyond the duration of most civilizations.

Faure imaginatively demonstrates the connections between his theorizations of cinematic time and cosmic time. Echoing Eberty, whose work had been translated into French upon its publication, Faure writes that through viewing film, "we shall be able to understand how it may be that the inhabitants of a distant star, if they can see things on earth with powerful telescopes, are really contemporaries of Jesus, since at the moment when I write these lines they may be witnessing his crucifixion, and perhaps making a photographic or even cinematographic record of the scene, for we know that the light that illumines us takes nineteen or twenty centuries to reach them."[53] In this passage, Faure's analogy to cosmic time points to the power of film as a medium that provides direct access to the past. Here, seeing cinematic images from the past can help us conceive of the way light's delay creates a disjointed time of celestial witness. Just as the projector allows us to see people and objects that have already disappeared, or at least changed, since the camera registered them, the light we see from distant stars comes from a past that has already faded.[54] The starlight we see emanates from the past and is thus the trace of a past that is lost to the star itself, just as the past that stars may now witness of Earth could place them in visual contact with a historical figure lost to us. As in Eberty's text, light archives here provide an imagined means of witnessing human civilization after its end.

Indeed, Faure quickly turns to envisioning the reversal of this cosmic gaze. Filmmakers of the future, he speculates, may access the immensity of space and time not just by turning cameras outward toward the heavens but by assuming the stars' perspective on Earth and its past and using a "system of interplanetary projection."[55] Film's ultimate potential would not be to *look out* at the majestic dance of planets but to *look back*, to capture a cosmocinematic gaze, to see events on Earth that transpired in a precinematic era. That Faure uses an imagined cinetechnological resurrection of Christ as his focal point is no coincidence; he places cineplastics at the heart of a new cosmology that interacts with a traditional religious one but draws on similar human needs for a sense of continuation beyond an individual lifespan and for a sense of a larger order in which our lives can become meaningful even after the end of a mortal life or a mortal world.

The cosmocinematic gaze as imagined by both Eberty and Faure is linked to world-ending in another sense, too. It closely resembles the kind of vision that Donna Haraway has called the "conquering gaze from nowhere."[56] This gaze, which has moved from myth to "ordinary practice" via surveillance technologies like the satellite, encapsulates what she terms the "god trick of seeing everything from nowhere"—of having the power of omniscient viewing without ever having to be seen. Associated with a Western, masculine gaze that seeks to subsume the world under its control, "this eye fucks the world," as Haraway puts it bluntly. Many other scholars subsequently link the aerial gaze as it has been mobilized technologically with precisely the racist and imperialist violence Haraway describes, not least Simone Browne with her analysis of bird's-eye-view diagrams of slave ships as a tool of abolition and empowered White gazes, and Paul Virilio with his description of how "eye and weapon" have become inextricably linked in aerial warfare and its cinematic documentation.[57] The fantasy of a God's-eye view is inextricable from fantasies of world domination and has been a key tool of Western imperialist projects of mapping and conquering, as Denis Cosgrove explores in depth.[58] The reality of cinema's historical attempts to document the world and its people, including through aerial perspectives, is similarly imbricated with these fantasies.[59] And yet, there is more to a cosmocinematic perspective than just a desire to conquer and to immortalize Western, White, male history. The possibility of a distanced gaze producing a cinematic record of history also holds the promise of reviving and redeeming precisely what such a history has consistently overlooked. Indeed, Patrick Ellis cautions against understanding aeroscopic media that adopt a bird's-eye view as "a transparently authoritarian viewpoint, one best made use of in planning and war."[60] He sees this take on aerial perspectives as ahistorical because of its failure to account for the pre–World War I democratization of such gazes via mass media and public spaces like observatories and panoramas. How aerial vantage points are understood is "determined by the varying ideologies" that shape the media through which they are encountered; what we now largely see as a "drone view," he writes, was once deemed a "celestial" one.[61] In this work, I take seriously the threats and destructive aspects of the cosmocinematic gaze, but I also seize on its imaginative potentials: the ways it invites fantasy, evokes longing, and even promises redemption—bringing to light aspects of the past that have been written out of history—through its capacity to traverse space and time. As such, this gaze is linked to the apocalyptic both in how it threatens and through its capacity to offer archives for after the end of the world.

Film theory's excitement about the cosmocinematic gaze takes on new meaning in the context of Siegfried Kracauer's post–Second World War *Theory of Film*. Kracauer cites Faure's reflections on cinema and the night sky in his discussion of historical fiction films, which he disdains for their attempts to falsely recreate a past time. He imagines an alternative filmic engagement with the past based on index rather than reenactment, drawing directly from Faure's earlier description of cinema as exemplifying light's delay at a cosmic level. Later in this book, Kracauer writes of the archival power of cinema as potentially "redemptive" and not just immortalizing.[62] His use of the word *redemption* in order to express the ways cinema salvages and restores aspects of history is not directly religious, in that he does not mean to suggest that film will somehow absolve anyone of their sins. But his use of the word powerfully evokes the language of biblical apocalypticism that promises redemption for those commonly overlooked: the poor and those who have been wronged, according to the Bible, "shall inherit the earth."[63] In Kracauer's imagined cosmocinematic history, those same figures regain their place within a visual record, a secular form of such redemption.

Like Eberty and Faure, Kracauer begins by imagining how a trip through cosmic light archives would enable a remote viewer to witness great biblical events.[64] Importantly, he continues, "Film being film, we would moreover be in a position to take in all the seemingly insignificant happenings incidental to those momentous events—the soldiers shuffling cards, the clouds of dust whirled up."[65] This image of the dust whirled up also recalls Faure, but for Kracauer, a turn to the less momentous happenings is precisely where the potential of cinema lies, and not just because it exemplifies the way the ephemeral gesture can be preserved. Film can expose material reality, rendering visible things long ignored.

The cosmic perspective Kracauer imagines adopting in *Theory of Film* is that of an observer outside of everything who can nevertheless know intimately the minutiae of Earth's history. This form of the cosmocinematic gaze fulfills what Cahill describes as cinema's "Copernican vocation," a sometimes-eccentric shift in perspective enabled by film's nonhuman gaze that, because of its displacement from human ways of looking, invites us to think differently about the planet and human histories.[66] Kracauer indeed idealizes such an extraterritorial vantage point for both historians and film viewers. In his book on historiography, *History: The Last Things before the Last*, he writes, "Evicted from our familiar surroundings," a remote, extraterritorial perspective on history thrusts us into an "open space where many traditional views and customary procedures no longer apply."[67] Engaging with the past "at a distance" forces the "crumbling of our idea-system," opening up new possibilities for understanding history. In his view, the exilic position that allows a historian to properly navigate the past is also the position a film can afford its viewers, allowing for a "close scrutiny of some minor event" that accesses "history's moving forces in full motion."[68] Kracauer's imagined cosmocinematic viewer of history, like the observer on a distant star, turns back to look from afar, seeing fleeting gestures and taken-for-granted infrastructures that are lost to those moving in the midst of them.[69] The movement of light through time, as Kracauer imagines it in *Theory of Film*, would permit a look at earthly events that would go beyond narratives of significant historical figures, enabling instead a view of history that equally includes the peripheral and provides the possibility of redemption. Gertrud Koch writes that this historical consciousness gives Kracauer an "anamnesic solidarity with the dead." Koch adds that "only by preserving them can we show our commitment to solidarity with dead things so that when revealed they shine forth in a different, perhaps more favorable light."[70]

This vision of how cinematic archives might work to investigate an overlooked past also aligns with the way Kracauer imagines photography in his famous essay "Photography." In it, he likens the accumulation of photographs in modernity to a total archive akin to a natural disaster that engulfs their viewer and makes it nearly impossible to discern major historical narratives. The image of such an inundation is striking: the proliferation of visual media spells a catastrophe for conventional modes of examining the past. Yet this overwhelming, catastrophic archive, perhaps precisely because it renders illegible vectors of history that might otherwise dominate narratives, is imbued with the possibility of accessing history anew without its familiar anchors. Cahill points out that this prospect is especially strong when the archive is animated through film, which, through "juxtaposition, montage, and spatial and temporal dislocations and rearticulations," bears the promise of deconstructing and reconstructing images and articulations of the world.[71] Cosmic archives of cinematic light, through enacting a preservation of small gestures as well as great moments, might bring a kind of justice to what has been historically wronged. This version of a cosmocinematic gaze shows the hope latent in apocalyptic thinking; the end of history as we know it marks an opening up to something new and perhaps more just.

This possibility of preserving and digging up the past in order to do justice comes up in the cosmic imagery that permeates Walter Benjamin's writing, too, providing another avenue through which to imagine the cosmocinematic gaze as something other than merely a "conquering gaze from nowhere." Writing before the Second World War but in dialogue with Kracauer's earlier work, Benjamin draws on another set of images that bring together cosmic and cinematic temporalities without fidelity to the temporal linearity of history presumed by Eberty's cosmocinematic gaze. Perhaps his most striking and well-known cosmic image is that of the Angel of History, looking back on the wreckage of the past as it moves away from the earth. Here, Eberty's vision of moving through cosmic archives to witness monumental histories turns nightmarish: looking back means having to confront the fact that "there is no document of civilization which is not at the same time a document of barbarism."[72] The way out from this look of horror is a view of time and history that does not succumb to a narrative of progress.

Benjamin writes repeatedly of the debt the living owe the dead to dig up their past—to remember. For him, the past has a powerful claim on the present, and the work of the historian is to undo the violence of traditional historical practices by allowing the past to puncture the present— to stage a historical encounter that allows involuntary memory to come through and that is not empathetic to a narrative of history that favors the victors.[73] At times he writes of this through the lens of a form of apocalypticism: only the blasting open of history can break through the continuum that perpetually favors a ruling class at the expense of others. Benjamin elaborates on this alternative temporality in "Theses on the Philosophy of History," in which he describes the possibility of messianic escape in every moment.[74] He espouses a messianicity without messianism—that is, he hopes for a discontinuous future that might promise the advent of

INTRODUCTION · 25

justice without resorting to a sense of predestination, the forms of exclusion, and the element of violence that characterize messianism.[75] In these theses, Benjamin advocates seizing the *Jetztzeit*, literally the "now time," not as an eternalized present but as a constellation of past, present, and future that ruptures a set, fatalistic trajectory of time: an apocalypse of sorts—an end, but also an opening to new, redemptive potentials. While he does not specifically outline a theory of film's relationship to these temporalities, one might guess that cinema, which he wrote about as having the power to reach mass audiences in their state of distraction, might also be able to pick up fragments of a discarded past and let them tear through the fabric of a complacent present: to stage an apocalypse that brings revolutionary potential to the deadened past that haunts us. Benjamin's insistence on constellating the present with the historically specific past gives new meaning to both history and the present. The present is indebted to the overlooked past, and the possibility of redemption resides within it. The figure of the constellation resonates here:

> It's not that what is past casts its light upon the present, or what is present its light on what is past; rather, image is wherein what has been comes together in a flash with the now to form a constellation. In other words, image is dialectics at a standstill. For while the relation of the present to the past is a purely temporal, continuous one, the relation of the what-has-been to the now is dialectical: not progression but image, suddenly emergent.[76]

Benjamin uses the word *constellation* metaphorically, of course. Yet this passage recalls an actual constellation: when we look into the night sky and identify a constellation in the stars, we are bringing together multiple temporalities to form one image that comprises moving celestial bodies that only appear as they do from one subjective perspective. The light we see from a single constellation spans millions of years, yet in the flash of an instant all of those pasts enter the present. Both photograph and moving image provide a shocking encounter with a constellation of pasts and the present, suddenly emergent.

The promise of preservation linked with promise of change that recurs in Benjamin's work and finds metaphor in the constellation summons a temporality not unlike what Slavoj Žižek suggests as our confrontation with the end of the world. Žižek writes that a new temporality exists in apocalyptic times, one in which the future has already been fated, and we must work now (the "past of the future") to retroactively rewrite that future: "One should accept the catastrophe as inevitable, and then work to undo what is already 'written in the stars' as our destiny."[77] These stars, with their twisting of time that makes the *now* the "past of the future" and accepts and defies inevitability at once, are a Benjaminian constellation, bringing into focus a rupture to all conventional teleologies: this disruptive now is a pure time of clairvoyance and action. This constellation is a form of dynamic preservation that holds onto a faith in the future while also acknowledging that it is, actually, too late. It has an attitude toward the past that is not nostalgic, not restorative, but embracing of the fragments that, when they come together, reveal something new, a future with the hope of not just replicating the past with all its wrongs. This vision of cosmic time is not a monodirectional reel of archival film with absolute fidelity to the original but light from the past recast in various presents, resonating in new combinations across the universe. As I move through the chapters that follow, the cosmocinematic gaze manifests in a wide range of ways, from the assertive omniscience Eberty describes to the politicized temporal constellations Benjamin conceives of.

Outline of the Book

My subsequent chapters address sets of films that have emerged around moments of global unrest that coincided with shifting technoscientific cosmologies, resulting in filmmaking that expresses apocalyptic anxieties around the sky and cosmos and allows us to see how the theoretical cosmocinematic gaze finds media representation. The first moment I discuss involved new astronomical and astrophysical developments around the buildup to and aftermath of the First World War, most notably Einstein's theories of special and general relativity and Hubble's discovery of the enormous universe beyond the Milky Way. The reformulation of human understanding of space and time that resulted from these revelations was enormous. Beyond their effects on scientific communities, these theories circulated widely and were reinterpreted in ways that reflect just how exciting, alarming, and freeing their shake-up of the universe could be and that echoed the existential uncertainties precipitated by increasingly global warfare. The films I analyze in the chapter respond to new astronomy and especially the formulation and reformulation of Einsteinian relativity, both scientifically and in the popular imagination. First, I discuss the role photographic media played in providing scientists with visual evidence of the phenomena Einstein had hypothesized. Second, I describe the ways Einsteinian ideas were subsequently taken up in educational films of the silent era that sought to explain astronomy and astrophysics while remaining entertaining, a challenge that resulted in liberal interpretations of science that reveal more about human anxieties about our precarious planet than about science itself.

My second chapter identifies the Second World War as another period of global and cosmic upheaval. The world wars demanded a reckoning with the world at a planetary scale even as it seemed newly splintered along geopolitical lines, and the domestication of the sky as a new terrain of political and military action changed the way people thought about the heavens. The documentaries, military films, and feature films that responded to these shifts found new ways to document and represent the scalar horizons associated with war and the technologies of the air that took shape around it. Chapter 3 centers on the shifting cosmologies triggered by the atomic bomb, which demanded new kinds of filmmaking in its wake. The experimental films I discuss here sought a cinematic language that could express the apocalyptic thwarting of dimensional stability associated with the bomb. As they drew on and reconfigured scientific images and modes of representation, these films also rejected science as a totalizing cosmology and expressed alternative ways of perceiving the universe. The Epilogue analyzes a surging cinematic fascination with the temporalities of outer space, evidenced in a spate of cosmic films in the past fifteen years. In large part, these recent films address a sense of despair at the impending demise of our planet due to climate change and a sense that the "end times," as Žižek deems our current era, necessitate an expansion into outer space, a mobility through time—a salvage temporality, we could call it—or both.

Each of the shifts I identify, associated with new astrophysical ideas, the catastrophe of global war, the detonation of the bomb, and the cataclysm of environmental collapse, has brought on not only new representational questions of how to register the changing ways humans thought about their place in the universe but also new experiments with how the medium of film, unique among arts in its union of space, time, image, and sound, could model cosmic systems and incarnate cosmocinematic gazes. In grappling with how to represent the scales, affects, and visual phenomena of evolving cosmic imaginaries, these films also experiment with their medium and reveal its multidimensionality, its profound temporal and spatial mobility, and its power to bring alive, and make newly resonant, constellations of light from the past.

1 LIGHTS ALL ASKEW

Relativity and New Astronomy on Film

"Lights All Askew in the Heavens," read a special cable in the *New York Times* on November 10, 1919. "Stars not where they seemed or were calculated to be, but nobody need worry." A British team of astronomers led by Sir Arthur Eddington had just taken a series of photographs and measurements of a solar eclipse, confirming Albert Einstein's groundbreaking theory of general relativity. The theory had enormous implications for how space and time were understood. The path of light was affected by gravity, meaning distant objects were not where they appeared to be, which had unsettling ramifications for faith in simple observation. The theory postulated that because the path of light bends in the presence of gravity, and because the speed of light is constant, space-time actually curves around gravitational fields.[1] This opened up strange spatiotemporal possibilities: the curvature of space-time meant a beam of light could actually return to its source, reencountering its origin in the distant future. The very fact that reporters felt the need to add to the news of Eddington's breakthrough that "nobody need worry" suggests how explosive these ideas were to existing notions of the cosmos and how imbricated they were with a sense of global instability.

Feelings of dimensional and existential volatility permeated the process of creating the images that confirmed special relativity and resounded in a spate of educational astronomy films that emerged in Europe and the United States as these new theories entered a popular vernacular from the early 1910s through the interwar period. The scientific theories themselves may not have been world-ending, but the visual media that documented and explained them evince how such theories added to a pervasive cosmic uncertainty within the United States and Europe that was affected by the upheaval of the First World War and the crumbling of imperial modernity.

In this chapter, I describe the photographic expedition that confirmed Einstein's theory, and then I explore how a broader set of silent-era educational films from the United States and Europe engaged with astronomy and astrophysics, making their discoveries accessible to lay audiences. I point to the ways these films reveal tensions between efforts to rein cosmic space and time into something manageable and comprehensible, captured by advanced scientific instruments at precise instants, and efforts to unhinge it from regularity and fully visualize the spatiotemporal disjuncture and the world-ending threats that the modern cosmos embodied. Running counter to every scientific attempt to define, measure, and categorize were various forces of disorder, whether associated with the limits of human perception, the unruliness of nature, or the incompatibility of rational equations with human experiences and fantasies of, and beliefs about, time and space.

In narratives of photographic expeditions and descriptions of astronomy film productions of this period, it is clear that the sheer magnitude of the cosmos, as well as its array of subtle and bright lights across this distance, presented a challenge to the rationalization sought through the technical mechanism of the camera and numerical approach of science. Photographers and filmmakers had to work creatively and with advanced equipment to register and contain cosmic light, movement, and scale. Overall, however, in the scientific, popular, and theoretical discourses around the photographic media I write about here, there was a strong sense that these media had the necessary properties to take on the cosmos and cosmic temporalities. I write about photography and film together in this chapter, though the two media and their uses are of course also quite distinct. Indeed, in 1914, Astronomer Royal Frank Dyson wrote a letter to an amateur astronomer who suggested that scientists use film to record a moving image of an upcoming eclipse, responding that the cinematograph was "not of any special scientific value," though its depictions of astronomical events could admittedly be "interesting."[2] Photography, however, transformed the field's ability to document phenomena in the sky, freezing astronomical bodies in their motion and allowing for precise measurements of their interrelations. And yet photography and film are more interconnected in the practice of astronomy than Dyson's letter acknowledged. The history of film is deeply entwined with that of astronomical photography, with one origin point of the moving image being traced to the time-lapse compilation of Pierre Janssen's photographs of the 1874 transit of Venus.[3] Astronomers viewed these images as a series of still photographs taken in rapid succession, valuable primarily for their halting of motion. But when animated, the images came alive for those who saw them. Film became useful to astronomical missions because it helped elucidate and popularize phenomena measured by photography. It could also overcome photography's perspectival limitations: until the first satellites were sent into space, all astronomical photography was grounded, or nearly grounded, on Earth. In a 1914 lecture, Eddington mentioned the difficulties of earthbound astronomy, bemoaning, "We must take our survey [of the stars and galaxies] from where we stand."[4] This meant that the earth's atmosphere clouded images of what lay beyond it and that the earth itself, let alone the entire solar system or galaxy more largely, could not be filmed as an astronomical body. But for films that sought to convey the place of the earth in larger cosmic systems, nonphotorealist representation brought new perspectives on the earth and its cosmic setting.

Film's flexibility as a medium that could document reality and stage cosmic voyages through fantasy was often associated with a loss of scientific accuracy. But film also possessed an ability to move across scales and take creative itineraries through time, making it an ideal medium for conveying and disseminating new cosmic theories—a task that was an inherent part of the work of scientists like Eddington, not alien to it. As one reviewer of a German film about Einstein's theory declared, "There is no other medium that could make the theory of relativity more vivid than the medium of film."[5] Yet, before film could do its part came the photographs that achieved visual documentation of this theory. These images, themselves a record of instability despite their stillness, enabled glimpses of new temporal possibilities that allowed a cinematic imagination to take hold and dynamize new astrophysical theories more fully. Before I turn to their story, I will explain the context of scientific discovery within which these media were received and understood.

New Astronomy and Its Visual Cultures

Einstein's theory of general relativity, confirmed by Eddington's expedition, joined his theory of special relativity, which suggested that time and space could not be parsed as separate dimensions but were rather extensions of each other. In the unified cosmos envisioned by Felix Eberty and Élie Faure, a single temporal reference frame governs the entire universe. In contrast, Einstein's theory of special relativity breaks time down into individual inertial reference frames, with each system in which everything moves at a constant velocity relative to each other operating according to its own clock—its *Eigenzeit*. Noting that "it is characteristic of Newtonian physics that it has to describe independent and real existence to space and time as well as to matter," Einstein proposes that in relativistic theory, time and space each only exist through the acceleration of moving bodies.[6] As soon as acceleration comes into play—which it does in the case of gravity, for example—so does another clock. This undoes a traditional sense of absolute simultaneity: now, events occur simultaneously only relative to a reference frame, outside of which they appear to be non-simultaneous. According to Einstein, "every reference-body (co-ordinate system) has its own particular time; unless we are told the reference-body to which a statement of time refers, there is no meaning in the statement of time of an event."[7] Time had become a kind of constellation, losing its sense of absoluteness. These revelations were deeply unsettling, associated as they were with the destabilization of time and dynamization of space. Einstein's theories challenged the solidity of Newtonian physics, with its concepts of universality and simultaneity, and Euclidean geometry, with its insistence on spatial uniformity. So even as time was standardized at the end of the nineteenth century, Einstein's special theory of relativity accentuated the superficiality of the concept of temporal unity.

Indeed, in Europe and the United States, Einstein's theories contributed to and were deciphered in the context of earth-shaking war and within a wider sense that space and time were not the stable dimensions they had seemed in the age of the Enlightenment. As German theoretical physicist Arnold Sommerfeld claimed at the time, "The belief in a rational world order was shaken by the way the [First World War] ended and the peace dictated; consequently one seeks salvation in an irrational world order."[8] Relativity has often been aligned with an end of rational order, despite Einstein's own stark objections that his system is fully rational.[9] Katy Price analyzes popular discourses around and appropriations of Einstein's theories within literature in 1920s England. She writes that the disorientation in space and time that is expressed in attempts to understand relativity gives way to a sense of "uncertainty as to what counted as a forward or backward development" in culture more broadly, contributing to a troubling of linear time.[10]

Within the world of modern art, Einstein's theories had enticing implications. Citing relativistic theory, a manifesto drafted in 1936 by a group of European artists including Marcel Duchamp, Wassily Kandinsky, and László Moholy-Nagy declared:

> We must accept—contrary to the classical conception—that Space and Time are no longer separate categories, but rather that they are related dimensions in the sense of the non-Euclidean conception, and thus all the old limits and boundaries of the arts d i s a p p e a r. This new ideology has elicited a veritable earthquake and subsequent landslide in the conventional artistic system. We designate the totality of relevant artistic phenomena by the term "DIMENSIONISM." . . . And after this a completely new art form will develop: Cosmic Art.[11]

Some filmmakers and theorists responded with similar enthusiasm to the introduction of new astrophysics, imagining how film, as a medium that also united space and time, could manifest the strangeness of relativistic dimensionality. For Russian filmmaker and theorist Sergei Eisenstein, for example, Einstein opened up the possibility of playing with time and defying a strict logic of progress, as did film, particularly through editing. In her analysis of how Einsteinian astrophysics influenced Eisenstein, Annette Michelson writes, "The manner in which film's elementary optical processes produced, through the use of acceleration, deceleration, freeze-frame and reverse motion, the visible suspension of causal relations within the phenomenal world gave hope that the cinema could be the articulate medium of the master theoretical systems of modernity: of psychoanalysis, historical materialism, Einsteinian physics."[12] One can see the influence of Einstein in Eisenstein's enthusiasm for the "complete remolding of nature" that montage enables, a power over time and space that he compares to Einstein's own remolding of the principles of the universe.[13] In his essay "The Filmic Fourth Dimension," a title with obvious reference to physics, Eisenstein describes how his editing process moves beyond "orthodox categories" and relies on a system that is "completely incomprehensible."[14] Even as the process seems devoid of any operative principle or intent, though, the effect produces a "fourth dimension," an almost musical overtone of rhythmic meaning, in the moving, projected film.[15] Eisenstein concludes this anecdote by exclaiming, "The fourth dimension?! Einstein? Or mysticism? Or a joke?" Einstein is on the brink of hilarity and of mysticism; his theories provide a way of expressing the incalculability of the relationship between space and time that lends cinema the capacity to work on a level unencumbered by reason, gripping audiences directly through feeling. The perceived end of reason becomes the foundation for new kinds of artistic freedom, ones that for Eisenstein were bound to filmmaking that was also revolutionary in content, celebrating the end of political world orders as well as scientific ones.

Other discoveries of modern astronomy similarly thwarted notions of progressive temporality and added to a sense of global instability, as well as anxieties around the planet's vulnerability in an enormous, indifferent universe. In 1924, Edwin Hubble photographed distant galaxies, convincing the scientific community once and for all that the Milky Way was just a minuscule system in an incomprehensibly large—and ever-expanding—universe; the earth's relative insignificance was astounding. In the aftermath of that revelation, news articles regularly addressed the "inconceivable magnitudes and distances" of the universe, as well as the unfathomable timelines of material existence in which the earth was a newcomer.[16] Harvard astronomer W. J. Luyten wrote in the *New York Times* of the universe as not a space of timeless scientific knowledge "but a vast ocean of space, all aglow with the light messages of countless galaxies," which in their variety of ages surround us with a "confusion of past, present, and future."[17] Recognizing the existential uncertainty precipitated by these confounded timelines and expanses of space, he added, "For some years at least we shall be safe, and we need not worry ourselves with what to do when we reach the limit. The outcome of all this new information? We have collected upon photographic plates a true record of the universe, past and present."[18] If the universe threatens with its incomprehensibility, its jumbled messages from distant bodies of light, reassurance lies in the ordered collection of all time on photographic plates that can be combed through, apprehending the unknowable. The discovery of the sun's deterioration also caused ripples of apocalyptic dread. One headline warned that the "Universe Is Wasting Away," adding that its demise due to radioactivity rendered humankind "like a polar bear on a melting ice floe"—an image that has particular resonances with the current moment, in which a polar bear on an ice floe has been used as a metonym for the perils of global environmental collapse.[19] Even as it seeks to rein in some of the apocalyptic anxieties the headline stokes by reassuring readers of the roughly "million million" years the sun will likely last, this article adds to a vision of the planet's deterioration. In the deep future, if humanity is still around, "the year will be a little longer and the climate quite a bit colder, while the rich accumulated stores of coal, oil and forests will be long since burned up." (A hint at how climate and the exhaustion of resources may loom even as the apocalypse is displaced onto the cosmos.)

The concurrent development of quantum physics, whose theories of how matter and light behaved at atomic and subatomic scales were "frequently in conflict with common-sense notions derived from observations of the everyday world," similarly disrupted a sense of stability and continuity.[20] Max Planck's initial description of light as both a wave and a stream of particles turned out to have wider implications for the workings of physical reality more broadly. As Einstein claimed in a talk in 1911, "These discontinuities, which we find so distasteful in Planck's theory, seem really to exist in nature."[21] Such new, liberating scientific perspectives were seemingly at odds with the increasing regulation and monitoring of time and space that accompanied industrialization and urbanization. Instead, they resonated with the human need to experience time outside of strict chronology—inventing possible futures or reclaiming foreshortened pasts—and to envision space that was not yet charted and subsumed under geopolitics.[22]

Even the circumstances of Eddington's expedition to confirm general relativity were shaped by undergirding anxieties around a deeply troubled world, an uncertain cosmos, a discipline in flux, and a medium—photography—that was also both materially and epistemologically unstable.[23] Eddington's voyage to Príncipe was a "rare occurrence" after the international networks of astronomical expeditions, which depended on easy crossing of borders to go wherever visibility of astronomical phenomena was highest, had been shut down during the First World War.[24] Eddington's desire to prove Einstein right is often held up as an attempt to unify Europe through common scientific endeavors.[25] Eddington and Einstein both were known as pacifists. Ernest Rutherford remarks on the significance of their scientific association, "The war had just ended, and the complacency of the Victorian and Edwardian times had been shattered. The people felt that all their values and all their ideals had lost their bearings. Now, suddenly, they learnt that an astronomical prediction by a German scientist had been confirmed by expeditions . . . by British astronomers. . . . An astronomical discovery, transcending worldly strife, struck a responsive chord."[26] A British expedition is assisted by the Portuguese government in proving a German man's theory, bringing Europe together in a moment of scientific unity and an attempt to "heal all wounds of war."[27]

But just as the cosmic theories Eddington confirmed did more to unsettle than to settle, a deeper look at his expedition shows how limited such harmony was. Indeed, these expeditions depended on and attempted to reinforce global networks of imperialism, with their emphasis on subsuming the world under Greenwich Mean Time. Eddington's report notes that the island of Príncipe was "covered with cocoa plantations," bespeaking the fraught colonial relations of a place where the stolen labor of enslaved people had continued unofficially to undergird the colony's sugar and cocoa industry until at least 1910.[28] Eddington and his fellow scientists stationed their telescopes and cameras at one such plantation, the headquarters of the Sociedade de Agricultura Colonial. Astronomy expeditions relied heavily on infrastructures of plantations, as well as those of transportation used by imperial militaries and even the global slave trade, and depended on the stolen labor of enslaved Indigenous and African people that sustained these infrastructures.[29] Imperial governments, such as the Portuguese government in Príncipe that allowed Eddington and his entourage to bring in thousands of pounds of equipment without having to pass through customs, were essential contacts for astronomers even as they continued to exploit local people and resources. When Eddington was stationed there, the government was still reliant on formerly enslaved people to produce the crops that fed the colony's economy.

Notably, the astronomers on this expedition and others of its time period documented the terrestrial world and the inhabitants of the places to which they traveled even as they went about their celestial missions. Scrapbooks of such expeditions, which can be viewed in the archives of the Oxford History of Science Museum and the Royal Astronomical Society, among other places, are primarily filled with postcards and photographs documenting the places and people astronomers encountered on their voyages. Page after page shows unnamed people lined up for the camera. There is very little to situate these faces within their larger story, and the visual similarity of each photograph's form, with its rows of anonymized people, suggests that the camera's gaze is more interested in cataloging than in investigating human experiences or histories. These scrapbooks demonstrate the expeditions' interest not just in looking up but in documenting the world from the removed perspective of a privileged foreigner, and thereby forming an archive of the world that plays precisely the "god trick" Donna Haraway associates with a gaze from above—a gaze that was used to justify devastating policies of imperialism.[30] One photograph, from an 1889 expedition to Cayenne, stands out though, complicating this hierarchical gaze even as one can imagine the hierarchies that underlay its capture. In it, a small boy, ostensibly a local inhabitant, looks through one of the telescopes astronomers have set up on their base (see Figure 3). The photograph takes the perspective of one of the White participants in the expedition and involves, at one level, a familiar colonial trope of "juxtaposing" modern Western technology with Indigenous people, not unlike the ostensibly comedic encounter between Nanook and a phonograph in Robert Flaherty's *Nanook of the North* (United States, 1922). This image conveys a defiance to the confines of that hegemonic perspective, though. The cosmic gaze here is not the sole province of White astronomers: this boy, too, has an understanding

Figure 3. A boy in Cayenne investigates a telescope during an 1889 expedition from Britain. Courtesy of the Royal Astronomical Society, ADD 94, no. 49.

of the sky above and its technological mediations, and the photograph, whatever its intent, invites us to think from his perspective. What does he see? Likely just an indistinct blur, given his distance from the lens and the fact that it looks to be broad daylight. Perhaps above all, he sees the mechanism itself—a mechanism about which his feelings may be mixed. Wonder? Frustration? Curiosity? The fact that it is impossible to know undermines the fixity of Haraway's god trick applied to such images. A gaze from "above" never sees all.

Despite the possibilities opened up by such a photograph, Western astronomers, including Eddington and his crew, often failed to view the constellations of earthly politics with the same sensitivity with which they registered the relations between cosmic bodies, writing of Indigenous populations in the same jocular and dismissive tone that they wrote of banana trees and other features of the natural landscape.[31] Political boundaries marked hurdles that had to be overcome for the sake of what they perceived as the universal value of scientific rationalism, and complicated, situated histories were ignored. Bluntly put, the expeditions participated in an apocalypse for Indigenous cultures across much of the world, even if only tangentially and without such an intent. Indeed, recent scholarship on imperial modernity describes this period and the destruction it brought—as it forged the global networks of the slave trade, spread decimating disease, and enacted genocidal violence—as genuinely apocalyptic.[32] This form of apocalypse runs counter to the narratives of world-ending so common in cosmic cinema: consisting of a singular cataclysmic event precipitated by a source beyond human control, the apocalypse has unfolded, and continues to unfold, in ways that are radically unequal and embedded within human systems of power. So many Western cinematic narratives stage the apocalypse as a future and as coming from some external, cosmic threat, and Western knowledge of that cosmos has been premised on perpetuating an apocalypse already brought by imperialism's devastation of Indigenous cultures in Africa, the Americas, and the Global South.[33] The specter of this apocalypse haunts the whole enterprise of Western astronomy's attempts to rationalize space, terrestrial and cosmic, threatening to undo all order.

The science of astronomy was fallible in other ways, too. The photographs Eddington took were famous for pinning down an elusive theory, their creation was frantic and fraught with uncertainties, and the results of his expedition, at first, seemed tenuous. The expedition followed on the heels of several failed ones: in 1901, equipment was badly "mauled" en route, the handle to one camera's shutter broke, and atmospheric tremors blurred the coronagraphs. Another camera yielded "no result," and many of the photographic plates proved to be "unsuited to the climate." Edward Walter Maunder, who headed the team, contracted malaria, delaying his analysis of the remaining photographs.[34] The results of Eddington's first eclipse expedition in 1912 to Brazil were similarly bleak. While he and his crew were the subject of "heaps of newspaper photographs," their own photographs were thwarted by "a regular tropical deluge" that struck just as the eclipse began.[35] Years of preparation and days of rehearsals were washed away with the rain. This heightened the sense of urgency associated with the 1919 Príncipe expedition: Eddington might not have another chance, and he knew just how singular and unreliable this opportunity was. Initially, the results from Eddington's Príncipe expedition too looked dubious. Once again, weather came in the way, clouding the cameras' perspective on the eclipse. In the whir of the moment, even as Eddington and his team sensed that, just as before, everything was going wrong, "we had to carry out our programme of photographs in faith."[36] Eddington described how, in the frenzy, "I did not see the eclipse, being too busy changing plates." Several days later, having developed and measured the majority of the photographs, he bemoaned the faulty weather, which had indeed made most of the plates entirely unusable and forced him to adjust his measurements to account for atmospheric effects. But there was a glimmer of hope: "The one good plate that I measured gave a result agreeing with Einstein, and I think I have got a little confirmation from a second plate." This tentative claim that one, maybe two photographs, taken in faith, might confirm Einstein's far-reaching theory, became the triumphant result that shook the world. Eddington's faith in the mechanism he had so carefully prepared was not misplaced, and the chance of nature was for once on his side.

New Astronomy on Film

In 1914, Eddington gave a public lecture in Perth titled "The Stars and Their Movements" that suggested the usefulness of film for animating the motions of cosmic bodies. His lecture depended on a series of twenty-three still magic-lantern slides, with images ranging from individual stars to nebulae to constellations. Calling attention to the shortcomings of these visual aids, he commented, "We have been trying to form some sort of picture of the dimensions and characteristics of the great stellar universe.

There is yet something to add to it. The picture must be a *moving picture*. All the stars that we used to call *fixed stars* are moving—*visibly* moving," in fact, if one is willing to observe for "a sufficiently long time, say thirty or forty years."[37] This comment reveals two vital roles that cinema could play, although Eddington's talk did not address these directly. First, moving pictures could dispel the illusion of stability that the lantern slides and other still images suggest, bringing cosmic motion to life for the curious spectator. Moreover, cinema had at hand the means to distill the results of thirty to forty years of observation into mere minutes, or even seconds, of screen time, effectively transposing time scales of the cosmos to those of human perception. In translating between these scales, cinema provided a means for bringing esoteric scientific knowledge to a larger public, extending the project of the popularization of science that many scientists themselves promoted through efforts like the Royal Astronomical Society's distribution of astronomical photographs and slides, as well as their own public lectures.

As I have documented so far, astronomers used photography as a tool for measuring the movement of planets, stars, and particularly the sun. For them, it was a mechanism that could help chart the unknown and define cosmic space and time more precisely than ever before, as well as document the places and people they encountered along the way. The mechanism was also imperfect, constantly susceptible to unknown factors like the weather, the human body that controlled it, and technical failures. The sense of cosmic and global uncertainty in the face of global war and shifting regimes of power that lurks in the background of Eddington's photographs emerges more explicitly in films of the period that address Einstein's theory and other contemporary astronomical and astrophysical concepts. As they reinterpret and reanimate astronomers' discoveries, these films hint at the apocalyptic threats of an unstable cosmos.

By September 1922, news of the "Einstein film," referring to a film by German filmmaker Hanns Walter Kornblum about Einstein's relativity, was spreading. The film, which had recently been purchased by Equity Films in the United States, was much anticipated. The U.S. version, soon to be released with added animations by Max Fleischer, was mentioned repeatedly in the press and in motion-picture trade publications. A brief article that month in *Film Daily* reported on the film's scientific relevance. "Edwin M. Fadman, who recently brought over the Einstein relativity film from Europe, has arranged to have the results of the Einstein eclipse expedition cabled to him."[38] An expedition was at that time underway in "the Southern Pacific and in the Australian wilds" to verify the results of Eddington's expedition in Príncipe. The direct line of communication between the members of the expedition and the head of a Hollywood production company lent some kind of assurance that the film, conceived for popular audiences, had real claims to scientific authority.

My discussion of this film and science-education films like it responds to a call for more work in film history that attends to the histories of "useful cinema." Charles R. Acland and Haidee Wasson draw attention to this concept.[39] To Acland and Wasson, "useful" films include those that circulated in places "beyond conventionally defined movie theaters," like "classrooms, factories, museums, community halls, and modes of transportation."[40] Through investigating nontheatrical contexts, they argue, we can unearth an alternative history of cinema's multiple functions that are irreducible to entertainment. Such purposes range "from transforming mass education to fortifying suburban domestic ideals." Building on the work of Acland and Wasson's volume, I want to suggest that the educational and scientific media I consider here draw on and contribute to the most advanced and diverse techniques cinema had to offer. That is, they were useful not just in the ways they implemented cinema to observe and disseminate scientific ideas but also in the ways they recalibrated what cinema was and meant.

Other scholars, including Eric Smoodin, Alison Griffiths, Oliver Gaycken, Devin Orgeron, Marsha Orgeron, and Dan Streible, direct their attention to the history of educational film in particular, considering exhibition spaces like schools, universities, museums, and even planetariums.[41] Furthering their work, I hope to contribute to a more expansive definition of educational cinema as a mobile medium that was not confined to any single exhibition space. The films I analyze were widely screened in diverse contexts, including the multiple spaces in which magic-lantern shows illustrating astronomical phenomena had taken place since the nineteenth century: classrooms, public lecture halls, entertainment cinemas, and even astronomy club meetings.[42] For example, Kornblum's film *The Einstein Theory of Relativity* (*Die Grundlagen der Einsteinschen Relativitätstheorie*, lit. "the principles of the Einsteinian theory of relativity," 1922) premiered in the grand lecture hall of the Physics Institute at the University of Frankfurt am Main and then was released in cinemas before winding its way into classrooms.[43] Thus, these films, like their magic-lantern forebears, were not "educational" in the narrow sense of being confined to classroom use. Rather, their mobility emphasizes that various kinds of audiences, from schoolchildren to science enthusiasts to entertainment seekers, formed a web of science publics, despite their indubitably different stakes in the material. In his history of science film spectatorship in silent-era German cinema, Scott Curtis writes that the boundaries between education and entertainment were quite murky, as cinema negotiated its identity between a medium of mass consumption and a medium uniquely suited to elevate children and the moviegoing public through mass education.[44] Makers of educational films struggled with the need to draw audiences to the theater and the need to satisfy educators.[45] The desire to attract diverse audiences is apparent in the approaches all of these films take to their scientific subject matter. It is also evident in their publicity: for example, *Our Heavenly Bodies* (*Wunder der Schöpfung*, lit. "the wonders of creation," dir. Kornblum, Germany, 1925), was advertised as "the greatest astronomical film of the Ufa-Cultural-Division" and starred several well-known actors and actresses of the period.[46] As they negotiated their genre-defying composition and addressed diverse audiences, these films faced two overlapping concerns: how to register cosmic time and space mechanically, in keeping with cutting-edge scientific theories and discoveries, and how to make cosmic time and space appeal to human responses to a world that felt more precarious than ever, between political tumult and these dramatically disruptive new theories about the universe.

From early in film history, there was a sense of anticipation about the ways film might represent the cosmos. I have already traced how film theorists like Faure and Jean Epstein imagined cinema as a cosmic medium, but this excitement also pervaded discourses about the uses of film for education that appeared in both trade journals and the popular press. In 1911, newspaper tycoon William Randolph Hearst imagined the promise of cinema to provide astronomical education in new, sensational ways that would grip children emotionally. He waxed, "How dull is astronomy as taught to the child today! How beautiful and entrancing it will be taught in the future with moving pictures!" He went on, rhapsodically envisioning how astronomical films could represent the cosmos:

> The child will see on the screen a great blazing central sun, with the masses of fire shooting up. And around this sun will be seen the family of planets, with their rings and moons and strange motions. The flaming comets will fly across the canvas, wiping out the light of the stars as they pass. The birth

and development of the nebulae, the processes that occupy thousands of millions of years, will pass before the eye of the child in pictures prepared by scientific men, fascinating, truthful. With such teaching of astronomy the child at fifteen will be as familiar with the marvelous universe, with the great celestial mechanism which alone illustrates Divine power, as he is today with the details of his father's front yard or the painful dullness of his school room.[47]

He was not alone in this kind of rapturous imagining of film's power to sublimate the banal educational enterprise. Ford W. Eaton, writing in *Motography*, enthusiastically predicted that film would allow students to experience and feel the universe and its vast scales of time and space, rather than just memorizing numbers that convey nothing of the awe of such scales. He wrote that astronomical films of the future would capture the same sense of discovery that prevailed in William Selig's 1912 film *The Coming of Columbus*: "In like manner in the schoolhouse of the future you will sail with the Columbuses of Space and see with your own eyes the million-jeweled panoply of the Pleiades; dive through the abysses of the Milky Way, and swing in a billion-mile circle through the mist-like streamers of the Great Nebula of Orion."[48] He emphasized that one need not leave the earth to have this experience, as cameramen were capable of transporting us across large swaths of time and space.[49] Eaton and Hearst both imagined that film might, through animation and models, facilitate extraterrestrial perspectives, offering a mobile cosmocinematic gaze linked to the language of colonization as well as what Zachary Horton calls "pan-scalar humanism," an impulse to mediate and master the alterity of phenomenally different scales.[50] But to reduce such an expansive gaze to one of simple mastery would be an error: it is a gaze of wonder and, when associated with the new medium of film and the new theories of relativity, a gaze of profound dislocation and vulnerability.

In the films I discuss here, the mission of illuminating scientific discoveries is brought together with a sense of excitement over the medium's own dynamic qualities—its ability to be cosmic and relativistic, not just illustrate cosmic and relativistic ideas. These films include the two German films I have mentioned, Kornblum's *The Einstein Theory of Relativity* and *Our Heavenly Bodies*, as well as the U.S. adaptation of the latter one, also titled *The Einstein Theory of Relativity* (United States, Premier Productions, 1923, animated by Max Fleischer), and two other U.S. films of the same period, *The Milky Way* (dir. Hoey Lawlor, Service Film Productions,

1920s) and *Romance of the Skies* (Bray Studios, 1925).[51] While this is not an exhaustive list of films that loosely adhered to the astronomy-education film genre, the films here are a representative sample. Other astronomical-education films from this period often reiterate the same visual and ideological tropes and draw on a similar array of techniques. Each of these films explains developments in astronomy and astrophysics by connecting them back to questions of earthly time and space. The films furthermore bridge the astronomical questions that drove expeditions to questions of filmic temporality, revealing dreams of manipulating and preserving time that exist both within a scientific (or pseudoscientific) imaginary and in the theory and production of film. As they do, they move between harmonious visions of the cosmos and the globe and visions that were disorienting, fragmented, and in upheaval, alluding to an apocalyptic uncertainty that haunted astronomical explorations of time and space.

The popularity of new astrophysical theories among European and U.S. publics meant that when these films were released, they garnered much more attention than most films designed to educate audiences in the sciences. When the U.S. version of the Einstein film was released in 1923, New York City's Rivoli and Rialto cinemas saw "long lines of patrons actually eager to learn more about this fascinating subject, standing in line during the coldest days of the winter waiting for the theater to open."[52] And when the Amateur Astronomers Association of New York hosted a public screening of a film on Einstein's theory of relativity in 1929, 4,500 people showed up to see the film, causing a riot as they stormed the gates of the Museum of Natural History.[53] The public craved access to the scientific theories that had flooded the news, and these films promised them such access with minimal effort. Particularly when it came to making films that were accessible to these mass audiences, various hurdles stood in the way of simply representing the cosmos as it was or achieving instant access to the "secrets" of the universe for audience members not educated in the sciences. One such problem was that the universe appears, at a human time scale, to be static, with the exception of slight twinkles, the occasional burst of a "shooting star," or, more seldom, a photogenic event like an eclipse. Planets and galaxies at a distance move too slowly for our eyes to detect and thus, in order to be visually stimulating, need to be set in motion via cinematic tricks, including time lapse and animation. Another challenge was that the relatively dim light cast by faraway stars is not conducive to film's fleeting exposure times, so films often relied on charts and artistic renderings. Because these films have to approach their subject creatively in order to represent it at all, they draw on a rich array of visual styles, including animated charts of orbits and trajectories, artistic renderings of cosmic views, stop-motion photography of scalar models, futuristic live-action visions of space travel or reenactments of the past, and explanatory intertitles. As such, their status as documentary-adjacent cinema is intriguing; they at once undertake to represent something of reality and sidestep that ambition for a dose of humor and fun. The archive of scientific knowledge they present is thus by no means that of the omniscient witness imagined as one province of cosmic cinema by the theorists I discussed in the Introduction.

In their oscillation between expository and narrative modes, these films sometimes lose coherence—fittingly, since they are bent on making sense of a seemingly incoherent universe. Scientists did not always approve of the ways these films altered the meaning of Einstein's theory and other astronomical concepts for public consumption. Einstein, for example, was enthusiastic about increasing popular understanding of his theories, and in 1920 he even published a book, *Relativity: The Special and General Theory*, intended to convey his theories to mass audiences. He happily consulted with the screenwriters of Kornblum's film about his theory as they began their project, but when the film was released, he was stern in his disavowal of the final product.[54] A reviewer of Kornblum's *The Einstein Theory of Relativity* commented that the film was "a bit technically uneven," an issue he chalks up to the fact that "the application of suitable trick techniques was only developed and fully realized through the process of production" of the film.[55]

Despite inaccuracies and technical challenges, these films are documents of a pervasive cinematic fascination with the universe and its dimensions. They are wonderfully experimental, employing innovative visualizations of realms that humans had been accustomed to viewing from a fixed position on the earth and within a fixed system of time and space. The films thus make visible not only the excitement and precariousness that new conceptions of the cosmos incited but also the contingency and possibility of the film medium itself. With its diverse representational strategies and its capacity for juxtapositional editing, film could evoke extreme mobility in space and time, achieving, to some degree, the dimensional flexibility envisioned by Eisenstein and the cosmocinematic perspectives imagined by astronomers and film theorists alike. As one reviewer wrote in response to the feature-length astronomy film

Our Heavenly Bodies, "Seldom have the special possibilities of film been exploited as they are here."[56] As they wrestle with these issues of mechanics and of appealing to human experiences, the films point to intersections between astronomical and cinematic conceptions of space and time. The next section of this chapter illuminates the affinities between the cosmos and the cinema that these films evince as they attempt to contain the magnitude of the universe and represent its seeming discontinuities.

Fragmenting and Containing the Universe

In the aftermath of Eddington's confirmation of general relativity, many films that addressed properties and theories of the universe sought to represent the particularization and fragmentation of time and space associated with the Einsteinian concepts of relativity and Eigenzeit. Even films that adhered to old Newtonian models of the universe still betrayed some uncertainties around the cohesion of time and space. The films I discuss here, with their array of visual tricks, were as much a source of perceptual mistrust as an objective lens to overcome it; frequently they play with the idea that the photographic image, too, may not be what it appears. The scenes I discuss here show how these new theories filtered into a popular imaginary that saw the cosmos as both a source of wonder and an existential threat. Notably, along with uncertainties about the universe came a distrust in human perception; if stars were not where they seemed to be, in what other ways were human senses being deceived?

The U.S. Einstein film, *The Einstein Theory of Relativity*, begins by defining the word *relativity* as "the principle of relating one thing to another"—a concept that barely "relates" to Einstein's theory. Expressing a deep concern with comprehending cosmic scales, the film emphasizes that our perception of size, speed, and duration are relative: "The earth is large when compared with the moon . . . but very small when compared with the sun" and "An hour for us may be a century for another planet, and vice versa!" While its engagement with the specifics of Einstein's ideas is in fact only fleeting, *The Einstein Theory* nevertheless provides a glimpse at how his theories permeated and percolated in a wider imaginary, opening up a sense of perspectival, spatial, and temporal mobility that was compatible with film's own transcendent ability to manipulate space and time and reckon with the failures of human perception in the face of cosmic dimensions.

Advertisements for the film consistently invoked the disorienting effects of Einstein's theories (see Figure 4). A full-page advertisement for the film featured in *Moving Picture World* emphasized the ways Einstein's theory thwarted a progressive timeline; according to the poster, directionality in space and time had become meaningless and "everyone's future is behind him." Any moral compass, moreover, was now similarly moot (see Figure 5)—everything was so unhinged from how humans had previously perceived it that there could be "no right or wrong." Playfully, film's own ontology is thrown into question too. "What is a feature?" the ad asks, suggesting that cinematic temporality and nomenclature is also relativistic. The question underscores the fundamental uncertainty of these films' relationship to fiction and documentary, as they turn scientific observation into entertaining feature. What is a feature? Perhaps a good deal of departure from an idealized, objective cosmocinematic gaze.

The Einstein Theory itself thematizes a sense of modern progress based on the technological advances of rational technoscience, but it embraces and even romanticizes the bewildering aspects of such rapid change. The film situates Einstein's theoretical achievement within a slew of scientific and technological developments of industrialized modernity: the steam engine, the automobile, the iron bridge, the train, the skyscraper, the airplane, the telegraph, and the x-ray. Each of these is described sensationally.

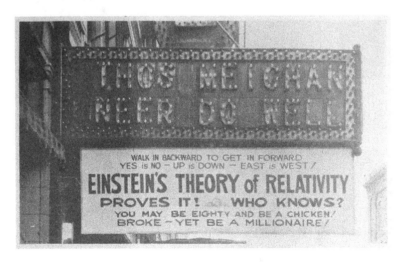

Figure 4. A sign outside the Loew's Palace Theater in Memphis suggests the reversal of reason associated with Einstein's theories. *Moving Picture World*, August 4, 1923, 373. Courtesy of Media History Digital Library.

WHAT IS A FEATURE?

Is it necessarily a 10-reel production—an 8 reeler, 6 or 5?

Einstein's Theory of Relativity tells us that an object's size, weight and importance can only be determined through its comparison with other objects. That's why

EINSTEIN'S
THEORY OF
RELATIVITY

in two-reels is more than a " short " feature. It's a sensational HEADLINER for any program.

Now Playing a Three Weeks Engagement at New York's Rialto Theatre after a week's Premiere at the Rivoli

To be released on

STATE RIGHTS PLAN

For Territorial Rights Communicate with

PREMIER PRODUCTIONS

EDWIN MILES FADMAN, President

229 West 42nd Street, New York City

Telephone Bryant 5421

Figure 5. "Einstein Says": A full-page advertisement that attempts to entice exhibitioners to screen the film as a headliner despite its "relative" brevity. "What Is a Feature?" *Motion Picture Daily*, March 10, 1923, 1,138. Courtesy of Media History Digital Library.

The x-ray is not simply a scientific device, it has "eyes that pierce solids"; the airplane, correspondingly, is "the magic carpet"; the automobile is "the mechanical demon"; and the train is "the thousand league boots." Bursting with a sense of technological accomplishment, the film declares: "The miracles of yesterday are the commonplaces of today." The telegraph and the x-ray are described as "the inventions dealing with the force on which Einstein's theory is based." The film, then, is as much about the sense of the achievements of technological modernity that surrounded the emergence of Einstein's theories as about relativity in particular. The changing conceptions of space and time that resulted from Einstein's theories were understood within a larger cultural shift, as modern technologies brought engines of increased speed and architecture of increased scale.

Each innovation in this film is, moreover, framed as recalibrating human sensation and experience, and Einstein's theory becomes another component of this recalibration. An intertitle proclaims, "To attain these inventions, many obstacles had to be overcome, one of the greatest being the deception of our senses": the x-ray reforms our idea of what is properly invisible, and the telephone muddles our assumption that sounds we hear must originate from proximate sources. Both the extension of vision and the divorce of sound from its origin are also attributes of film, an invention that is implicit in this film's catalog of perception-altering technologies. *The Einstein Theory* makes use of various illusionary cinematic tricks to illustrate how our senses may be deceived: what appears to be a boulder is revealed, with a zoom, to be a small rock in the palm of a hand; a circle that appears white against a black background appears gray against a white one; what appears to be moving forward moves backward relative to a faster-moving object. Relativity similarly requires overcoming sensory deception, the film tells us. Like cinema that draws on these devices of visual deception, these theories do not adhere to intuitive, linear conceptions of time and space.

The representations of cosmic models in educational films of this period more generally also betray the discomfort that surrounded fluctuating conceptions of the globe and its cosmic context in the interwar period. They highlight how Einstein's theory in particular was seen as warping conventional notions of space and time, but a sense of unease permeates explanations of other astronomical and astrophysical concepts as well. For example, *Our Heavenly Bodies* primarily represents a Newtonian model of the cosmos, focusing on the ordered movement of the earth and planets according to the universal principle of gravity and eschewing more complex Einsteinian notions. An early image depicts the earth, with a giant deciduous tree emerging from one hemisphere and a giant palm tree sprouting from the opposite one (a balance that creates a sense of yin-yang-like harmony across the globe), slowly rotating as the moon circles uniformly around it. The film goes on to state that just as the moon circles around the earth, the earth rotates around the sun. A series of animated charts demonstrating this motion—white dotted lines tracing the paths of the orbits—is punctuated by intertitles, in a familiar pedagogical mode characteristic of all of these films.[57] The film projects an image of a rational, unified cosmos operating according to age-old principles. Yet despite its adherence to this ordered model of the universe, this section of the film also includes a bizarre sequence that threatens to unsettle this order. Exiting a merely pedagogical paradigm, the film bursts into live action. The ensuing scene imagines a world without gravity, informing us via an intertitle, "If this force suddenly ceased, nothing could remain on earth." A man who in a previous frame was sitting under a tree, perhaps echoing the apocryphal inspiration behind Newton's theory, suddenly finds himself dangling from one of the tree's branches, legs flailing upward, away from the earth. In order to convey the effects of such an upheaval viscerally, Kornblum draws on film's ability to disorient, its versatile perspective enabling a convincing vision of an impossible upward fall. Shifting visual modes again, now to an illuminated model of the globe, another title informs us that without gravity "the earth herself would burst into fragments," and a striking image of the earth exploding follows (see Figure 6).

While the film then resumes its account of the Newtonian cosmos in which gravity is fully functioning, this image conveys a sense of the earth's precariousness, playfully visualizing the fragmentation that was part of the experience of the globe in the twentieth century. By simulating what would happen without the literal force of gravity to hold the material earth in place, this scene gestures, unconsciously or not, to the metaphorical fragmentation that occurs without Newton's unifying, stable principle to hold the world together conceptually in the wake of Einstein's theoretical intervention. The insertion of this scene also functions as a spectacular display of the medium's mechanical and experiential possibilities—film's own ability to afford us an extraterrestrial perspective and to simulate the absence of gravity at a planetary scale—rather than simply the elucidation of scientific phenomena. But it is also something more: a

Figure 6. The earth explodes without gravity to bind it together in *Our Heavenly Bodies* (1925).

visualization of apocalyptic anxiety that is latent in the cosmos and its cinematic representations.[58]

Close to the end of this feature-length film is another scene that envisions the end of the world, this time in a more prolonged, chaotic sequence that combines biblical prophesies, human melodrama, and scientific models. Having explicated the earth's origins in a more pedagogical vein, the film asks, "And what will be the fate of the earth? Cold death when the sun loses its warming, life-giving power?" Staging astronomical plight as

LIGHTS ALL ASKEW · 51

human melodrama, the film cuts from a black-and-white title frame to a blue-tinted image of a man and a woman staggering through a tundra and dying of cold. It then poses another possibility, claiming that because paths of planets and stars are not permanent, the earth faces the threat of explosion in collision with another planet or star. Emphasizing the calamity to an embodied experience of such an apocalyptic moment, this sequence unfolds discontinuously, both temporally and chromatically. From a perspective remote from earth, much as in the earlier, zero-gravity sequence, we see a simulation of a star hitting a model of the earth, followed by an explosion. The earth is engulfed by a cloud of smoke, suddenly tinted red. This abruptly gives way to an untinted live-action scene staged at an observatory, where people are frantic as they see the star approaching. The image of the star colliding with the model earth then repeats, moving us backward in time as the star approaches again, pre-explosion, this time crosscutting with the scene at the observatory before again staging the collision. Stylistically, this repetition from multiple perspectives also echoes the famous reiteration of the image of the spaceship hitting the moon in *A Trip to the Moon* (dir. Georges Méliès, France, 1902). First, we witness the collision from a distance at which we see the entire moon and then from a closer perspective that allows us to see the contours of the moon's surface and experience the landing from the perspective of a human scale. In both cases, the repetition at different scales serves to heighten the experience of human drama even while contextualizing it within a larger, cosmic space (see Figure 7).[59]

The repetition also gives us the chance to imagine the human drama behind the astronomical event that, when viewed from the perspective of the distant camera's omniscient, alien gaze, appears spectacular but not tragic. The program that was distributed to audiences at theatrical screenings of the film proclaims of this scene, "Thus with merciless candour and logic of science the dark future of the earth is laid bare to us."[60] The idea of science is mobilized here to strike an apocalyptic nerve. The temporal and visual disjunction of this sequence, along with the narrative of demise, intensifies a sense that the universe is both enigmatic and menacing in its indifference to life on earth. The cosmocinematic gaze, in this film, allows the audience to enjoy the spectacle of our own destruction even as we dread it—to experience this destruction both from the perspective of one embedded in the experience of annihilation and from an external, indifferent positionality of the nonhuman extraterrestrial.

Figure 7. People in an observatory watch in horror as a star careens toward the earth in *Our Heavenly Bodies* (1925).

These examples show that as educational astronomy films departed from pedagogical approaches to accepted scientific theories, they often tested the limits of mechanical temporalities and spatialities and attempted to appeal to human concerns about cosmic space and time, giving way to the anxieties of a world on edge after being engulfed by the First World War. But at other moments, the films sought to rein in a sense of the universe as unwieldy and threatening and the earth as vulnerable within it. By representing incomprehensibly great movements with simple charts of motion and anchoring the universe to familiar discourses like scientific rationalism, the films present the viewer with a universe that submits itself to human comprehension. These visions of the cosmos push back against the sense of uncertainty that surrounded popular interpretations of Einstein's theory.

The rationalization of cosmic theories and movements within the visual schema of the cinematic apparatus is one way these films contain a sense of cosmic disorientation. Just as science breaks down the immense universe into a set of interlocking principles and laws that describe all possible phenomena, the "interlocking mechanisms" of the camera and the object on which it focuses can capture and define movements at nearly incomprehensible scales.[61] This harmonious interplay of camera and universe comes through in a pamphlet that was provided to German audiences of Kornblum's film *The Einstein Theory of Relativity*. In it, Kornblum elaborates on the difficulties of registering cosmic scales of time and space and representing relativity's complex temporalities on film. He details the new production techniques demanded by a theory that had similarly demanded new equations and principles to model the cosmos and sophisticated technical mechanisms to prove their accuracy. In Kornblum's description of his setup, there is no trace of the disorienting effects of relativity proclaimed so boldly in advertisements for the U.S. version of the film. Rather, his notes in this program focus on the intricate, precise choreography of human gestures and mechanical motion that allowed the filmstrip to represent cosmic temporalities. It is worth quoting at length:

> When they see the images of the film run past their eyes in their methodical, seemingly self-evident order, the audience can hardly imagine the difficulties that had to be overcome technically. . . . Entirely new methods of filmic representation had to be found . . . in order to make comprehensible the speed of light. . . . New equipment had to be built that permits complicated adjustments of models or drawing with minute exactitude. The production of this film required approximately 80,000 individual exposures in total, with

each exposure differing from the one that preceded and the one that followed it, sometimes by only a tenth of a millimeter. Because 10–20 adjustments had to be made simultaneously between many exposures, the seamlessly moving film comprises a count of more than a million individual manipulations. A whole system of moving belts, whose mechanism runs without a tremor, had to be rigged in order to render the changes in scale demanded.... The preparation of the models and diagrams, calculated down to the smallest fraction of a millimeter, took even longer than the difficult recording process. Thus a film that runs for barely 2 hours before the eyes of the spectator, and that shows him images that appear to have come organically into being in their logical sequence, emerged from one and a half years of belabored work.[62]

The narrative mobilization of Einstein's theory in the film—at least in the U.S. version whose footage has been preserved—dwells on the ways relativity reflects a sense of temporal irrationality. But this description of the process of manipulating the planetary models reveals the highly rationalized temporalities that allowed for the theory's representation. The organic viewing time of the spectator, the belabored production time of the filmmakers, and the condensed cosmic time of actual planetary and stellar motion were calibrated to come together in a seamless harmony.

The reliance on facts and figures also provides a gravitational center to these films, allowing filmmakers to stake claims to scientific knowledge grounded in comprehensible measurement. The films are frequently obsessed with scale, emphasizing the relation between the sizes of various cosmic bodies, the speeds of various trajectories, and the various spans of time over which cosmic events unfold. Lawlor's *The Milky Way*, a short educational film from the United States, exemplifies this fixation on scale, and is in fact almost exclusively a catalog of scales.[63] After summoning us into a familiar cosmos with an intertitle reading "Twinkle, Twinkle, Little Star, How I Wonder What You Are," the informational portion of the film begins, noting where various stars are situated within the Milky Way. To give a sense of scale within the limited frame of the image, an intertitle informs us of how long a train would take to travel from Earth to Venus: fifty-eight years. This trip is animated, with a train slowly moving across the screen—but of course, as much as the interplanetary space is condensed, so too is the time, and only seconds go by before the train arrives at its destination. The film continues by comparing distances and sizes of planets: Jupiter is 51 times farther from the sun than Earth and is 308 times larger than Earth. A trip from Earth to Neptune would take a train 5,055 years and a cannonball 285 years. The film attempts to convey the grandeur of cosmic scales, emphasizing the unbelievable distances and durations the film covers with the use of capital letters and exclamation marks in all intertitles. The sublimity of cosmic magnitude is better captured by fantastic images than a list of numbers, though—which may account for the complete lack of journalistic attention to this film at the time of its release. A study published in the *Transactions of the Society of Motion Picture Engineers* advised, "Explanatory titles, if used at all, should not be painfully exact. . . . Details are wearying," and reactions to films that lingered over such exactitudes bolster this study's conclusions.[64] One reviewer called the portion of the Fleischer film that deals with scale "just a labored exposition of the obvious," a sentiment that seemed to be widely shared.[65] The straightforward recitation of numbers, while reassuring in its reinforcement of categorical knowledge, failed to appeal to more complicated experiential sentiments around space and time.

Other films found more compelling approaches to bolstering faith in the rationalizing force of science. Like astronomical expeditions, many of these films were invested in projecting a positive view of Western scientific rationalism and in placing such rationalism as the orienting center of a modern understanding of the world. The 1925 educational film *Romance of the Skies*, like *The Milky Way*, retains a scientific, objective approach to the universe at its core. The film was part of the Bray educational film series and was included in the *Educational Film Catalog*'s list of astronomy films as late as 1939 (albeit with the note "Old. Authenticity doubted by some").[66] In *Romance of the Skies*, reliance on scientific rationalism becomes a celebration of the totalizing belief system science affords, one that is wondrous and that does not resort to a recitation of numbers. Rather than attempting to impart scientific knowledge, the film posits science as a new kind of religion, replacing earlier modes of human engagement with the universe. In this way, it reinforces the bridge between science and religion characteristic of Newton's cosmic model, which retained the structures of Christian cosmology. Just like monotheistic religion, scientific reason tries to maintain a system of belief that is ordered and coherent, in stark contrast to the ways scientific theory comes to life with the disorientation theorists like Jean Epstein attribute to relativity.[67] Asserting a timeline in which scientific knowledge is the ultimate emblem of progress, an intertitle praises science as the antidote to "prehistoric man's" understanding of cosmic events as religious signs, claiming that "astronomy lifted from man the dread of the unknown." This notion of scientific progress is premised on differentiating science's supposedly objective methods from the mythical narratives of the stars that are relegated to "primitive" man and, on expeditions, local people.[68] The next intertitle announces: "This is the Romance of the Skies—that science can peer into the depths once believed unfathomable, and tell man something of the secret wonders of the Universe." In contrast to "primitive man," modern (presumptively Western) man is "armed with the facts of science." The film thus rejects any sense of the cosmos as unknowable: science is so powerful that it renders our wonder or terror in the face of the unknown universe irrelevant. Instead, science itself is a miracle, and awe is reserved for its unfathomable feats.

In a similar vein, some of these films turn to religion as a coherent center from which to explore a universe that otherwise looms threateningly. In these moments, science as a totalizing belief system resembles religious cosmologies. *Our Heavenly Bodies* in particular draws on both religious imagery and scientific lessons, bringing the two together in an uneasy accord. Notes accompanying the film's screening remark, "Astronomy is perhaps the oldest science in existence and as such it is closely connected to religion."[69] The film stresses these connections. The intertitles often quote biblical verses, even as they serve as the launching point for astronomy lessons. The seventh and final "chapter" of the film, called "Werden und Vergehen im Weltenraum" (Growth and decay in outer space), begins with the verse from Genesis "In the beginning God created the heaven and the earth" and then provides a scientific explanation for the birth of our planet within a larger solar system and galaxy.[70] In a fantastical animation, the film summons the evolution of the solar system out of a spiral of dust, with gravity pulling together debris and forming the dense spheres we recognize as the earth and its fellow planets. This scene provides a visual modeling of a scientifically explicable phenomenon, but it is also a marvelous spectacle, in part because of the immense swath of time that is condensed into mere minutes. Animated time lapse becomes a cinematic mechanism for translating a cosmic timescale to a human one— an impressive condensation of the cosmocinematic gaze's ability to move through deep spatiotemporal registers. It also reveals a primordial time that is almost impossible to fathom, a time before human existence that implies the possibility of a symmetrical time after us. Karl Clausberg writes about how the concept of the time lapse was imagined as capturing the viewpoint of an all-seeing God, who observes history pass on a scale that makes our human timescale seem trivial.[71] The compression of a cosmic scale of time contributes to a sense of being able to access a perspective of the world that may replicate a God's-eye perspective, positioning the cosmocinematic gaze as an omniscient and omnipotent one that shores up a sense of permanence and certainty in the face of apocalypse. *Our Heavenly Bodies,* in setting up this cosmic history with a passage from Genesis, invites us to view this compression of cosmic time as in some way paralleling a godly vision of creation. Here, creating a parallel between the cosmic timescale and a theological perspective on time anchors what might seem dizzying—the scale of time and space represented by the universe—in a familiar Judeo-Christian narrative. Aligning the viewer with that of a creator reasserts the power of human subjectivity—much like the cover of *American Cinematographer* with its extraterrestrial camera looking back at the earth—even as it hints at the pre- and posthuman.

Our Heavenly Bodies tends to resolve into such reassuring, familiar narratives just when it has stirred up a vision of the universe that is out of control. For example, just after the apocalyptic sequence in which a rogue star annihilates the earth, a cheery intertitle tames the audience's fears: "For now, though, the ancient earth stands steadfast, and safely on her, mankind." We are shown a banal scene of farmers in a pasture tending to cows—an image that, especially to a German audience, would have evoked the *Heimat,* or homeland, and all of the familiar, seemingly timeless comforts associated with it. Contradicting the scenes of explosion, terror, and demise, a title tells us, "Above us, though, the stars move in their paths in eternal harmony according to ancient laws." The cosmos is once again restored to a Newtonian model in which everything operates smoothly, predictably, and harmoniously. The film concludes with a passage from a well-known poem by Johann Wolfgang von Goethe: "No being vanishes to nothingness / The eternal pushes on in everything. / Persist in being with delight! / Being is eternal, for nature's laws / safeguard the living treasures / which adorn the universe."[72] We are reassured that eternity is not lost to us: we can and will continue on, even past our individual deaths or the demise of our planet. The film thus draws on astronomical principles while recentering religious rhetoric in the face of apocalyptic dread, assuring viewers of the ultimate benevolence of the universe in which the earth came to be and will be destroyed.

Archives of Light

Throughout this chapter I have referred to philosophical, aesthetic, and technical affinities between chronophotographic media and astronomy.

These affinities are evident in the use of photography to confirm astronomical and astrophysical theories, as well as in films that foreground astronomical temporalities. In sequences that visualize the limits of the speed of light or that seek to render Einstein's theories comprehensible, cosmic and cinematic conceptions of temporality converge. But these sequences also take on cosmic temporalities that move beyond the mechanistic understanding of the cosmos that astronomers often strove for. In addition to restaging the past to convey outmoded cultural and scientific beliefs about the heavens, these films suggest how time itself, in light of new cosmic theories, could be conceived of as allowing for preservation of or movement through the past, bolstering some trace of human history in the face of possible, even inevitable, obliteration. The films manipulate time in ways that align with Eberty's more regimented cosmocinematic imaginary of moving through space to uncover illuminated histories, as well as with the manipulations of time that were associated with the disorienting effects of Einstein's theories. In doing so, these films provide a gateway to the past, both in their reenactments and—because we now view them almost a century later—the glimpse they provide of 1920s engagements with the cosmos. These films thus imagine cosmic voyages that activate deeper pasts. They also reveal the creative visions that unfold at the limits of the philosophical and technical affinities of astronomy and the cinema. Film was not as useful a tool for astronomers as was photography, but these films expose a very human longing for temporal mobility that was projected onto the cosmos and realized in the filmstrip's archives of light. Cosmic time, associated with a quest to understand origins and the path to the present, and to secure some sense of continuity into an unknown and terrifying future, becomes deeply personal. In the conjunction between cosmos and the mechanics of film, a cinematic time emerges that is concerned with bringing the past into the present.[73] These sequences of temporal mobility realize an imaginatively rich cosmocinematic gaze that resembles the backward voyage through archives of light that Faure and Siegfried Kracauer describe.

Toward the end of the U.S. version of *The Einstein Theory*, we are presented with a prime example of how the cosmocinematic gaze opens up to a fantasy of spatiotemporal mobility. A shadowy globe hovers at the right edge of the frame as the years roll by to the left, indicated by a banner of sequential numbers emanating outward in a line: 1920, 1921, 1922 ... (see Figure 8). The earth casts out light, shedding the traces of its history into the sky's archives: the limit of the speed of light means these indexes are always caught in an outward motion, never lost entirely. The film reaches its apex as it envisions the possibility of a retreat through earthly history as it is preserved by light in space. Suddenly a rocket shoots out from the globe, overtaking the light of the passing years. An intertitle declares of the man on the speeding projectile: "Racing forward at tremendous speed, he flies backward through the centuries. He looks behind and finds / His former *Past* is now his *Future*!" The projectile stops only after it has rushed back to 1492, when it turns backward to look at the earth and witness Columbus "in the act of discovering America." This scene's creative take on relativity imagines the possibility of defying the law of temporal irreversibility, taking an excursion through outer space and the earth's past via a spatially and temporally mobile cosmocinematic gaze.[74] Echoing the descriptions of new cosmic theories that appeared in the popular press, here, the boundaries between past, future, and present are eroded, and the measured, progressive flow of years that begins the scene gives way to a dynamic, nonlinear temporality.

Einstein's theory hinges, in actuality, on a constant—a speed, 299,792,458 meters per second—that can never be overcome. A constant is an odd starting place for a theory that was seen as troubling all order. But the theory could not be contained by the scientific community or by scientific reason; its proclamation of constancy became a departure point

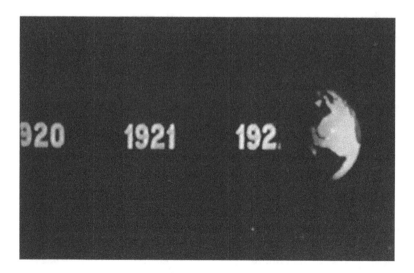

Figure 8. Depiction of the earth casting out the light of passing years in *The Einstein Theory of Relativity* (United States, 1923).

for interpretations that invoked the opposite. This film ignores the constant entirely, propelling its animated projectile right past the speeding light, which is left behind in the trudge of ordinary time. The film, that is, stages what the universe cannot, even as it lays claim to explicating the theory that it sheds in favor of a more comprehensible and creative version of astrophysics.

A similar sequence in *The Milky Way* connects this cosmic form of preservation directly to film's own preservation and reincarnation of the past. The sequence details how light takes its time to travel to various destinations in space: first Alpha, the closest star to the sun, and then farther reaches, including Sirius and the Polar Star. A moving image of a "girl" lighting a cigarette is superimposed over a hovering image of the earth. A dotted line emanates from her cloud of smoke, and we follow it to Alpha, where, in a massive condensation of time on the part of the film, it is now four years later, and the same image of the girl reappears. The ephemeral gesture is repeated, both in the light of the sky and, for the film audience, on the reel of film. This repetition emphasizes the connection between the preservation of human gestures on film and in the cosmos, through which such gestures can be viewed again as if in the present. As viewers of the film a century later, it is easy to imagine that we are simply positioned on a star one hundred light-years away, turning our cosmo-cinematic gaze back to the early twentieth-century United States.

Our Heavenly Bodies, too, has a sequence that imagines travel through space as allowing for backward travel through time, in the process calling attention to the way film plays with time and represents the past. In the chapter called "At the Gates of Eternity," a spaceship that has traveled to a distance four light-years away from the earth connects to an image of earthly happenings via a *Fernseher*—a television of sorts. This screen shows a horse galloping, then suddenly rearing up, and its rider tumbling off. The accident seems unremarkable but takes on an air of historicity when an intertitle informs us: "This took place four years ago! / Indeed: for light, despite its speed of 300,000 kilometers per second, needs ten years to speed through the 95 billion kilometers from earth to here." Here we see an overlap between a futuristic fantasy of space travel and a scientific model of how the past might be accessed. Suddenly, as the spaceship surpasses the speed of light, the scene of the man falling off his horse reverses: the man seems to defy gravity, floating back to his position atop the horse, who gallops backward, receding to the horizon. Another intertitle adds, "Now we are flying at twice the speed of light, so the same light beam that overtook us is now gliding past backwards, and we must see everything in the opposite order. Time is moving backwards for us." In addition to drawing attention to the way light archives time and imagining an impossible trip through this archive, this provides an opportunity to show off the temporal flexibility of film as a medium. Even if a spaceship cannot, in actuality, allow us to view time in reverse, film can. Running the image of an indexed moment from the past backward through the projector allows for its apparent reversal, defying the progressive temporality to which we seem, ordinarily, to be bound. The sequence concludes by describing the "monstrous" distance to which the spaceship has by now propelled itself—3,500 light-years from Earth—"We no longer glimpse the occurrences of the recent past, but rather those from a gloomy prehistory." The past is preserved and documented for the future, but despite the film's staging of time travel, the notion of progress persists in this vision, like that of *The Einstein Theory* with its focus on Columbus's supposed discovery. It is only through the advanced technologies of the spaceship, within the diegesis, or the cinematic mechanism, in the hands of the filmmakers, that this contact with the comparatively gloomy past can occur. This past, which the film stages at several points—with people from the Middle Ages interpreting comets as omens, Babylonians and ancient Chinese constructing observatories, and ancient Greeks tracing the movements of heavenly bodies—consists of "primitive" engagements with phenomena that now, according to this film, have been fully explained by science.

The U.S. version of *The Einstein Theory* operates similarly, elucidating a theory that the film associates with a challenge to universal order and human perception of that order, but settling back into familiar tropes. The trip through history that the film envisions stops at a momentous occasion in Western global colonialism that here serves as a familiar benchmark in the threatening depths of outer space, even as it in fact precipitates an apocalypse for Indigenous peoples of North America. The film thus anchors its exploration of time in a version of the past that complies with a dominant narrative of enlightened European expansion across the passively awaiting globe—a narrative that also, of course, justified the kinds of expeditions in which Eddington participated. In this way, the film staves off for its imagined White, Western audience some of the bewilderment that would result from the complete upheaval of the perception of space, time, and morals that the film attaches to Einstein's theories. It is as if this film wants to tame the cosmos that Einstein's theory might let get out of hand and to subsume his model under an understanding of the universe that replaces uncertainty with certainty, fragmentation with stability, the marginal with the dominant, and even relativity with the absolute. In doing so, this scene alleviates apocalyptic anxieties for its intended audience while erasing the apocalypse wrought by Columbus and the settlers who followed in his wake, thus securing the perpetuity of one version of human history in the face of another and embracing an incomplete cosmocinematic archive. The ghosts that haunt from beyond the frame of "Columbus's discovery," who exist in the dark space cinema has not successfully illuminated, speak of the limits of this archive as it has been incarnated, so far, in celluloid. But even so, the fact that the film offers the chance to return to the deep past via the archive of the cosmos hints at the possibility of a reinterrogation of that past—a reinterrogation that could realize Walter Benjamin's vision of vindicating the victims of history.[75]

The films I have discussed here often suggest aspirations for the global and cosmic harmony that Eddington, an Englishman proving the theory of a German so shortly after the First World War, was credited with creating. Their grounding of cosmic theories in progressive historical narratives and in celebrations of modern technologies and rationalism signals a desire intrinsic to Eddington's effort: to stabilize, to move forward in a linear progression, and to reopen a sense of depoliticized awe of a space beyond human strife. Yet, these films allude to the instability of time and space—and the instability of the earth as a planet in an indifferent universe—even as they shuffle backward to more comforting paradigms. These simultaneous impulses to stabilize and destabilize are also fundamental to the ways these films reflect on cinematic time: film operates, on the one hand, to preserve historical traces for the future and realize the triumphs of progressive modern technologies and, on the other hand, to visualize concepts of temporal manipulability that trouble such progressive narratives. The medium can fluctuate between bringing cosmic temporalities down to earth through mechanical processes and using such temporalities as a starting point to probe human dreams of mobility in time and preservation of the past even beyond the time of human existence. What happens when these dreams become subsumed by political regimes and co-opted for propagandistic causes will be the purview of the next chapter.

2 NEW CONSTELLATIONS

Aerial Cinema in the Second World War

IN A 1946 ESSAY ON THE FRANK CAPRA SERIES *Why We Fight* (1942–45), André Bazin describes with some alarm the scope of wartime documentary filmmaking. He is concerned with "the craze of war reports" that had reached a "cosmic scale," proliferating images and facts with such rapidity and ubiquity that "the days of total war are finally matched by total history."[1] Cameramen were deployed alongside armies, Bazin elaborates, and cameras were positioned in bombers, capturing every movement of the plane and "taking aim" and "shooting" along with the machine guns. Newsreels and a perpetual stream of propaganda films brought this footage to mass civilian audiences, who experienced the war with unprecedented visual access to remote fronts. In this new reality, in which film technologies were increasingly omnipresent and automated in an attempt to bear witness to and document the enormity of destruction, film came close to creating a totalizing vision of earthly history as it unfolded. "We live more and more in a world stripped bare by film," he writes, "a world that tends to peel off its own image." This image recalls Felix Eberty's description of the archives of earthly light being shed into the universe, expanding outward and inviting a cosmocinematic gaze, and the similar image in *The Einstein Theory of Relativity* of the light of past years rolling from the earth and into outer space. Bazin pursues the implications of this cosmocinematic gaze further, however, noting that "hundreds of thousands of screens make us watch, during the news broadcasts, the extraordinary shedding performed each day by tens of thousands of cameras. As soon as it forms, history peels off again." Unlike a passive, uniform cosmic absorption of all of earth's light, the history being shed and stored in the form of wartime films was situated and framed in ways that lent them political agency and made no claim to unbiased witnessing. The cosmocinematic gaze now belonged not to some distant, disembodied onlooker but to any cinemagoer who consumed the sloughed images of recent history.

Aerial footage in particular challenged any romantic vision of an innocent cosmocinematic gaze in another way, linking archives with obliteration: so often, the moment something was witnessed and put on film, it also became a target and was destroyed. Rey Chow writes that by the end of the war, seeing from above was no longer an act of witnessing and archiving but an act of erasing archives—in part by literally decimating what had been seen.[2] Bazin's notion that the world was "stripped bare" by the filmic archives it produced underscores this strange relationship between cinematic preservation and destruction; the very act of archiving on film did violence to the cinematic subject, exposing it at once to light and to the surveillance that entailed. As aerial perspectives abounded in the filmmaking of the Second World War, a cosmocinematic archive of destruction and suffering complicated the cosmocinematic fantasy of time travel through images of earthly splendor, instead recalling Walter Benjamin's angel of history and its implication that all archives serve as evidence of barbarism. Early film theorists' excitement about cinema's capacity to bestow eternal life was tempered with the recognition, voiced here by Bazin, that what was emanating outward was at least in part an archive of violence building to potentially apocalyptic ends.

At the same time that the omniscient gaze from above became tinged by an association with violent surveillance, the sky itself became a site of potential terror, its constellations no longer held at a sublime distance. The whole cosmos seemed filled with apocalyptic dread rather than wondrous potential. Benjamin, writing of the expansion of warfare to the air in the First World War, used imagery of the cosmos being "wooed" down to earth:

> Human multitudes, gases, electrical forces were hurled into the open country, high-frequency currents coursed through the landscape, new constellations rose in the sky, aerial space and ocean depths thundered with propellers, and everywhere sacrificial shafts were dug in Mother Earth.[3]

This imagery only became more potent as warfare by air became central to all theaters of the Second World War.[4] Benjamin's passage echoes the apocalyptic visions of Saint John's Book of Revelation, in which stars are cast down to the earth repeatedly as the world below is decimated: disaster as *dis astro*. With the advent of aerial bombing, lights really were all askew in the heavens, in both astrophysical theory and tangible experiential reality. The cosmos was coming undone. Fittingly, international astronomy was similarly jostled. The International Astronomical Union, which was founded in 1919 at the heels of the First World War to "facilitate the relations between astronomers of different countries where international cooperation is necessary or useful" and "to promote the study of astronomy in all its departments," was dispersed.[5] The Second World War made communication among scientists difficult and in some cases impossible. In the late 1930s, several Soviet members were cut off from the community by their government, and with Germany's invasion of Poland in 1939 and occupation of Holland in 1940, the vice president of the union was imprisoned and the secretary was severed from all communication with those in Allied territories. The union had to move to the Mount Wilson Observatory in California, and it struggled to maintain funding as membership flagged. Astronomical research as a global endeavor that relied on international collaborations was stalled. The scientific projects that thrived were primarily undertaken in the name of individual states and included aerial engineering, the development of radar, medical experimentation in the name of eugenics, and, in Albert Einstein's case, the promotion of research into the potential of nuclear chain reactions to produce explosions at colossal scales.[6] Accordingly, I turn my attention now away from the scientific endeavor of astronomy, instead looking at how cinema engaged with the sky as a new theater of war.

In this chapter, I focus on a number of wartime films from Great Britain that have to do with the sky, flight, and aerial warfare. Whether they take the perspective of an air-bound bomber in flight or give a glimpse of the havoc wrought below, they show how military technologies reshaped the sky as a new site of human vulnerability and menace. At the same time, these films frequently project a sense of the sky as a boundless space filled with possibility, and perhaps even home to the cosmocinematic gaze of some celestial witness—whether benevolent or linked to new and violent technologies of surveillance. A great number of documentary and propaganda films about aerial warfare were made during the Second World War, emerging from the Ministry of Information and the War Office Film Unit, the General Post Office (GPO) Film Unit and its successor the Crown Film Unit, the London Fire Brigade Unit, the Air Ministry Directorate of Public Relations, the Royal Air Force Film Production Unit, and newsreel production companies, including Gaumont British News, Universal News, British Paramount News, and British Movietone News, in addition to commercial film production studios.[7]

Like new astronomy, warfare in the air was an appealing cinematic subject. Filming aerial warfare made use of new technological developments, including the camera gun and other lightweight cameras designed for flight. While aerial action posed a challenge to filmmakers in part because of the tendency toward night raids, not to mention the bureaucratic hurdles involved with filming military action in the midst of war, the ability to capture aerial perspectives exemplified the forefront of technoscientific modernity. Even as they celebrate this technological feat, though, the films I consider here frequently grapple with the need for omniscient, archival media—media that witness, document, and testify—in a world where a God's-eye view is overtaken by a camera gun, seeing at a cosmic distance becomes linked with surveilling to kill, and the world seems to be crumbling. If astronomy of the early twentieth century had to imagine a cosmocinematic gaze turned back to Earth, aerial warfare embodied one complex reality of that perspective.

This chapter responds to a wealth of literature on the aerial gaze and its links to violence. Numerous scholars, including Paul Virilio, Caren Kaplan, Rey Chow, Lisa Parks, and Peter Sloterdijk, consistently demonstrate how the reality of aerial vision as it has been embodied technologically is inextricable from surveillance and violence.[8] These voices echo Donna Haraway's description of the god trick intrinsic to a gaze from above and its association with imperialism and its damaging power. But I also take heed of Paula Amad's call to consider the gaze from above as not just destructive: even in wartime, when it is so closely aligned with militarism, the cosmocinematic gaze is not simply an "all-seeing emblem of power" and violence.[9] It still contains imaginative horizons and possibilities of seeing the planet with sensitivity to human interconnections and the larger natural environment, including that beyond the atmosphere. Aerial perspectives linked to the media of wartime aviation embody the tension between "celestial" and "authoritarian" that Patrick Ellis describes and that is intrinsic to the cosmocinematic gaze more generally.[10]

I have limited the purview of this chapter to Great Britain in order to delve more deeply into the way film production unfolded in one particular and highly influential context, but the burst in production of films about aerial warfare was by no means confined to Britain.[11] Rather, Britain provides a particularly salient example of trends in wartime filmmaking for two reasons. First, it had a strong documentary film culture in the interwar period, which inspired other documentary film movements around the globe. This allows us to see how ideas of documenting and archiving reality, so central to dreams of the cosmocinematic gaze, took shape under institutional, political, and narrative pressures—documentary film, after all, is not simply a neutral look at everything that unfolds, and its institutional and aesthetic history converges often with fiction filmmaking. Second, the British Empire in this period covered a great geographic expanse, and its films projected a strong global imaginary that was often in tension with a countervailing sense of England as an insular culture. This friction makes Great Britain a compelling site in which to explore how films mapped regional identities across various scales, including the cosmic.

The British documentary film movement that provided the training ground and theoretical backbone for many of Britain's wartime filmmakers found its first home in the Empire Marketing Board (EMB). The film unit was formed out of a perceived need to reinforce the ideological cohesion of the extensive economic networks of the British Empire. British documentarians traveled to various outposts in the empire, making films such as *Song of Ceylon* (dir. Basil Wright, 1934), *Cargo from Jamaica* (dir. Basil Wright, 1933), and *Windmill in Barbados* (dir. Basil Wright, 1933) that documented the empire's diverse cultures and depicted "the survival of a traditional way of life side by side with the modern complexity of commerce and labor."[12] In many ways, this documentary film movement was part of the expeditionary culture I described in relation to Sir Arthur Eddington's astronomical voyages in the previous chapter, relying on imperial infrastructures to bolster a specific vision of global order. These filmmakers were thus greatly affected by the restrictions of the war on global mobility. Like scientists, filmmakers also faced new institutional pressures during the war, when leaders became increasingly aware of the power of film to reinforce national ideologies and identities. As scientists became consumed with their contributions to the war effort—or sidelined as government resources were redirected toward the war effort—the documentary movement in Britain also switched gears. Pedagogical impulses that manifested in British documentary earlier in the century, including popular science films akin to those I discussed in chapter 1, were also repurposed to serve the interests of the military.[13] In the process, new debates about film emerged, raising questions about the role cinema could play in terrestrial politics and shifting cosmologies, as well as how cinema should represent the realities of war.

John Grierson, largely regarded as a central figure in the history of documentary film, took the helm at the EMB Film Unit and later led the

GPO Film Unit, conceiving of the units as educational bodies with the power to teach and inform a diverse British citizenry and unite people across divisions of class and nation.[14] In the context of war, Grierson saw documentary as a tool to harness objective real-ity in the service of shaping public consciousness in favor of the war effort. Effective cinema, Grierson wrote in 1942, required an "objective and hard" manner that could instill in the viewer a sense of certainty and purpose.[15] This approach would delve into the realities of industrial modernity and war and forge a totalizing call to action. Meanwhile, Alberto Cavalcanti, who took over as head of the GPO Film Unit in 1937, expressed disdain for this approach to documentary, which to him "smell[ed] of dust and boredom."[16] Arguing that "there is not such a big difference between documentary and feature," Cavalcanti helped to embolden a lasting tendency in the GPO toward "documentary" driven by a fictionalized story or by an associative logic that was closer to poetic reflection than to expository essay or politicized argument. Both philosophies shaped the ways aerial visions were shaped into propagandistic messages and narratives of personal and global violence, healing, and loss during the war. They each correspondingly put pressure on the idea that documentary film could just be an impartial witness of history aligned with an omniscient gaze. Filmic archives of war were carefully crafted to tell specific stories.

The GPO Film Unit was at the heart of these debates about the evolving role of cinema, and documentary in particular, in national and global politics. Before the outbreak of the Second World War, the unit had already established an interest in documenting and explaining the complex technical and industrial tools and systems that characterized modern industrial England, through films like *Night Mail* (dir. Harry Watt and Basil Wright, 1936), *Locomotives* (dir. Humphrey Jennings, 1934), and *Introducing the Dial* (dir. Stuart Legg, 1934). Such films advertise the wonders of industrial modernity in ways that recall the science films I discussed in chapter 1, especially the sequence of *The Einstein Theory of Relativity* that extols the x-ray, the airplane, the telephone, and other modern technologies. During the war, such technological innovation was geared toward military purposes, and the documentary films of the period reflect the pressures of the British Ministry of Information to display such innovations to the British public and its allies, in part in hopes of promoting a sense of optimism about Britain's technological prowess and military might. Wartime documentary films also revealed a new perspective on the world, much as magnifying lenses did in the earlier science films: again and again, films from the interwar period through the end of the Second World War adopt the gaze of a bomber in the sky, a view afforded by new aeronautic technologies.[17] So, just as archives and destruction became linked, so did documentary and the war effort; cinema was associated with violence in multiple senses.

Even with the suspension of astronomical endeavors and the move of pedagogical filmmaking toward the task of solidifying state interests rather than revealing the marvels of nature's cosmic spheres, cosmic thinking did not disappear. Rather, it found new configurations and expressions, new entry points into the popular imaginary and new articulations in science. The kind of rationalization of time and space that astronomical endeavors entailed, which included conceptualizations of the globe and its aerial and cosmic context, continued in new forms as the sky was increasingly militarized. The cosmocinematic gaze, too, persisted and mutated in aerial films from wartime Britain, as did the technical and formal experimentation with space and time in the field of the sky associated with new astrophysics. In this chapter, I turn away from the scientific practices of astronomy and continue to find the "cosmic," more broadly construed, in this set of aerial films. As the camera took to the sky, and Britain's young, enthusiastic group of novice filmmakers experimented with novel forms of filmmaking that expanded documentary and spilled into fiction, new engagements with the cosmos and its dimensions emerged.

In considering filmmaking that spans documentary, quasi-documentary propaganda, and historically situated fiction, I am also thinking through how the realities of filmic archives challenge the idea of a total archive, invoked at the beginning of this chapter by Bazin. Throughout this chapter, I want to demonstrate the entanglements between fiction and documentary filmmaking, both institutional and in terms of how they reflect fantasy and reality at once. Documentary's association with propaganda filmmaking during the war evinces the ways even film that relies on an indexical archive bend truths to privilege certain narratives. Like the projectile in *The Einstein Theory of Relativity*, which zips through history to view Columbus's supposed discovery of America, any film takes a particular lens on historical material that alienates it from the project of total testimony. Yet, this is also what gives film redemptive potential—one can trace a trajectory through archival material that brings to life stories yet untold.

I begin with an analysis of a story-driven semidocumentary propaganda film produced by the GPO, *Target for Tonight* (dir. Harry Watt, 1941). The film was one of several films of its period to move between documentary footage and a loose narrative to promote a particular image of the war for largely British audiences. It features the Royal Air Force (RAF) and demonstrates the reshaping of vision from above that aerial warfare entailed. I conclude with a discussion of two fiction films, *Dangerous Moonlight* (dir. Brian Desmond Hurst, RKO Pictures, 1941) and *A Matter of Life and Death* (dir. Michael Powell and Emeric Pressburger, Eagle-Lion Films, 1946), both of which revolve around the psychological and romantic lives of individual RAF fighters. In each case, I consider how dreams of temporal, spatial, and perspectival mobility expressed in interwar astronomy educational films transformed in wartime, when the sky could seem as much a place of menace as of escape and could be a source of apocalyptic fears. I am further interested in how the cosmocinematic gaze and the appeal to its celestial witness adapted and found embodiment under these conditions, as military forces, exemplified by the British RAF, took hold of cosmic dreams and mobilized them for national—and sometimes transnational—interests.

The wartime films I consider here reckon with a new sense of how people might think of and interact with the cosmos spatially. This change was partly precipitated by aviation, which brought the sky into the sphere of human influence, shrank the globe by decreasing travel times, and made national boundaries more easily surmountable. Lisa Parks writes about the militarization of the circumterrarium, the area of space within which objects can orbit the earth, which has become one of the primary stages for global warfare with the proliferation of military observation satellites and drones. The use of this space, Parks argues, intensifies global disparities even while extending the reach of an individual state's power around the entirety of the globe through surveillance and the possibility of targeted violence.[18] The films I discuss in this chapter provide a glimpse of the prehistory to the occupation of this "vertical space" by drones and satellites that Parks describes.[19] James Hay maps debates around the politics and legal categorizations of vertical space in the early twentieth century, as it became clear that it could come under human influence and control and influence to a new degree. The central question in these debates was whether the sky would function as an extension of the political territory of the country beneath it or be defined as res communis, equally open to the people of any nation-state. Crucially for the air battles of the world wars, the airspace overhead was subsumed under the sovereignty of nations below, making the sky a space of extended geopolitical influence. Outer space, beyond the atmosphere, remained res communes.[20]

New camera technologies like the camera gun linked evolving film technologies with this militarization of the circumterrarium as well. This device consisted of a camera mounted on the wing of a fighter plane that could be triggered by the pilot in order to produce a series of photographs of the plane's targets during an attack. According to a training manual, it was a "gun which instead of firing bullets 'shoots' a series of positions of the target aircraft when in actual combat a gun would be firing bullets. In combat, the camera gun is synchronized to the gun firing button and is automatically set in operation when the pilot opens fire."[21] Thus, the cinematic apparatus was bound up with the mechanics of aerial warfare in addition to its representation.[22] As the sky opened up to the interrelated technologies of flight, warfare, and cinematography, films of the Second World War represented evolving cosmocinematic gazes and perceptions of the heavens.

Before examining how such perspectives were analyzed and narrated within the context of propagandistic documentary and fiction films, it is worth a look at what raw aerial footage from the period suggests about a gaze from above. In addition to many newsreels, documentaries, and narrative films, there exists a sizable amount of footage related to the RAF that was never molded into narratives, providing instead a glimpse into how cameras were used as part of military training, strategy, and self-documentation. The archives of London's Imperial War Museums and the Royal Air Force Museum contain many simple reels of films of planes taking off, looking down, dropping bombs, and landing. While some of this footage found its way into newsreels, propaganda films, and fiction films of the era, the reels in the archives are largely unstructured. There are no voiceovers to direct our vision, just a shaky frame that suggests the precariousness of our aerial vision. Over and over, as I sat in these archives, I watched as the camera focused on some unlabeled patch of earth, releasing missiles onto unspecified targets. I saw flashes of light reminiscent of asteroid belts in science-fiction films erupting spectacularly across the sky and land. If there were people down below, their suffering went unspoken and unwitnessed. The view from above was largely indifferent, responding only to cues of the terrain while allowing little space for imagining the terror of what it might mean to be on the receiving end of these constellations of light. The very existence of these archives reveals the enormous cleft between the cosmocinematic gaze as it was imagined romantically in the early days of cinema and the reality of what archiving from above has entailed, especially in wartime. To view archives of aerial warfare is to take a cosmocinematic perspective akin to that imagined so enthusiastically by earlier theorists of cinema and to witness the absolute partiality of that gaze, its embeddedness within human structures of knowledge, and the link between that perspective and destruction. Caren Kaplan, in her history of aerial perspectives, writes of how limited they actually are: they require "let[ting] go of the desire for totalized vision that requires a singular world, always already legible."[23] Indeed, any image of what lies below is largely illegible, except in its "ephemeral, utilitarian function in military practice."[24] The reels of film are a testament to how such a gaze may nevertheless preserve a partial fleeting past; I see, as they spin on the desk in front of me, what this pilot saw, how this little patch of earth looked from the sky at one brief moment decades ago. But I also witness that moment of preservation as one of annihilation: seeing means bombing, capturing on camera what is moments later blasted to nothingness. Thus the glorious trip through the past that Eberty and Élie Faure envision becomes more wholly spectral, more indelibly marred by loss—an archive of apocalypse at some scale.

As partial and limited as these individual reels of aerial footage are, the expansion of aerial imagery on the whole is associated with an increasingly global imaginary, an awareness of the earth as planet. Within documentary and fiction films, these aerial perspectives were framed in ways that situated the cosmocinematic within a larger context. Viewed from above, and with terrestrial boundaries more easily breeched by air, the earth could be better accounted for at a planetary scale; the interconnectedness and interdependence of nations across the globe was more urgently apparent even as its fragmentation along national lines was starker than ever. In the films I discuss, both the view afforded by the aerial camera and an array of animated maps that leap across scales from local to global reveal this concern with planetary scale. Charles Wolfe, writing on Capra's *Why We Fight*, highlights how the series maps a world that was at once more interconnected and characterized by a sense of "dislocation and displacement."[25] Tracing the ways Capra's films use editing to compress time and space, various kinds of footage to construct meaning, and animated maps to orient, provide historical perspective, and measure and rationalize nations and "zones of combat," Wolfe argues that "the films traded in a particular capacity of motion pictures to construct complex battlescapes defined by sudden shifts of scale, perspective, and time."[26] The films I consider in the remainder of this chapter, which seek to position aerial perspectives within larger narratives of global warfare, draw on a similar visual vocabulary and likewise wrestle with the problem of imagining the globe as a coherent whole at the moment when that coherence seemed threatened on every front. As they do so, they often refer to the cosmos within which this precarious globe is situated.

Narrativized aerial films, wherever they fall on the continuum from fictional to documentary, engage with temporal aspects of the cosmos and those of cinema itself. Rather than embracing a simple, passively observed progressive timeline, they take on temporalities that at times recall Benjamin's constellation, an amalgamation of past, present, and future that is at once apocalyptic and full of potential. They exhibit a renewed investment in questions of origins, the place of the earth and human life in a cosmic order, and of the meaning of afterlife in the wake of physical and spiritual destruction at scales from personal to global. The films raise questions concerning how the traumatic erasure of human memory and destruction of human life associated with the war can be adequately witnessed and archived. Even as propagandistic films present an order in which systems operate according to interlocking protocols and regulations, that order frequently becomes frayed. The soundtracks of these films, their adoption of aerial perspectives, and their use of maps to leap between scales and define territories display how uncertainty, violence, and a sense of apocalyptic anxiety permeated the new visual perspectives and constellations brought about by the mechanisms of war.

RAF on Film: Mapping a New Cosmic Vision

As the Second World War began, the Royal Air Force became a popular topic for British filmmakers, who were fascinated with how the unit navigated two worlds—the seemingly boundless world of the air and the nationalized world of conflict.[27] Since the end of the First World War, air power had developed into an ominous threat. When Britain declared war on Germany in 1939, what would happen in the air was of utmost concern to a nation renowned for its navy and protected from land-bound troops by its insularity. The development of a strong air force became a crucial topic in the eyes of the Air Ministry, which wanted film to bolster the image of the RAF as a formidable entity capable of conquering the German forces. In 1937, the Air Ministry formed a publicity committee aimed at expanding public consciousness of the RAF.[28] In many ways, films featuring the RAF attempt to recuperate a sense of security and stability: audiences are assured that global space is manageable and that the watchful eyes and bold wings of the Royal Air Force are here to ensure and restore that manageability. Much as educational films about astronomy sought to rein in the seeming unruliness of Einstein's theories and the expanding universe with an emphasis on numbers, charts, and scales, the films produced under the supervision of the Air Ministry repeatedly refer to numerical data associated with the scale and activities of the RAF in order to reassure audiences.

In *Target for Tonight,* just as we see how easily efforts at documentary testimony slide into partial and fictionalized accounts, we also see how the cosmocinematic gaze becomes embodied in the form of a fighter jet, and the distanced, omniscient view from above that bears passive witness to great moments of human history is replaced with a situated aerial perspective that, like the raw archival footage, is always partial, often linked with violent intent, and subject to the interference of weapons, shadows, and atmospheric conditions. *Target for Tonight* advertises its ties to the RAF in its opening credits, boasting that it was "filmed with the full cooperation of the Royal Air Force—Music by the Royal Air Force Central Band." Accentuating the authority that comes from such direct access, another frame informs viewers that this is an "authentic story"; every person we see is an actual RAF member going about his "daily life on the job." The film, which follows one flight crew as they bomb a target in Germany and return to their base, focuses on the new relationship to terrestrial space forged through the mapping and bombardment that are the daily work of these men. The opening scene shows us an officer thumbing through a set of aerial photographs of a potential industrial target in Germany. His careful inspection of the photographs using a magnifying glass guides the viewer's interpretation of them, pointing to particular features that indicate the site's strategic importance. In the background, other officers measure and draw on maps and aerial photographs, creating a distinct sense that these images primarily exist to provide topographical data. Far from providing a way of witnessing the progressive unfolding of human history, these snapshots from above are tools for a military machinery, allowing earthly locales to become abstracted into mere targets characterized by specific physical attributes and devoid of any sense of being lived places. This scene is followed by one in which the officer introduces the night's mission to the crew of the bomber *"F" is for*

Freddie. In a moment that underscores the film's own pedagogical aim, the officer points at a screen on which photographs of the target are projected, describing to the crew—and to the film's audience—what they are seeing. We are receiving a lesson in parsing this particular visual field, which needs to be measured and deciphered by those trained to understand it. From there, we watch as the crew takes off, using cues from maps and reconnaissance photographs to locate their target and successfully bomb it before returning home. The image exists as an index of what must be erased—much as cinema as a whole has been conceived as an interplay between presence and absence, time "embalmed" (per Bazin) and therefore always a kind of spectral resurrection.[29]

Much like the images Eddington produced of the eclipse in Príncipe, the photographic images we see in *Target for Tonight* were subject to specific algorithms and modes of analysis to reveal the data they contained. For example, shadows would be analyzed to determine the precise orientation of vertical images, and manuals detailed how to process photographs depending on the weather and other circumstances surrounding their production.[30] Aerial photographs were meant to observe what pilots could not and to establish whether or not bombs dropped or shots fired from the planes had hit their target.[31] They were also used, as in this opening sequence, to determine enemy vulnerabilities and set new targets. Air Council workers were provided with charts that showed what familiar objects would look like from above, and the photographs were plotted onto extant maps in order to highlight differences and expose new trenches or other developments. As a manual from the Air Council outlines:

> In order to accurately make deductions, it is essential that all objects appearing on the photograph shall be recognized. The continued study of aerial photographs under different lighting conditions is therefore necessary, always bearing in mind that objects are viewed from directly above. It is useful to compare well-known objects on the ground with objects in an aerial photograph taken in the same district.[32]

Only in this way could human vision be trained to recognize familiar objects from this new vantage point, as we see in the crew's eventual recognition of their target because of its position relative to a known body of water that is easily seen at night.

The aerial camera thus became a "calculating machine," according to Kaja Silverman, rather than the source of a direct, uncomplicated replication of reality for posterity. Even as the terrestrial landscape below *"F" is for Freddie*'s crew is dissected visually, the decimation of the landscape by the crew's bombs, as in other military aerial footage, occurs without any sense of the human loss unfolding there. As a result, the images only document a sliver of the scene below, despite containing a wealth of information for analysis by RAF crew and their officers. This film thus underscores the abstraction and alienation often linked with a militarized cosmocinematic gaze, which takes on a purposeful, embodied viewing that suggests the limits of any archive from above for understanding lived human history.

In opposition to this mechanized vision of aerial power, *Target for Tonight*'s emotionally charged soundtrack compels us to see the uncertainty and humanity at work in aerial bombardment. The crew's voices, inflected with an array of accents from within Britain, are compelling in their diversity, expressing a sense of coming together across lines of class and geography. The score takes us along on their journey emotionally. As their plane ascends into the sky, and again as it returns to the shores of England, it is accompanied by a thick, romantic symphony of strings and harp that instills a sense of cosmic grandeur. But in the moments of greatest anxiety, as the crew completes its dangerous mission, we are left with the sounds of reality: the nervous hum of propellers, the blasts of bombs exploding below, and the percussive shots fired at the plane by German guns. This anxiety was very real indeed. As director Harry Watt recounts, the shooting of the film was troubled by the fact that "we'd shoot with a boy in the morning and he'd be dead by the afternoon. Of the twenty-four, eventually nineteen were killed, and it was utterly hopeless because there was no continuity."[33] The film tells a commercially viable, highly fictionalized story about the success of the RAF's careful scientific calibration and application of aerial vision.[34] Yet discontinuity is at its heart. Satisfying as it may be to see the bombs hitting their targets, the vision and its accompanying sound recall Benjamin's imagery of the cosmos being lured down to earth. The film hits on two cosmic registers, celebrating aerial power as a cosmic force while conveying the fears of cosmic collapse that surrounded the implementation of this burgeoning force.

Flight, Trauma, and Cosmocinematic Time

As I have suggested, the raw footage of aerial war provides a new kind of cosmocinematic archive, one that is situated, partial, and linked with destruction. Documentary and semidocumentary propaganda films often mobilized this archive to affirm a sense of modern progress leading to eventual triumph. Fictionalized aerial film could examine yet more fully how cinematic time intersected with the new cosmic temporalities this introduced. The two following films that narrate wartime experiences of aviation allow us to see how memory and visions from above were narrativized in this new context. How did cinema—particularly fictional cinema—grapple with its own relationship to archives, memory, and a backward look through history? How were these questions situated within imaginaries of an increasingly uncertain and fragmented cosmos? In the films that follow, we also see how apocalyptic anxiety at a planetary scale is mapped onto the individual scale, with individual psyches reflecting the tumult, rupture, and nonlinearity of apocalyptic time. The figure of the airman, one who is situated among the stars and who looks down at the fires of the earth, provides this window onto the apocalypse as individual mental breakdown.

I focus my analysis here on two films. One, *Dangerous Moonlight* (dir. Brian Desmond Hurst, 1941), was a U.S./U.K. coproduction from RKO British Pictures that screened in both countries leading up to the entry of the United States into the war. The other, *A Matter of Life and Death* (dir. Michael Powell and Emeric Pressburger, 1946), was produced just after the end of the war and was also exhibited widely in both the United States and the United Kingdom. While *Dangerous Moonlight* can be read as making a case for U.S. involvement in the war, *A Matter of Life and Death* might be seen as firming up a global allied vision of democracy at the close of the war. Both films center on the struggles of RAF airmen who fall in love with American women and who straddle two worlds of sorts. In *Dangerous Moonlight*, the film's hero is caught between a world of transnational solidarities that requires him to fight and the insular world of domesticity that removes him from the urgent concerns of his professional life. In *A Matter of Life and Death*, the hero navigates between worlds of fantasy and reality—not unlike the films that form the basis of this chapter—both of which forge certain ideals of transnationalism that aim to make the world cohere in a moment of apocalyptic uncertainty. And in each case, a plane crash, an instantiation of the unpredictability and failure always latent in modern technologies no matter how advanced, precipitates a temporal disjunction that requires the hero to sort through his individual identity within the global and cosmic shifts that are occurring around him, including the push-and-pull between rational order and irrationality and cataclysmic destruction.

Dangerous Moonlight was a box office success in the United States and became a point of reference for subsequent collaborations between the two countries.[35] The influence of propaganda films is strong, from the tone of some of the dialogue about serving one's country, to RAF Film Production Unit footage of air battles and planes overhead. Released in 1941, *Dangerous Moonlight* explores wartime aviation through the fictional story of an individual airman, Stefan (Anton Walbrook), who is a member of the Polish division of the RAF and is also a concert pianist. The story is about duty and heroism and revolves around Stefan's willingness to put his life on the line for the cause of his country and its allies, even though he has an easy way out through his music. After seeing his country bombarded by the Germans, Stefan has joined the RAF to aid in the international effort to defeat the Germans, but he still plays piano by night, accessing a romantic part of himself that is not caught up in the battles of war. The central tension of the film is between Stefan and his American wife Carol (Sally Gray), as she tries to justify his break from military action through her claim that his music does greater good for the morale of the Allied powers than his active military service could do to win the war.

Music plays a crucial role throughout the film. It is a cosmic force, powerfully associated with love—he composes the film's central melody on the night he meets his wife—that draws people across the world together with a common sense of transcendent meaning. The popularity of the score of *Dangerous Moonlight* in Britain and the United States is a testament to the music's unifying power beyond the diegesis, in which Stefan's music inspires everyone who hears it, providing a temporary escape from a world that was in the midst of war. In reviews, the score of *Dangerous Moonlight* received at least as much attention as the film itself, and in the time since the film's release it has been performed and recorded independently multiple times, giving it a reputation of its own.[36] Composed by Richard Addinsell in a style reminiscent of Sergei Rachmaninoff—indeed, Rachmaninoff was Hearst's first choice for the job, but he was unattainable—the score is lush and romantic, with swelling melodies and a close interaction between the solo piano and orchestral string parts that lends a sense of fullness. Addinsell's "Warsaw Concerto," the piece whose melody Stefan composes spontaneously when he meets his wife and that recurs in various iterations at multiple points in the film, was quite popular with audiences. A review of a later recording summed up the piece as "totally irresistible—a juicy compression of everyone's Romantic daydreams into nine minutes."[37]

While not always articulable, there is a persistent link between music —an art form whose emotional effects are at times ethereal or ineffable, seeming to touch a realm beyond human language—and the universe, whose scale and meaning defy human efforts to bring it entirely into the realm of human understanding.[38] Einstein, with his lifelong passion for violin, saw this affinity, writing of Mozart's music that it "was so pure that it seemed to have been ever-present in the universe, waiting to be discovered by the master."[39] Composers and astrophysicists, by such thinking, are engaged in the same task of discovering and bringing out the secrets already latent in the universe. Meanwhile, many of the film theorists whose work I foregrounded in my introduction use musical terms to describe the cosmos that film can evoke. Epstein celebrates the "harmony of interlocking mechanisms" through which film creates a "sort of euphony, an orchestration, a consonance"—a cosmic dance at multiple scales that is undeniably musical. And for Eisenstein, music could provide a contrapuntal "fourth dimension" in film. That is, it could inject space with the dimension of time, contributing to a "mysticism" that also recalls Einstein's theories of the universe.[40] Both scientists and film theorists thus recognize the ways elements of the universe may be evoked through music, musical language, and the purity of musical principles.

In the film's story, music also functions as a distraction from Stefan's other calling, which provides another form of cosmic experience. In an intimate scene in which all music stops and the camera tracks in on his face, luminous in an otherwise dark room, he articulates this experience to his wife, describing the feeling of embodying a gaze from above:

> When I was a flyer it felt like being in another world. There's something so cold and clean up there, and so beautiful too. You come out of the darkness of the clouds to clear bright sun. Underneath are the tops of the high mountains. You are high above them. Sometimes at night you can almost touch the stars. You feel you belong with them. You almost forget that you are fighting a war. It seems so far away. Miles and miles below you.

Despite the fact that his reason for it is inextricably linked to the war, flight allows Stefan to be boundless, to transcend the war and its fraught terrestrial geographies. In that regard, flying occupies a very similar role to that of music. In both his musical and his aerial occupations, Stefan is able to find an escape from the realities that are tearing Europe apart and leaving his homeland in tatters, finding instead a cosmos that unifies mountaintops and stars, individual love and global harmony. Crucially, when Stefan's flying career ends with a dramatic crash, his ability to find wholeness through music is also lost. Music, in the framing narrative that explores the effects of his plane crash on Stefan's mind, is used to express his trauma as well as heroic successes.

In the opening sequence, the score of *Dangerous Moonlight* creates an atmosphere of dissonance and confusion that contrasts sharply with the romantic melody of the "Warsaw Concerto." The scene takes place in London in 1940, after the main action of the film, told as a flashback leading up to this point, has transpired. We learn from a doctor that Stefan has had a complete mental breakdown caused by his traumatic injuries in a plane crash. He sits at the piano, playing jarring and disconnected chords. We see the back of Carol's head as she approaches him at the piano, trying to hum a tune to him, but he is utterly in his own world. Stefan is suffering from amnesia, unable to recall what brought him here or to play the concerto that made him a world-renowned pianist. The film's temporal structure, plunging viewers into this scene in medias res rather than showing us what has brought Stefan to this state, aligns us with his mentality: like him, we experience this moment as unhinged from a rational trajectory and unmoored from the past. Speaking to the doctor, Carol says, "I'd like to know what he's thinking about." At that moment, the camera tracks in on Stefan's face, and the image dissolves into a scene of Warsaw as it is being attacked from the air by the Germans. Time collapses as explosions illuminate the sky, and a crucifix rattles on the wall of a church that is nearly reduced to rubble. The scene spatializes the shambles of the past that Stefan is now experiencing; his memory is lost as his home lies in ruins. Both time and space are dimensions of disorder—hardly the calming vision of the cosmos that characterizes his description of flying before the accident that took away his memory and experience of temporal continuity.

Like music and flight, the cosmos occupies a dual place in the film, at times romanticized and unifying, as in Stefan's idealization of the stars as removed from global conflict, and at times menacing. The title, *Dangerous Moonlight*, suggests this more negative valence of the cosmos, which is revealed in a scene that unfolds at the beginning of the prolonged flashback. In the midst of the air raid on Warsaw into which Stefan's vision dissolves, taking us away from the film's framing narrative, we find him playing piano in an unlit room. Entering his life for the first time, Carol walks into the room, seeking shelter from the action outside. He berates her for having exposed herself to the gaze of the enemy planes overhead:

"It's not safe to be alone when the moon is so bright." Moonlight is thus implicated as complicit in the efforts of enemy aircraft, allowing them to detect movement below and aim at it. Recalling *Target for Tonight* and the darkness in which the landscape below is shrouded, one can understand well the role a bright moon could play in determining the presence of targets below. Harkening back to Bazin's vision of the earth peeling off a film of light at every instant, creating an archive of humanity's violence, here the casting of light is directly linked with the act of violence: an exposure of one's image is an exposure to an aerial eye that is itself a weapon. The moon becomes an ominous cosmic force, providing an avenue for a surveillant and violent gaze. Yet even as it is charged with a role in illuminating people as moving targets, the moon nevertheless retains a hint of the romanticism with which it has so long been associated. The moon's intense light is the justification for the encounter that brings this couple together, as she escapes it by seeking shelter in his parlor, and hovers visibly in the background of this scene, casting a romantic glow. Its importance in this regard is underscored by the recurrence of his line—"It's not safe to be alone when the moon is so bright"—at the conclusion of the film, when suddenly Stefan is released from his altered mental state, regaining his memory, and, most importantly, his ability to play the concerto he composed at this first encounter with his wife. The light of the moon is thus also associated with escape from the realities of war and with a continuous experience of time and space that Stefan regains in accessing this memory again. This ambiguity of the cosmos as alternately romantic and threatening, which resonates with Stefan's experience of the war that is at once romanticized and the source of his psychological breakdown, features in *A Matter of Life and Death* as well.

Michael Powell and Emeric Pressburger's immediate postwar film *A Matter of Life and Death*, in its spirited exploration of the psychological aftermath of one airman's plane crash, expresses the incommensurability of progressive narratives of history, including those so often embraced by military propaganda, and the fragmentation of experience in the midst of war. Here, as in *Dangerous Moonlight*, music plays a significant role. Disjunctions of time are also prominent, conveyed through visual cues—from the alternation between black and white and color, to the freezing of movement—as well as in the script, which frequently refers to the passing and suspension of time. This film is more sophisticated than *Dangerous Moonlight* and benefited from the luxury of having more resources at its disposal, not least the color film stock that enables the visual separation between life and the afterlife in the film's plot. Produced after the war had ended, *A Matter of Life and Death* is able to tell the story of a crashed airman in a way that is more reflective, nuanced, and for the most part unbound by the kinds of moral messages about heroism and duty that pervade most propaganda films, as well as the ultimately sentimental *Dangerous Moonlight*. Perhaps in part as a result of the alleviation of the pressures of conveying such morals, the film opens up more explicitly to cosmic questions, probing the conjunctions of real and imagined worlds and human and cosmic scales at a moment that is globally and personally catastrophic.

A Matter of Life and Death follows the story of Peter (David Niven), who is supposed to have died in a plane crash but survived because the fog masked his fall from the eyes of the heavenly emissary sent to collect him. The film begins by introducing the "two worlds" in which the action unfolds. Over a dark-blue-painted background studded with white dots of stars, scrolling text informs us, "This is a story of two worlds, the one we know and another which exists only in the mind." These two worlds model two competing worldviews, one premised on the primacy of human love that transcends all boundaries and the other on the absolute necessity of temporal and spatial order. When we are first introduced to Peter, he is falling in two senses: falling out of the sky and falling in love with June (Kim Hunter), the young American air-control officer who talks with him over the radio in an emotional frenzy as his plane plummets to the earth. When a messenger from heaven comes to tell him he should by all rights be dead and is defying the order of the cosmos by remaining alive, Peter invokes this love as justification for remaining on the earth. The drama concludes in a trial in which June's tear, ejected outside of time, is admitted as evidence of their love's boundless power, allowing Peter to recover from his traumatic brain injury and rejoin human civilization for at least a while longer.

These two worlds take the viewer on a scalar voyage that ranges from that individual teardrop to the expansive universe. Just after the opening text concludes by telling us we will be seeing the story of a "young airman whose life and imagination have been violently shaped by war," a voiceover begins to describe to us the scale of the universe in which this personal story unfolds and across which the camera is panning. The personal imagination and the cosmic scale of the universe are thus already entwined. To convey this scale, the voice tells us, "This is the universe: big, isn't it? Thousands of suns, millions of stars, separated by immense distances and by thin floating clouds of gas." In a turn that recalls the educational films of the interwar period, the voiceover details what we see—a simple, painted representation of the universe—in more clearly scientific terms.

> The starlight makes the gas transparent, but where there are no stars, it appears as dark, obscuring clouds, like that great black cone over there. Hello! There's a supernova. Someone must have been playing around with a uranium atom. No, it's not our solar system, I'm glad to say. Ah, those are called a globular cluster of stars. . . . And down here . . . it's a massive cluster of gas expanding at thousands of cubic miles a minute.

At the same time, the film's score, which at this point is largely atonal and disconnected, summons up a more ethereal, mystical dimension to the image, guiding us by sonic metaphor through the seeming irrationality of the universe with shimmering tremolos, undefinable pitches, and sudden clangs.

Like the astronomy films of the interwar period, *A Matter of Life and Death* hinges on this tension between the rational and the irrational—between an urge to pin down the universe as a place of stability that operates according to discernible principles, and a terrible sense that everything is precarious and unknowable. The whole story revolves around Peter's experience as he alternates between his continued life on earth, which he owes only to an accident of the atmosphere, and the disruptions in this life that occur as he interacts with those from the afterlife who have come to take him to his rightful place in the heavens. The universe with which the film begins is fully rational, with terminology and numbers to describe its features and scales. Yet a pan across this universe reveals that it contains, spatially, both the rational, external earth and the heaven that exists in Peter's imagination, which, we have been warned, has been "violently shaped by war." The cosmos is at once a product of the imagination and an external entity that scientific observation can record, define, and explain. And bizarrely, the cosmos that we are told is a product of Peter's delusional imagination is an extremely rational one, governed by strict laws, attentive to precise timing. Scenes of this heavenly afterlife are undergirded by a musical score that mimics a ticking clock or that consists of the "Staircase Motif," a piano part with a "remorseless beat," in Powell's words, that looms ominously as it goes up and down a Phrygian scale—it can be no coincidence that scholars of baroque music have identified a consistent link between the Phrygian mode and songs about moral and spiritual condemnation.[41] Played most often in parallel octaves, the left and right hand of the pianist moving in tandem in neither unison nor harmony forbidden by traditional Western music theory, the theme is unsettling and jarring. This is a place where, the voiceover assures us, "there hasn't been a mistake for 1,000 years," a statistic that speaks to an almost spooky regimentation.

Earth, which we see from an objective perspective external to Peter's imagination, seems by contrast to lack the clear moral, judicial, and temporal structure of the imagined heaven. Here, Peter experiences radical discontinuity as the heavenly emissary suspends time, allowing for their tête-à-tête to take place in literally no time at all. As this cosmic messenger, Conductor 71 (Marius Goring), tells Peter, "We are talking in space, not time." This clash of immiscible temporalities—something akin to the timeline-rupturing *Jetztzeit* of Benjaminian constellations—is visualized by the freezing of all other elements of the frame, including other characters not experiencing such a temporal gap, as Peter and Conductor 71 interact. Earth is also freed from the ascetic visual world of the heavens, which is constrained to a black-and-white palette that reinforces a sense of rigidity and discipline contrasting with the lush Technicolor of the earthbound scenes. A comic moment in which Peter awakes the morning after his plane crash to find himself on a splendid beach plays with the sublimity of this earth, which evokes a much more mystical and timeless cosmos commonly associated with the heavens. This beach, on a grand scale that contrasts with Peter's isolated body and is cast in a gentle mist that feels otherworldly, is coupled with the bucolic scene of a naked boy piping a tune as he shepherds his goats, and Peter is convinced that he has died and gone to heaven.

Refulgent as it might be, this earth is also a place where the chaos of war has broken loose. Powell's description of filming this scene tells just how contingent and marred by war this seemingly pristine and eternal setting was. The beach was in fact filled with "unexploded mines, bombs and barbed wire," and the crew was unprepared to begin shooting. Yet the moment was right, and like Eddington capturing a photograph of a solar eclipse just as the clouds began to part, Powell seized the moment at hand. Timing was everything. In his recounting, Powell mentions that that very day Japan had surrendered to the United States, marking a crucial moment in the end of the war. "It was a glorious day," he writes, and his subsequent description conjures an auratic, cosmic vision in which the sky opens up and everything, for just that moment, is right.

I looked at the vast expanse of the Burrows, a wilderness of sandhills stretching for several miles. It had the look of an English August morning, like nothing on earth, which was just as well because David Niven thought he was in Another World. As we stood upon the cliffs above the sands and looked directly down onto where the waves were lazily breaking, we could see the blue sky and the cirrus clouds reflected in this enormous mirror made up of sand and water. "Quick!" I said to Jack Cardiff. "We must shoot at once!"[42]

They jostled to get the equipment set up and Niven into his costume, and like Eddington shooting the eclipse, they managed to preserve an ephemeral moment of sublimity that seemed somehow linked to the end of the war whose traces were all around.

Earth is consequently a space that is susceptible to the eruption of both the sublime and utter apocalyptic destruction, at the scale of the planet and of the individual psyche. In the film's initial introduction to the universe, as the camera takes us closer to our planet, the music becomes more ominous, with a dissonant chord swelling in a long crescendo, which then gives way to the sound of an explosion. From the voiceover's commentary that "here's the earth, our earth, moving around in its place, part of the pattern, part of the universe—reassuring, isn't it?," we move with a crescendo of eerie music to a different cosmic reality: rather than a glowing star, the "point of fire" the voiceover points us to now is a "burning city," freshly raided by a thousand bombers. The cosmos is indeed being wooed down to earth, as Benjamin puts it. The view from above that has carried us through the universe ever closer to the surface of the earth now suddenly becomes obscured by fog; far from being a perspective of omniscient witness, it is hazy, partial, obscured, and, we quickly learn, situated within an aircraft that is itself on fire and plummeting, carrying one dead airman alongside our evidently doomed protagonist. The distanced cosmocinematic gaze barrels down to earth, as vulnerable as any other embodied perspective. The chaos of our transition from intergalactic to earthly is evidenced by the pandemonium of sounds the voiceover encourages us to attend to. The air is as dense with noise as with fog; as we listen, we hear radio broadcasts, beeping signals, humming engines, blasts of bombs, and the urgent voices of pilots communicating with bases. This array of sounds is associated with modern technological progress, but we are exposed to it as a bath of noise, and what is more, as technology on the brink: the sequence concludes with the plane crash in which Peter is supposed to die. Time, too, is unstable in this sequence, far from the steady measure it provides in the cosmic sequences of the film. Quoting a Sir Walter Raleigh poem over his radio to June, Peter says, "At my back I always hear / Time's winged chariot hurrying near; / and yonder all before us lie / deserts of vast eternity." Whether she simply cannot comprehend the poem or the signal is lost in the cacophony of the air, June responds, urgently, "Cannot read you!"

The intermingling between the rational and the irrational that abounds in these scenes is also a confounding of scales, temporal—as the Raleigh quote suggests—and spatial. The human mind is able to summon up an entire cosmos, and as this voiceover suggests (however jestingly), an atom can wreak havoc on a galactic scale. This scalar conflation represents a domestication of the cosmos, or an example of the "panscalar humanism" Zachary Horton describes as an effort to rationalize and contain the alterity of inhuman scales.[43] Rather than the cosmos being subsumed simply into the mind of an individual, the individual mind structures the cosmos according to the mechanization of time that characterizes modern culture, and it places it under a system of governance that echoes those on earth. Edward S. Casey, in tracing a philosophical history of the concepts of space and place in the West, shows how the cosmos has been linked to the personal scale, writing in his concluding remarks, quoting French philosopher Jean-Luc Nancy, that "if 'it is granted to us to see the limitless openness of space,' we shall see it most surely in the undelimited localities of our concrete bodily movements, that is to say, in our most engaged experiences of being-in-place."[44] Indeed, the human body and the universe are often conceived as reflections, extensions, or scalar models of each other. We see this in texts ranging from a description in the Hindu scripture the Bhagavad Gita of the moment when "Arjuna saw the entire universe, divided in many ways, but standing as (all in) One (and One in all) in the body of Krishna, the God of gods"; to Paracelsus's writing of the universe as a kind of bodily extension in *Astronomia Magna: A Philosophy of the Great and the Small World*; to Kant's location of the sublime not in the cosmos itself but in the human mind's comprehension of it.[45] *A Matter of Life and Death* participates in this philosophical legacy, with the cosmos emerging from the troubled mind of a man. Whether fantasy or a reality that simply exists elsewhere in the "real" universe, this entire other world is contained in Peter's mind. The whole of the world is rationalized in a sequence in which Peter's doctor (Roger Livesey) explains away the fantasy in highly technical language as he urges a surgeon to operate immediately. "The x-ray is inconclusive; you'll see in the ocular reports.

Highly organized hallucinations coupled with a sense of smell. Everything points to arytenoid adhesions involving the olfactory nerve in the brain." Peter's mind takes on sublime proportions, while the heavens are reduced to a madman's nightmare. There are notable parallels here to the apocalyptic Book of Revelation: an entire cosmic order emerges frenetically from the mad dream of one prophetic individual. By the logic of the medics in this film, the damage done by war has intercepted Peter's ability to exist in the regular trudge of everyday time, much as the plane crash prevents Stefan in *Dangerous Moonlight* from finding his continuous melody.

Cosmocinematic Time in Aerial Film

In addition to reflecting on the human mind and its divorce from chronology under the duress of war, *A Matter of Life and Death* also revises the cosmocinematic gaze, showing how cinematic perspectives can connect us to the complex and apocalyptic spatiotemporalities of the universe. Perhaps most tellingly, the way the doctor describes Peter's vision, as a "series of highly organized hallucinations, comparable to an experience of actual life," strikingly recalls the cinematic. Just as Peter's "hallucinations" grant him access to another world, the cinema takes us in, allowing us to traverse multiple worlds. When we are first introduced to the doctor who takes on Peter's case, he is in his camera obscura—an optical device associated with both the cinema and the observatory. The device projects the image of the scene outside onto a circular screen in his dark room, lending him an omniscient perspective on the town that resembles the vision from above afforded airmen but vested here with a tenderness toward what he sees that aligns him more with a benevolent deity. June, who has befriended him, comes into his room to tell him about Peter and remarks that she sees he is "surveying [his] kingdom." She remarks on how different it is to see the world from this perspective, and we could take this comment too to remark on the various perspectives, including aerial, provided by film, a device often put in a technological continuum with the camera obscura. Like the mobile vision the doctor accesses through this device, the vision film gives us can seem omniscient and even voyeuristic, and it can pan smoothly across space to give us glimpses of what lies beyond our ordinary field of vision. As the doctor tells June, echoing the cosmocinematic omniscience ascribed to a distant star in Eberty's cosmology, this perspective is exciting "because you see [the town below] clearly and all at once, as in a poet's eye."

The film is also self-reflexive in its dexterous play with time and space that defies the clear order of the doctor's cosmocinematic gaze. Throughout the film, Conductor 71 acts as a more arbitrary deity. In some ways, he plays the role of a film editor, stopping time and resuming it at will. One scene, when Conductor 71 comes to visit Peter and time is suspended for the other characters, is particularly clearly a wink at the audience. As we see June and the doctor stuck midmotion in the background, Conductor 71 points at a pile of books that has fallen to the ground and, with the filmstrip reversing, makes them spring back into place, defying gravity. "After all, what is time?" he says to Peter in the same scene. The answer, it seems in this moment, is that time is a medium that film can manipulate. This comes up again in the film's closing scene, as the court of heaven decides whether or not the budding love between Peter and June is strong enough to warrant his defiance of death. In an amusing moment, the jury realizes it is nearly impossible to gauge this love when the glimpse they are provided of it is entirely static—love, it seems, depends on duration and motion. Inspecting the scene of the doctors and June huddled around Peter's body as he undergoes surgery, which has all the animation of a wooden nativity, a jury member speaks, "There is no reason to deprive ourselves of the dimension of time. The jury feels it would help provide us with a picture of the true conditions." The film releases its cast of characters into motion, and we are reminded of the power of cinema to provide this temporal dimension of witnessing.

The profound temporal mobility and access to varying scales and perspectives of space that we see in this film, as well as the others I have discussed here, suggest a more complex cinematic archive of war than the one Bazin imagined as a constant sloughing off of images of violence. Instead, this set of films provides us with a cosmocinematic archive that connects us dynamically to the pasts it portrays, allowing us, like Peter's jury, to see "a picture of the true conditions"—albeit injected with fantasy, whether under pressures of governments or under the freeing influence of imagination. The films of the various film units that documented the Second World War reflect the ways changing military technologies, and the airplane in particular, affected daily life and global warfare. But they also provide a record of crucial developments in cinema itself, as cameras took to the air and offered new perspectives of the sky and of the earth, and documentary cinema found definition even as its overlap with fiction filmmaking remained strong. If Einstein's theories and Hubble's observations had shaken the scientific foundation of understanding the cosmos, global war and the expanding domain of aerial warfare cemented a sense that the sky had lost its innocence, that lights were askew, and that gazing upward—and imagining a returned gaze from above—could be cause for terror as much as respite. Filmmakers accordingly reckoned with both the medium's new aerial perspective and a pervasive uncertainty about the future of the earth at a planetary scale. By the end of the war, it was clear that scientific rationalism was no guard against cosmic breakdown. The pull between rationalism and its opposite becomes most apparent in *Dangerous Moonlight,* with its simultaneous yearning for cosmic harmony and exploration of disintegration, and *A Matter of Life and Death,* with its alternation between two cosmic visions, one in which time and space are thoroughly rationalized and one in which warfare threatens all order.

When Siegfried Kracauer revised the cosmocinematic imaginary of Faure and Eberty, he envisioned a cosmic look backward that would enable a reinterrogation of history, not an uncritical embrace of past spectacles. Ultimately, this is what the archives of aerial warfare, whether unedited, compiled into propaganda films, or entirely fictionalized, demand. Their testimony to human life on the ground is partial, even tangential, their role as witness restricted by their complicity in obliteration and their political intent. But in the shadows of these films, in their pauses that resist linear time, in their probing of human psychology and all of its messiness, lurk unseen presences that reach across time, haunting and hinting at what can be neither archived nor annihilated, what never reaches illumination and instead persists in the dark matter of the universe. While these absent presences are in the unprobed shadows of archives of aerial footage, in fiction films they are evoked differently. Both *A Matter of Life and Death* and *Dangerous Moonlight* use sound to evoke what lies at the limits of visual representation. Sound, that added "dimension" of film, gropes at the intangible and the unknowable, counterbalancing the objective knowing that pervades the military rhetoric surrounding aerial vision. In *Dangerous Moonlight,* sound stands in for both the universal and its breakdown—trauma and the erosion of memory that cannot be reconciled to standard narratives of progressive history. In *A Matter of Life and Death,* sound betrays the menace and uncertainty that pervade the universe and the air. Both suggest the limits of visual representation, packaged in narratives of any persuasion, to access the reality of what the apocalypse of war means at a human level. As the war came to a close with the shocking detonation of atomic bombs at Hiroshima and Nagasaki, those limits were to be tested anew.

3 DESTROYER OF WORLDS

Cinema of Atomic Experimentation

ON JULY 16, 1945, a group of scientists led by J. Robert Oppenheimer gathered in the aptly named Jornada del Muerto desert in New Mexico to test the experiment they had been working on for the past five years: the world's first atomic bomb. Armed with simulations but never having seen the results of their work, the scientists took measures to document this detonation, known as the Trinity test, in every way they could. It was filmed by multiple cameras serving different scientific purposes, as well as by three newsreel cameras whose footage was intended for mass consumption and has since become iconic. Each camera was nearly six miles from the site of detonation and used varying lenses and frame rates to capture the tests. One such test, filmed at a frame rate of 119 frames per second, presents an image of thick, billowing clouds illuminated dramatically from behind. Slow-motion cinematography reveals the morphology of the forms, whose profoundly elemental quality evokes the wonders of creation. The scientists, when witnessing the initial test bomb firsthand, described a visual force that utterly overwhelmed their senses: they were "completely blinded by the flash"—as if "the whole world was gone up in flames," and then came an "unearthly hovering cloud."[1] A verse from the Hindu text the Bhagavad Gita came to Oppenheimer's mind: "If the radiance of a thousand suns / were burst into the sky, / that would be like / the splendor of the Mighty One. / Now I am become Death, the destroyer of worlds."[2] The atomic bomb had seemingly harnessed the divine power of the cosmos, creative but also spectacularly destructive, and the vision inspired in Oppenheimer a sense of his own godliness. He immediately knew that "the world would never be the same."[3] Remarkably, as scientists began to discuss whether or not to implement the "gadget" they had created, they focused most intensely on the visual impact of the atomic bomb. Oppenheimer wrote that "the visual effect of an atomic bombing would be tremendous," and the other scientists speculated that such an image would serve to incarnate an absolute power in the face of which any enemy could only surrender.[4] There was some discussion of simply filming an atomic test as propaganda to provoke surrender of the Axis: the visual impact alone, some postulated, would be enough to end the war. While politicians soon resolved to use the bomb itself instead of its visual record, this discussion leaves lingering questions about how film could be used to document and convey the cosmic scale and power of the bomb.

Just as the extreme power of the bomb itself entailed a rethinking of warfare and, in the words of secretary of war Henry L. Stimson, a "revolutionary change in the relations of man to the universe," the enormity of the bomb's visual impact demanded new filmmaking techniques.[5] Akira Mizuta Lippit suggests that the "radical visuality" of the atomic explosion's blinding light made it "the last form of light, perhaps, that anyone needed to see."[6] That is, its total annihilation of all visual information into one white flash not only was literally blinding but also triggered a crisis of representation in which earlier visual tactics were insufficient. As I discussed at more length in the previous chapter, the violence of this impact on visual representation also underscores the violence *of* visual representation, particularly through photography and film. Paul Virilio writes of the nuclear bomb as a "*light-weapon*," an extension of both weaponry and photography, whose histories have been entangled in the form of photographic military technologies such as the camera gun and the drone.[7] Harun Farocki probes this connection between technologies of visual documentation and those of war in his 1989 documentary *Images of the World and the Inscription of War*, demonstrating that capturing images has often been a strategy of inflicting or condoning violence. The association between the flash of the camera and the flash of the bomb was historical as well as visual. Filmmakers who wished to overcome this history of violence would have to find strategies of representation that would move markedly away from conventions of a documentary cinema that had been complicit in warfare.

In 1945, the film theorist Jean Epstein—who, in 1926, had written ecstatically that cinema "unites all the kingdoms of nature into a single order, one possessing the most majestic vitality" and "inscribes a bit of the divine in everything"—grappled with the need to rethink what cinema should be in light of the totalizing ruin associated with nuclear bombs.[8]

The bomb's confounding of scalar hierarchies and stark displacement of science as the stabilizing, rational framework it had previously seemed to him necessitated artistic appeals to a "second reason."[9] This reason was fragmentary rather than totalizing, diffuse rather than centered, and disordered rather than systematic. Cinema, with its capacity to traverse different temporal and spatial scales, to upend a sense of normalcy, and to give sensory expression to the uncertainties of the postatomic world, struck Epstein as the prime medium for the postatomic moment, if used well. He argued that filmmakers needed to experiment with the plastic possibilities of the medium to manipulate space and time in order to access this second, alternative reason, inaccessible through traditional representational modes. In 1946, Japanese film theorist Nakai Masakazu wrote similarly of the need for film to respond to the enormous leaps of scale associated with the bomb: "With the help of electron microscopes or telephoto lenses we can even insert our eyes, our film or 'kino-eye,' into the interior of an electron or the structure of a constellation." Film's ability to move across scales and to work against linear time also primed it to represent the postwar human ego, which was itself "dismembered and fragmented in time within the cosmic essence."[10] These ruminations suggest the need for a more dispersed cosmocinematic gaze, working against the omniscience and omnipotence of earlier cosmocinematic positionalities that were now associated with destruction.

The need for new kinds of filmic representation is evident in the footage of the 1945 film *The Effects of the Atomic Bomb on Hiroshima and Nagasaki*, which was used by the U.S. Strategic Bombing Survey to report to the U.S. government the precise impact and residual effects of the bombs on infrastructure, human life, and other life-forms. Withheld from public distribution until the later appearance of some of the footage in the short documentary *Hiroshima–Nagasaki, August 1945* (prod. Erik Barnouw, 1970), *The Effects of the Atomic Bomb* reveals the limits of representability as it works to convey the unfathomable scope of nuclear destruction and the invisible forces of radioactivity that remained in the bombing's wake. Accompanying footage that pans across decimated shells of buildings, which was taken under the direction of Japanese filmmaker Akira Iwasaki, is the commanding voice of an unseen narrator who invokes numbers of lives lost, square miles affected, and buildings destroyed. Animated maps appear, drawing concentric circles around the areas of impact in an attempt to convey the scope of destruction. But many of the effects of the bomb can be neither revealed nor articulated through the cinematic devices at hand. Trond Lundemo writes, "Nuclear radiation is invisible, inaudible, intangible, without taste or smell. This makes it elusive to photographic representation, as the inscription of the radiation is on the vital organs of the body, forming an embodied memory of the bomb."[11] The tension between the bomb's totalizing visuality and the invisibility of its effects is also central to Lippit's conception of "catastrophic light"—light that flashes so brightly and with such obliteration that it leaves only shadows in its wake.[12] In *The Effects of the Atomic Bomb*, we see the camera seeking out traces of radioactivity, probing rocks and wreckage to try to show us what cannot be detected without a powerful magnifying lens— the microscale decay induced by radiation. And even with the voice- over, maps, and images of destruction, the extreme scale of the damage wrought by the bomb defies any totalizing audiovisual accounting. As the somber voice of an off-screen narrator (Paul Ronder) in Barnouw's later documentary tells us, "Near the center, people became nothing. Near the center, there was no sound.... The light of the bomb flashed whiter than any white.... Eyes turned up to the Sun melted." The ultimate experience of the bomb, then, was characterized by the absolute incapacity of the senses to register the scale of what was occurring, and filmmakers were left with the challenge of summoning an emotional experience out of this failure. The images of rubble are unnerving in part because, even as they document the nothingness that the bomb left behind, they bespeak the absence of visual record that can adequately convey what has been lost. Lippit proposes that the atomic bombs dropped on Hiroshima and Nagasaki "threatened to destroy the trace, to destroy even the shadows," citing Jacques Derrida's claim that the possibility of nuclear war "is obviously the possibility of an irreversible destruction, leaving no traces."[13] Jennifer Fay, responding to Derrida, suggests that the threat of nuclear obliteration goes hand in hand with the proliferation of archives, including cinema that bears witness to nuclear violence.[14] This tension between documentation and erasure bespeaks the difficulty of creating an archive of ruin and recalls Walter Benjamin's Angel of History with its backward look at history as a voyage through rubble.[15] Some experimental filmmakers at a postatomic moment sought to use the medium to animate reality without simply documenting and repeating violent acts and historical injustices and without echoing the modes of representation—not least propaganda films—that had supported them. And at the same time, other forms of filmmaking sought to bear witness to nuclear detonations precisely in order to develop their strength as weapons and rhetorical devices.

Two distinct but surprisingly intersecting kinds of experimental filmmaking arose around the nuclear bomb that, I argue, pushed past this representational impasse and provided visible evidence of the magnitude of nuclear explosions in an age Lundemo describes as one "where physical processes elude visual inscription."[16] The first is a mode of scientific filmmaking. Between 1946 and 1962, the United States performed 210 atmospheric nuclear bomb tests, each of which was recorded by an average of fifty cameras to produce a total of approximately ten thousand atomic test films.[17] The U.S. military used film as an experimental device, recording aspects of the explosions that the human eye and other devices could not detect. Drawing on film as a means of documentation and as an experimental tool, atomic test footage is a prototypical light-weapon, its creative vision inseparable from the violence of the bomb itself. Meanwhile, avant-garde filmmakers, including Maya Deren, Bruce Conner, and experimental documentarians Roman Kroitor and Colin Low, integrated nuclear images and undercurrents in their own work, using experimental techniques to alter the ways in which science served as a creative force in contemporary society, in keeping with Epstein's and Deren's visions of cinema's future.[18] In this effort, Deren and other filmmakers did not simply work against scientific endeavors. Rather, they often sought to counterbalance the science that produced the cosmic force of the bomb with imagery that combined scientific and spiritual cosmologies, using theories like Albert Einstein's relativity or the images of planetary motion to express rhythms and temporalities antithetical to that of nuclear apocalypse.

I focus on the period from 1945, when Deren articulated the theoretical thrust of the avant-garde in the United States, to the early 1960s, when, at the time of Deren's death, the avant-garde movement was in full swing in New York, Los Angeles, and the Bay Area. In addition to spanning the arc of Deren's postwar career, this period covers the emergence and decline of Cinema 16 (1947–1963), a central node of the American avant-garde scene; the first atomic bomb detonation in 1945 through the last of the U.S. atomic bomb tests in 1962; and the publication of related commentaries on the pertinence of the plastic or redemptive qualities of cinema to postatomic thinking by Deren, Epstein, and Siegfried Kracauer. This period was also one of immense geopolitical change. My attention to these filmmakers marks a geographical shift from the previous chapter, which centered on filmmaking that emerged from Britain, the dominant global empire of that time. My shift of focus responds in part to the enormous upheaval and reconfigurations of global centers of power in the post–Second World War era. The old order of European colonial expansion across the globe was ending, with new nations declaring sovereignty and imperial governments withdrawing, having been battered by war.[19] At the same time, the influence of the United States, which had dramatically asserted itself as the world's leading military power with its bombings in Japan, was ever expanding. Already, when the war erupted, the center of astronomical sciences had migrated away from Britain to the United States. The International Astronomical Union found a new home in Los Angeles, where Edwin Hubble had made his discovery of the existence of galaxies beyond the Milky Way. The geography of experimental and documentary filmmaking was also migrating, as the avant-garde film movement in Europe had largely faded away around 1931. At that time, the political situation in Europe caused many avant-garde filmmakers—including Alberto Cavalcanti—to join filmmaking groups, especially documentary film units, with more explicitly political goals.[20] In the United States, meanwhile, a group of young filmmakers, influenced by European film movements and staking a space for film outside of Hollywood's commercial structures, began to coalesce. These filmmakers included Maya Deren, James and John Whitney, Douglass Crockwell, Marie Menken, and Mary Ellen Bute. In 1939, as the U.S. nuclear bomb program took shape, John Grierson moved to Canada to start up the National Film Board (NFB), which became a major center of documentary and animated film production with lasting influence. When the war ended and the demand for a regular supply of propaganda films receded, the NFB increasingly provided funding and resources for innovative approaches to filmmaking.[21] Film Unit B, whose activities I will discuss in more detail below, became especially admired for aesthetically inventive approaches to instructional and educational subject matter.[22]

Meanwhile, rising competition between the United States and the Union of Soviet Socialist Republics for political spheres of influence, coupled with the arms race between the two nations, birthed new forms of imperialism. Where the flourishing of astronomy in the nineteenth and early twentieth centuries depended on expeditions that made use of imperial infrastructures, new superpowers used their global networks of influence to bolster scientific experimentation that would in part aid in the assertion of their power. Imperialistic contestations over influence and territory now extended into outer space as well. During the period I consider in this chapter, as the space race took off, satellites were launched into orbit, and preparations were made for the first moon landings, dreams of imperialism were mapped onto space, including through science-fiction filmmaking.[23] Visions of extending human presence beyond the atmosphere were entrenched in nationalist logics and Cold War rhetoric. While of course many scientists continued to work from positions of genuine curiosity and hope for societal betterment, scientific and military images were entangled during this period on the whole, with many branches of scientific inquiry including astrophysics and astronomy increasingly linked, via funding and various by-products of their research, to space race technologies, as well as to ever more destructive weaponry.[24]

Accompanying mainstream images of heroic journeys into outer space came countercultural strains of filmmaking that probed cosmic visions, whether scientific or not, in ways not wedded to the universalizing ideologies of communism or capitalism. As they wrestled with the consequences of the totalizing vision science could produce, the experimental filmmakers I discuss here explored the more generative aspects of current scientific thinking and imagery, as well as its alternatives. The existential uncertainty of the atomic age required a search for new ways of articulating the connection between the personal and the cosmic, and this search entailed a rethinking of scientific inquiry as one among many sets of cosmologies, beliefs, practices, and modes of visual representation. These filmmakers played with the cosmic imagery produced by scientific and military efforts, juxtaposing it with other images to create new associative logics or examining existential questions that opened up terrains of uncertainty within scientific discourse. As they absorbed, reframed, or rearticulated scientific modes of observation and representation, the films I discuss also directly engaged with questions of how film could shape perception, document and manipulate reality, and summon visions of real and imagined phenomena at the microcosmic and cosmic scales whose bearing on phenomena at the human scale had been thrown into stark relief, threatening all order.

Setting the Scene: The American Avant-Garde, 1945–1963

I have chosen to isolate the period of avant-garde filmmaking from 1945 to 1963, though many of the filmmakers whose work I mention continued to make films well after that period. In part, this is because of political bookends that shaped American countercultures more broadly during this time. At the beginning of this period, as I have mentioned, the atomic bomb's detonation fomented new approaches to film as a medium that could express scalar and temporal disjunctions and the moral confusion of the era. By the end of this period, the United States was sending troops to Vietnam, inciting a new wave of countercultural movements. The avant-garde efforts I describe here thus occupy a period of ambiguity: on the one hand, the United States had come out of the war victorious; on the other hand, the specter of the atomic bomb haunted U.S. and international politics. And while the avant-garde scene was certainly robust from the mid-1940s to the early 1960s, it was also still finding its footing. Initially centered in New York, the movement was also taking hold in San Francisco and Los Angeles. This period of expansion, characterized by institutionalization but precariousness nevertheless, is particularly ripe for analysis in relation to the experimental use of cinema to reflect changing views of the cosmos.

Disparate as their ideological intentions and imagined audiences were, the scientific and avant-garde modes of filmmaking I discuss here were both connected through their deep association with documentary filmmaking traditions. Scientific photography and film have been associated with the development of cinematic objectivity and influenced the aesthetics of the Griersonian documentary movement that took shape in England in the late 1920s and 1930s (even as Grierson himself disavowed these earlier films as exposing, rather than revealing, reality).[25] Oliver Gaycken convincingly argues that early science films must be considered in the genealogy of nonfiction cinema and even that they fit Grierson's famous definition of documentary as "the creative treatment of actuality."[26] Furthermore, as Timothy Boon traces, documentary filmmakers under Grierson's influence returned consistently to topics like machines and rational systems, building on a tradition of scientific actuality films made by Charles Urban and British Instructional Films, among others, in the preceding decades.[27] The atomic test films, with their roots in exposing scientific fact and their simultaneous realization of a creative vision, thus share some elements of the history of more canonical documentary film. Avant-garde filmmaking, meanwhile, developed largely in tandem with nascent documentary modes and heavily influenced Grierson and other filmmakers of the 1930s documentary film movement, as has been well established in documentary studies. Bill Nichols in particular demonstrates how documentary developed out of a "modernist aesthetic" of fragmentation and defamiliarization that characterized 1920s and 1930s avant-garde filmmaking.[28] Joris Ivens, writing in 1931, went so far as to suggest that documentary was the only mode in which avant-garde filmmakers could work as they battled "Big Companies" and sought to be the "standard-bearer of cinematographic sincerity."[29] The compilation film, which I will return to in my analysis of Bruce Conner's A MOVIE, exemplifies shared aesthetics and histories of documentary and avant-garde practice, drawing on archival footage to make new meaning out of images of the past.[30]

Experimental cinema also had something in common with scientific modes of experimentation, which were similarly invested in questions of the properties of space and time. Even as avant-garde filmmakers wrestled with the implications of some militarized scientific practices, scientific filmmaking contributed techniques and exploratory and revelatory impulses to the avant-garde. Historian and scholar of avant-garde cinema Scott MacDonald commented to Amos Vogel on the intriguing mix of cinematic experiments represented in Cinema 16's programming, "The only place I can think of where there seems to be a consciousness of science film *as film* is among avant-garde filmmakers."[31] Several historians touch on the interest of avant-garde filmmakers in scientific ideas and images, including William C. Wees and P. Adams Sitney.[32] In 2001, Robert A. Haller curated a film series called *Galaxy: Avant-Garde Film-Makers Look across Space and Time*, for which he wrote a catalog introduction that traces a sense among avant-garde filmmakers that "cinema is a privileged place where this wider, deeper vision of the cosmos can be given full expression."[33] Haller offers a brief overview of cosmic imagery found in films by Oskar Fischinger, Jim Davis, Stan Brakhage, Roman Kroitor and Colin Low, Ed Emshwiller, Charles and Ray Eames, Jordan Belson, Steina Vasulka, Chris Welsby, Monika Pormale, and Bill Morrison. This catalog provides a compelling case for the consistency with which avant-garde filmmakers across the twentieth and early twenty-first centuries have turned to cosmic themes and images. Indeed, the number of avant-garde filmmakers whose work engaged with cosmic themes could be expanded to include John and James Whitney (*Five Film Exercises*, 1943–44; *Yantra*, 1955), Gregory J. Markopoulos (*Psyche*, 1947), Kenneth Anger (*Rabbit's Moon*, 1950), and Marie Menken (*Moonplay*, 1962), among others. Haller stops short, in his piece, of examining the specific textures of these diverse films and the precise ways they take up, distort, reframe, or reject scientific approaches to the cosmos. He describes avant-garde engagements with the cosmos as free of the apprehension that plagued philosophers like Friedrich Nietzsche. These filmmakers, he argues, embrace the cosmos with "curiosity" and a "sense of wonder" characteristic of scientists like Hubble and Einstein.[34] While curiosity and wonder certainly are part of how these films engage with the cosmos, the films' underlying concerns and anxieties merit analysis as well. The entanglement of scientific questions with military ones, and especially the overlapping imagery of nuclear explosions and cosmic images such as films of solar flares, led filmmakers to appropriate scientific cosmologies that were imbued with political force. Recontextualizing scientific research was crucial to the process by which countercultural filmmakers depicted the bombings at Hiroshima and Nagasaki as a culmination of Western rationalism and expressed an urgent need to escape the logic that had led to that calamity.

As I move through my analysis of these films, I also point to new ways the cosmocinematic gaze is manifested. Building on previous chapters, the tensions between documentary as a medium of observation, witnessing, testifying, and preserving, documentary as a medium of persuasion, and other forms of filmmaking that draw on those same practices but without purporting to be documentary are at the heart of how this metaphorical gaze bears out in actual cosmic cinema. If earlier theorists envisioned cinema as cosmic by virtue of inviting an unproblematic trip through linear archives of progressive history, the filmmakers whose work I address here set cinematic cosmoses in motion with less fidelity to the idea of a stable archive or a stable viewpoint, whether looking up or back down, through history or into the future. The cosmocinematic gaze here becomes a way of moving across scales and resisting linearity or totalization, aligning more closely with the discontinuous temporality of Benjamin's "constellation" and taking up Einsteinian relativity as a central ideological and aesthetic influence.

Maya Deren: Visions for a New Cinema

Deren was at the forefront of avant-garde filmmaking in the postwar period in the United States and heavily influenced the movement as a whole. She fostered the work of many other filmmakers of the experimental film movement in the United States, including through her frequent presence at and involvement with Cinema 16 and, later, her founding of the Creative Film Foundation.[35] In addition to making some of the most widely screened and artistically inventive films of the immediate postwar period, she inspired other filmmakers through her theoretical writing about film. Like Epstein, Deren wrote with conviction of the need for a different approach to filmmaking at a moment of cosmic disorder. Her body of writing about film attempts to articulate a new kind of filmmaking that responded to the conditions of the world and universe and departed from the stale narrative conventions of Hollywood fiction. In a passage that refers to her own film *At Land* but speaks to film and narrative more broadly, Deren writes:

> The universe was once conceived almost as a vast preserve, landscaped for heroes, plotted to provide them the appropriate adventures. The rules were known and respected.... Errors of weakness or vanity led, with measured momentum, to the tragedy which resolved everything. Today the rules are more ambiguous, the adversary is concealed in aliases, the oracles broadcast a babble of contradictions. Adventure is no longer reserved for heroes and challengers. The universe itself imposes its challenges on the meek and the brave indiscriminately. One does not so much act upon such a universe as react to its volatile variety.[36]

For Deren, this volatile universe required filmmaking that actively manipulated space and time.[37] The universe no longer seemed to invite an impartial, remote gaze; instead, it could be a platform for spatiotemporal experimentation. *At Land,* she writes, explores "20th century-minded time and space" through the "curious dislocation of the individual in a suddenly and actually relativistic world."[38] The woman at the center of the film cannot cope with the "fluidity" of this world "or achieve a stable, adjusted relationship to its elements." Dislocation and instability are conveyed through a combination of camera movements, repetitions, and the "repeated technique of relating two unrelated places by a continuous movement of the character." Rather than analyzing *At Land* at length, I wish to draw on Deren's account of it to point to the conditions of the world and universe to which she thought filmmakers were compelled to respond. Deren's own aesthetic response was frequently to turn away from the material universe, instead filming her characters in "a world of the imagination" that was independent of the laws that govern the physical universe.[39]

Deren's treatise *An Anagram of Ideas on Art, Form, and Film* contains a gripping diatribe on the necessity of a new kind of filmmaking in a postatomic moment in which many people had acquiesced entirely to the consequences of militaristic scientific innovation, including the mass decimation of human life in Hiroshima and Nagasaki.[40] According to Deren, science had become the dominant creative force in contemporary society, capable of observing and manipulating reality in ways that art had to surpass if it hoped to remain relevant.[41] She describes how scientific developments had, over the course of the past four centuries, reconfigured the cosmos, supplanting the "central, absolute consciousness" of a deity with the figure of the scientist. The scientist, in this conceit, was now godlike, with powers of perception and creation—the ability to change nature in addition to observing it.[42] Though Deren does not single out Oppenheimer explicitly, one can well imagine him as a central figure in such a cosmology, which echoes his own reaction to the detonation of the atomic bomb. The scientific process, according to Deren, imbued the scientist with the power to deconstruct the creations of nature with the help of scientific instruments and then recombine the elemental structures to produce a new, "miraculous" whole that transcended its constitutive elements.[43] Deren uses the atomic bomb as an example of the ultimate reaches of this creative experimentation, culminating in "man's great dream": after isolating atomic particles, the scientist adds them back together in new configurations. "The relationship may be simple—as when water emerges from the interaction of hydrogen and oxygen. But let a third element be added, which transfigures both; and a fourth, which transforms the third—and the difficulties of analysis and creation become incalculable."[44]

Described in this way, the atomic bomb becomes for Deren both a model and the negative impetus behind the new approach to filmmaking for which she advocates. If her imagined stance of a scientist is akin to Élie Faure's or Felix Eberty's cosmic onlooker, that of the avant-garde filmmaker embraces new cosmocinematic possibilities. The paramount calling of filmmakers in the postatomic moment, Deren claims, is to explore thoroughly the unique properties of cinema as a vehicle of temporal and spatial mobility.[45] Moving past Hollywood film's dependence on temporal tropes like flashbacks and parallel action, which only serve to reinforce narrative chronologies, new experimental filmmaking would embrace techniques of genuine temporal manipulation. These include slow motion, which she analogizes to the scientific process: "Just as the telescope reveals the structure of matter in a way that the unaided eye can never see, so slow motion reveals the structure of motion—events that occur rapidly . . . so that they seem a continuous flux are revealed in slow motion to be full of pulsations and agonies and indecisions and repetitions."[46] In her essay "Cinema as an Art Form," Deren remarks on the cosmic sensation slow-motion cinematography can conjure. In the "agony of its analysis," slow motion "reveals in the most casual incident a cosmic constellation."[47] Deren catalogs a range of techniques that can produce sensations of temporal and spatial relativity: time-lapse, the reversal of the filmstrip, spatial disorientation through the stitching together of disparate spaces, and the changing orientation of the camera. Flipping the camera on its head, she notes, allows the subject of the image to appear to defy gravity. This kind of play with film form stands in contrast to the godlike perspective of her imagined modern scientist and to the god trick of other kinds of cosmocinematic gazes.

Deren's 1958 film *The Very Eye of Night*, while chronologically removed from this writing, provides an example of how she integrated her earlier theory into her work with film and goes beyond the techniques listed in *Anagram of Ideas* to test the possibilities of the medium.[48] *The Very Eye of Night* demonstrates how Deren adapted scientific imagery for her own aesthetic purposes, as well as how she used diverse techniques to upend film's narrative propensities and instead reveal its rhythmic, ritual potentials. Rather than dismissing scientific inquiry, she instead allows it to become the platform for a more ideologically pure engagement with the cosmos. In a later lecture, Deren recalls finding inspiration in a film she saw at the Natural History Museum:

> It was a scientific film. . . . It had no pretensions. . . . But here was the moon, and here were the stars, and here were Jupiter, and so on, and all these things in this great black space were revolving. It was really the most beautiful abstract ballet that I've ever seen in all my life. And it was beautiful because the bodies were really related by gravity—they were not falsely related by artistic decisions—the moon came closer or farther for real reasons, not for made up reasons, and therefore the balance of the frame . . . was perfect! The balance of the relationships of all these bodies was at all times perfect.[49]

Deren was drawn to the harmonious planetary relationships she saw in this film and used them as her artistic model. Scientific analysis of cosmic movement became a template for the movement of human bodies in *The Very Eye of Night*. Deren's film, like the scientific one she describes, features white bodies moving in relation to one another against a black backdrop whose depth is not perceptible. The human forms are portrayed in negative, and as Keller remarks, "the actors illuminate the negative filmstrip like stars rising in a night sky."[50]

After an opening credit sequence that introduces each participant in the ensuing dance, the film begins with the chime of a single note on a xylophone set to a black background dotted with bright white stars. As the stars move across the depthless black background, the chime strikes repeatedly at different tones, piercing the silence like the sharp points of starlight. The sequence was critiqued for its simplicity and seeming failure to capture a sense of verisimilitude: "Oh, you can see that those stars are just sequins on a scrim of some kind that are being shakily moved along. . . . It's like a child's little theater," Stan Brakhage quotes audiences as complaining.[51] Yet that simplicity and childlike quality is "exactly the point," according to Brakhage. It captures "a child's vision," rather than attempting to present a replica of actual star movement, and in so doing it makes the cosmos into a ritual space rather than one with specific properties to be observed and measured. Upon this backdrop Deren superimposes dancers, whose movements are optically manipulated to obscure any horizontal, gravitational axis. As the figures dance in orbits that recall the planets, they drift across the frame, propelled by a larger motion they cannot control. Thus Deren incorporates the intricacies of planetary motion—rotations, revolutions, and orbits, all relative, without a singular, constant center—but does not attempt to explain it. Her universe is at once rationally balanced and set free from the constraints of scientific documentary vision.

Atomic Experiments: Test Films and Bruce Conner's A MOVIE

Toward the end of her life, Deren's work drew on a wide spectrum of cinematic devices to operate at a remove from everyday time and space. *The Very Eye of Night*, for example, draws minimally on the indexical quality of film, decontextualizing the human figures from their filmed environment and displaying them in a colorless negative form that depersonalizes and abstracts them. Yet the fact that it was inspired by a science documentary shows that even this film, like avant-garde filmmaking more broadly, was engaged with documentary filmmaking practices. Indeed, the programs of Cinema 16 evince the persistent overlap between the worlds of avant-garde filmmaking and documentary film, including documentary with scientific leanings. One program, from March 1951, included *The Atom Strikes!* (prod. U.S. Army Signal Corps, 1945)—a rather conventional documentary about the effects of the atomic bomb on Hiroshima and Nagasaki that draws on the test footage from the Trinity test of 1945—alongside animated cartoons by the U.S. studio UPA, films of psychological experiments, and an oneiric experimental film by Curtis Harrington.

Atomic test footage, because it combined scientific data with arresting apocalyptic visuals, straddled scientific and artistic experimentation and has been appropriated by numerous filmmakers who have drawn to varying extents on its documentary value. The ten thousand U.S. atomic test films produced between 1945 and 1962 reflect the interconnectedness of avant-garde and scientific efforts, as both experimented with the temporal and spatial limits of film form.[52] Taking the effect of slow motion to its extreme, the cameras used for the atomic test films in this period recorded the explosions at a speed of 2,400 frames per second. This allowed for an event that transpired in one second to be stretched out to over a minute and a half at normal projection speeds. The resulting films are astounding, revealing the striking, beautiful, and fearsome forms produced by the release of unthinkable amounts of energy.[53] As the gargantuan clouds unfurl, one can see precisely what Deren meant when she described the creative force of scientific experimentation, and the footage perfectly illustrates her argument about the cosmic power of slow-motion photography, which exposes something primordial within the spectacle of the bomb's sheer force. But these films, unlike the newsreel footage taken by Oppenheimer's team, were not originally created for their aesthetic merits; they were visual data for scientists to analyze in their work calculating the precise effects of nuclear detonation. William Shurcliff, a scientist who was involved in the U.S. nuclear tests in Bikini Atoll in 1947, recounts how film exposed to scientists the otherwise undetectable properties of the explosions. The extreme speed at which the explosions took place made them difficult to analyze except through the use of slow-motion film, which could capture and display exactly how they unfolded.[54]

The Trinity test films do not just document scientific phenomena; they recall the very essence of cinema as described by early film theorists Epstein and Faure in their ruminations on the cinematic quality of volcanic eruptions. Faure, in 1923, writes of the volcano as a cloud in which "enormous masses of ashes assumed form and became formless unceasingly, all sharing in the modeling of a great sphere and producing an undulation on the surface, moving and varying, but sustained, as if by an attraction at the center, in the general mass, the form and dimensions of which nothing appeared to alter." This provides him with a metaphor for what cinema "doubtless holds in store for us, namely a moving construction ceaselessly reborn out of itself under our eyes by virtue of its inner forces alone."[55] In a cosmic vein not so different from Oppenheimer's reaction to seeing the bomb explode, Faure writes, "It seemed to me as I looked upon this phenomenon that I had grasped the law of the birth of planets, held by gravitation around the solar nucleus." The experience of immensity and totality is stirred within this smaller-scale phenomenon, evoking a cosmic resonance that, to him, is also cinema's calling. Epstein, writing three years later, describes something similar in his account of watching the eruption of Mount Etna: the volcano summons a sense of "absolute power and divine authority," affecting everything from the minute—the leaf on a tree—to the immense sky above.[56] It is in this context that Epstein invokes the cinema in such rapturous terms, writing that it, like the volcano, "unites all the kingdoms of nature into a single order," and "inscribes a bit of the divine in everything."[57] For both Faure and Epstein, properly cinematic imagery is explosive and expansive, evoking cosmic origins and destruction at once, and thwarting any sense of linear scale. The test films have precisely this arresting visual power. Ironically, then, the atomic bomb fulfilled Epstein's early vision of cinematic potential and, in its explicit revelation of the violence of such a totalizing cinematic image, caused him to recoil from that vision, advocating for a new turn in cinema instead—a turn away from the cosmocinematic gaze as an archive of destruction.

Despite their visual sensuality, the atomic test films were a utilitarian tool of visual data for scientists to analyze in their work calculating the precise effects of nuclear detonation. They documented the small-scale data of destruction along with the immense power of those in possession of nuclear energy. Shurcliff describes the intricate process of planning and coordinating the atomic tests, which involved the collaboration of 550 scientists and engineers and thousands more military personnel. Scientific instruments of various kinds were installed on ships and airplanes from which scientists would make their measurements, and among these instruments was an array of photographic equipment. Airplanes were mounted with normal-speed and high-speed motion-picture cameras, as well as gigantic still cameras that required eight camera operators per unit (73). The high-speed cameras were aimed in every possible direction and triggered automatically and sequentially to make a record of the entire explosion from all angles. Shurcliff emphasizes the importance of these high-speed cameras, writing, "The changes would occur hundreds of times too fast for the human eye to notice—even if the eye were not momentarily blinded" (76). Intriguingly, the proliferation of perspectives on the detonations, the use of so many cameras and mechanisms to record this event, belies the totalizing vision the bomb seemed to provide: the cosmocinematic gaze here is in fact a disjointed panoply of gazes.

Nevertheless, Shurcliff contrasts the shortcomings of the human eye with the all-seeing power of the camera to detect the unfolding of a cosmic-scale event. For the test films, the mechanical timing of the camera was carefully calibrated to match the incredible speed at which the visual phenomenon unfolded. Echoing earlier language comparing cinema's timescales to cosmic ones, Shurcliff extols the power of his cameras to capture phenomena that unfold at rates illegible to human perception:

> The rate of growth of the fireball was to be measured principally by cameras. . . . Each of these had microsecond resolution; that is, each could distinguish what happened from one millionth of a second to the next millionth. . . . Each was capable of charting the fireball's development from birth to old age, a total span of only one or two seconds. (78)

This passage evokes the profound disjunction between human timescales and the "life span" of the explosion, which can only be reconciled by the mediation of cameras developed by scientists specifically for this kind of detection. Such cameras enabled scientists to review the explosions at speeds they could register, allowing them to develop a vocabulary with which to describe and categorize the different patterns nuclear explosions followed.

Scientifically advanced photographic equipment was also employed for detecting other aspects of the bomb's effects. Shurcliff explains that underwater cameras documented the impact of the explosion on oceanic fluid dynamics, and photographic emulsion badges, which could detect beta rays, were placed on structures and animals at varying distances from the site of detonation in order to map the zone affected by radiation (82–83). But interestingly, Shurcliff also mentions the integral use of "nontechnical photography" alongside these highly technical apparatuses. He was keenly aware that footage intended to appeal to mass viewership was as important to the purposes of the "expedition" as the scientific footage. "In the Nucleonics Age it is still true that a picture is worth a thousand words," he waxes, and it was vital that "the world at large could see vicariously all that security could permit" (38). Much like Sir Arthur Eddington, Einstein, and other astronomers and astrophysicists of the pre–Second World War period, these scientists wanted their work to be seen and known, and they recognized the power of film and photography to disseminate scientific research in ways that could capture some of the cosmic wonder experienced by those present.

It is clear that Bruce Conner, whose work beginning in the late 1950s returned obsessively to footage of atomic bomb tests, saw something similarly powerful in the image of the bomb. The test films' scientific explorations are also explorations of cinematic possibility in similar ways to those Deren outlines in *Anagram of Ideas*: they exploit and demonstrate film's ability to expand and contract space and time, to transport across scales, and to evoke otherworldliness and cosmic sublimity within a phenomenon enabled by militarized technoscience. Conner, a Midwestern native who had started his art career in New York and whose work was screened frequently at Cinema 16, pursued cinematic experimentation, including with images of nuclear explosions, in ways that departed markedly from the aesthetic and political intentions of the test films. Conner had moved to San Francisco to find more artistic freedom and inspiration, becoming a "representative of a Bay Area counterculture."[58] As he describes the scene in San Francisco, people "stopped going to church, and they stopped believing that the army and the scientists were good guys. . . . The scientists were always inventing something really bad that got out of hand."[59] In using film to comment on this political situation, Conner experimented with new film forms that defied any genre conventions.[60] Like Deren and Jordan Belson, whose work heavily influenced his own, Conner drew, at times, on Eastern cosmologies, seeking an alternative to Western science.[61] The recurrence of mandala images across his films and other artwork is one indication of this persistent fascination. As an artist who worked in various visual media, Conner was also invested in exploring the qualities of film that differentiated it from other arts. He is most known for his compilation films, which edit together archival footage in new and surprising combinations to address, in his own words, "issues of violence in American culture, the objectification of the female body, and nuclear holocaust."[62]

Conner's CROSSROADS (1976), which lies outside of the period I address here but culminates the themes and formal qualities of his work from the previous decades, draws on the very footage Shurcliff and his team used in 1947 to develop this vocabulary, presenting us with an artistic rather than a scientific take on the morphology of the blasts. The ever-morphing and expanding clouds of smoke that follow a nuclear blast had by that point become a leitmotif across his work, including notably A MOVIE (1958) and COSMIC RAY (1961). For Conner, like Oppenheimer, there was a cosmic quality to these images, which were shot through with a mystical power. As Diedrich Diederichsen puts it, the image of the atomic blast "combines overly bright illumination with the reality of the illuminated public and removes light from its abstract role as a filmmaking tool, linking it directly to one of the central aspects of the human condition in the postwar period."[63] Conner's use of the atomic image thus foregrounds the light that is the basis of film's ontology, displaying it as a shock that is at once political and linked to transcendent insight. He seizes the cinematic quality of the bomb and shows that film is an ideal medium for capturing the shadows of the clouds, the bright flashes of the explosion, and the hypnotic morphology of the smoke.

In A MOVIE, which was released the same year as *The Very Eye of Night*, Conner recontextualizes atomic test footage in ways that undermined the seeming absoluteness of the atomic bomb's power and, at the same time, the completeness of any cinematic archive. In doing so, he reconfigures an earlier cosmocinematic gaze by moving through archives nonlinearly, without fidelity to a historical narrative and without any illusion of impartiality or completion. Conner's first foray into film, A MOVIE thwarts expectations of continuity while commenting on the very concept of "a movie." The film begins with his name projected in stark white capital letters for over thirty seconds, accompanied by the frantic, galloping opening to Ottorino Respighi's 1924 tone poem *Pines of Rome*. This sustained frame is interrupted by a cascade of numbered frames typically found at the beginning of a reel of film, followed by a frame declaring "end of part four." We then see a brief clip of a woman undressing, followed by "THE END." A series of found footage clips, including car races, Western cowboy chase scenes, and women carrying fruit in Bali, are punctuated by the repeated title frame, "MOVIE," at first projected upside-down, and, again, "THE END." Only after two supposed endings and the elapsed time of four minutes does the sequence of opening frames appear in its proper order (A / MOVIE / BY / BRUCE CONNER). Conner continues to intercut old footage playfully, for example creating an eyeline match between submarine sailors and a sunbathing woman. And then, as Respighi's march reaches its most suspended, lyrical section, a missile is launched and a mushroom cloud spreads across the frame. It is an eerie moment of visual and sonic beauty that is at odds with the horrifying reality of the bomb's effects. The images that follow undercut the emotion of this moment, depriving the bomb of its power: a surfer continues to surf, visually connected to the water in which the bomb has exploded but clearly at a spatial remove. The disjunction between the image of the bomb and the continuation of images of everyday life visually reinforces Deren's observation that most people entirely ignored the cosmic rupture that the bomb signaled. Conner does not let viewers rest easy, however. The film's next section is haunting, moving back in time to show footage of tanks plowing across battlefields, the *Hindenburg* exploding into flames, and military planes dropping bombs onto targets below, some plummeting to their own demise in the process. As the musical march builds to its dramatic, unrelenting climax, we witness an execution and track across a pit of human corpses before seeing, again, the explosion of a mushroom cloud. We are not allowed to extricate the bomb's majesty from the history of violence of which it was one instantiation. But what happens next is surprising: Conner lets go, where the musical score does not. As the music continues to mount to the end, we are released into the sea, where we see a manatee swimming, a diver exploring, and, as if mercifully, a glimpse of the sun shimmering through the water.

Using precisely the kind of footage so frequently featured in documentaries and newsreels of the Second World War, not to mention *The Atom Strikes!*, Conner tests the limits of the image's testimonial quality. Here, taken out of their historical chronologies, images of human carnage are unnerving simply because they show the brutality of war; no voice-over is needed to convey the horror, no justifying narrative provided to excuse or aggrandize what we see laid bare. Conner would never purport to be a documentarist, and the absence of any narrator, intertitles, or visual cues to explain to viewers what they are seeing defies any documentary conventions. Conner's explicit resistance to chronology—within the structure of the ever-ending film and between its fragments of footage—and geographic leaps also position him firmly outside of any documentary efforts. Nor did he, like Shurcliff, value the military footage for its scientific merit. Yet there is a profundity in his integration of footage that had served propagandistic, informational, and scientific purposes into an entirely different context. The film's resistance to a coherent message testifies to the fragmentary nature of the world more aptly than any documentary could. A MOVIE subverts the earlier test film images by making them speak of the devastation to which they are inextricably bound: the devastation of human life but also of a world that can no longer be made whole—a world that necessitates the fragmentation of time and space. Where scientific experimental films of the atomic bomb used the medium to manipulate time in order to bear witness to its astounding power and to overcome human fallibility and translate phenomena of minute and massive scales to the human eye and mind, the kind of experimental filmmaking in which Conner took part manipulated cinematic time in order to break down any notion of omniscient witness, any simple, disembodied cosmocinematic gaze from above, and take seriously human experiences of time in the atomic age as incontrovertibly disordered, irrational, and at risk—at any moment—of flickering "THE END."

Documentary Experiments

Experimentation with film form and the representation of scientific and nonscientific cosmologies also persisted in the arena of documentary filmmaking. The 1961 film *Universe* (dir. Kroitor and Low, Canada) finds a remarkable open-endedness within a wholly scientific cosmology based on astronomical observation. Rather than seeking to undermine, destabilize, or decontextualize scientific rationalism, Kroitor and Low explore the sometimes-unsettling implications of the truths about the universe that astronomy exposes. In the process, *Universe* also reflects on the temporal vicissitudes of outer space and explores the ways a cosmic cinema, through the footage this film comprises and the amalgamation of the various embodied gazes of the world's many astronomers, allows for a kind of time travel.

Universe follows in the tradition of earlier astronomy education films in that it combines a recitation of numbers in the service of conveying scale with a reflection on how human life figures in an unfathomably large universe. The film is also visually and aurally experimental, drawing on a wealth of cinematic devices—including the film's sonic dimension—to summon a sense of a cosmic realm that threatens with its vastness. And like the earlier science films I discussed in my first chapter, the uncertainties inherent to that realm are balanced by recitations of scientific fact.

Kroitor and Low made the film with the oversight of the National Film Board of Canada, an institution founded by Grierson in 1939 after his departure from England. The establishment of the NFB was predicated on the need to forge a stronger sense of national identity among a populace spread thinly across a large and diverse territory.[64] Grierson was drawn to this country that seemed to him to be unburdened by the weighty tradition of intellectualism in England, and he saw an opportunity to develop a documentary filmmaking center oriented toward public welfare and responding to political necessities. At the NFB, Grierson's style solidified into a "tough-minded realism" that took seriously the intelligence and curiosity of the audiences his films addressed without appealing exclusively to an educated, intellectual class. As in his work for the GPO Film Unit, Grierson encouraged experimentation with technique and style in the service of appealing to and molding the opinions of film audiences. He also strove to face the genuine upendedness of war head-on, which required some stylistic ingenuity. "If our maps look upside down," he wrote, "it is because it's time people saw things in relativity."[65] The exigent situation of war demanded new perspectives on the world, and filmmaking had to adopt new techniques to access such perspectives. Grierson maintained a global outlook on film and politics and insisted on imagining the reconfiguration of transnational politics after the war.[66] His "antiaestheticky fever," which had put him at odds with Cavalcanti in his time with the GPO Film Unit, was countered with a consistent openness to new filmmaking approaches.[67]

Unit B, the NFB group with which Kroitor and Low were affiliated when they directed *Universe*, was known for cultivating aesthetically and formally experimental filmmaking on a wide range of topics. With the high degree of freedom afforded to its filmmakers, the unit produced "sponsored, scientific, cultural, and animated films," and the filmmakers approached its subjects liberally and with a sense of exploration.[68] The confident and "authoritative" voiceover narration characteristic of wartime films was in *Universe* and other NFB films replaced with the more understated and sparing voice of Stanley Jackson, who seemed to pry open questions more than provide answers.[69] After the Second World War, Unit B adopted a style that was more personal and ambiguous than the NFB's wartime films, which had a "didactic expository style" inspired by Grierson's pragmatism.[70] Unburdened of the concerns of the war, the filmmakers could prioritize "aesthetic fulfillment" over the conveyance of information and the shaping of national and transnational identities.[71] This resulted in a pervasive "quality of suspended judgment, of something left open at the end, of something left undecided," in Peter Harcourt's words, in the many films produced by Unit B.[72] Unit B was technically experimental as well, contributing to innovations in lightweight cameras that have been credited with enabling the more spontaneous, less staged documentary style of cinema verité, which was one of the greatest aesthetic movements to emerge from the NFB.

Universe is characteristically experimental. The film required unfamiliar techniques, and at the outset the filmmakers simply did not know how they would shoot certain scenes the planned project required. D. B. Jones reflects on the "adventuresome" process of making the film in the absence of expertise in creating the kinds of cosmic images they needed.[73] One of the workers on the film remarks, "We couldn't say, 'to shoot these solar prominences we'll have to do this and this and this'; we just didn't know yet how to achieve what we wanted."[74] As a result, the film was novel not just in concept but in its technical specifics, much like the educational films of the silent era that had to find new means of cinematic representation to capture their astronomical subjects. Kroitor's interest in scale, evidenced in his eventual founding of IMAX, is apparent in *Universe*, which uses a range of techniques to register the immensity of the universe within a cinematic semiotics. *Universe* begins by creating a visual resonance between the stars in the night sky and the lights that illuminate the city skyline by night. The narrator, with his subtle, probing voice, sets the cityscape in the context of the solar system and universe, destabilizing any sense of anthropocentrism or groundedness in the process. "The ground beneath our feet," Jackson's voice tells us, "is the surface of a planet twirling thousands of miles an hour around a distant sun"—which is only "one out of billions of such stars."

The disembodied voice invites us to see our position as cosmic viewers who participate in a long history of such viewing. When Mars enters the scene, we are told, "This is the planet men have looked on and wondered whether they are alone in the heavens." Rather than merely reciting information, the film thus instills a sense of the importance of the objects of astronomical study to humankind at large; these cosmic bodies connect people across time and space in their call to reflect on otherworldly horizons, whether emotional or material. The voice of the narrator itself opens up to a cosmic register, forming a sense of expansive collectivity beyond the individual astronomer whose daily work frames the documentary's narrative. In this case, the fact that no visible body gives form to the voice allows the narrator to seem to speak from a position beyond individual knowledge, giving voice to the collective call of cosmic questions across the ages and inviting us to share a disembodied, omniscient cosmocinematic gaze. This time, though, that gaze emerges out of a sense of the unknown and unknowable. We share in its vision, but we know we do so from a position of uncertainty, of questioning rather than commanding.

The musical score composed by Eldon Rathburn, who also worked with Kroitor on other films, adds to the sonic dimension, forging transitions from human to cosmic domains and expressing both permanence and ephemerality.[75] The steady beat of a bass drum in many sections seems to correspond to a cosmic pulse of orbits that keep their pace even as other cosmic phenomena, gestured at by more fleeting musical gestures that lack a tonal center, present us with uncertainties. The narrator at times emphasizes the inhospitable nature of the universe and the fragility of human life within it, but at other moments he holds up the hallmarks of scientific practice as a means of steadying an incomplete human grasp of the universe. "With data sifted over countless painstaking observations," the narrator tells us, "astronomers are now filling in the details of a pattern so vast, that everyday distance and time cannot encompass it." The film itself also takes on the task of filling in gaps in knowledge: it takes data provided by scientists as the basis of a visually rich, simulated universe.

Through this process of creating something out of an absence, the film explores the possibilities of cinematic representation and of a cosmo-cinematic gaze, in particular. Where scientific visualization reaches its limits, a cinematic imaginary can take over, extrapolating from data to envision unexplored terrain. For example, in one sequence, the camera seems to sweep across an unending field of stars, then to plunge into a blackness that lies beyond them. Summoning the familiar vision of a cosmocinematic voyager, the narrator tells us, "If we could move with the freedom of a god, so that a million years passed as in a second, and if we went far enough, past the nearest suns, beyond the star clouds and nebulae, in time they would end, and as if moving from behind a curtain, we would come to an endless sea of night. In that sea are islands, continents of stars." Science, of course, had not (and still has not) afforded us the possibility of actually traveling beyond the nebulae. Because of the limit of the speed of light, it would be physically impossible, in the span of a human lifetime, to go any farther than a hundred or so light-years away from Earth. But Kroitor and Low, drawing on scientific speculation and extrapolation, are able to stage this journey—to harness the creative capacities of film to document what has not yet been seen.

Even as the film takes us on an infeasible journey, the narrator makes clear that it is not a flight of fancy: it is backed by scientific observation. "Enough is now known that we can, in imagination, journey into these spaces," we are told, as a spinning replica of the moon, with vivid, accurate contours, comes into view. But rather than situating this gaze within a single viewer, the film makes clear that the vision we witness is the product of a dispersed global scientific effort. The film sets the stage by guiding us into an observatory and watching an individual astronomer—alone in the grandly arcing and hollowly echoing dome of the observatory— prepare for his night's work. Though this lone figure is visually isolated, the narrator provides a more expansive sense of the astronomical endeavor of which he is a part, telling us that at any given moment, "scattered throughout the world," hundreds of men and women are observing the heavens and "gathering data about the universe." Each astronomer gains only a fragmentary view of the universe, with its astounding scope and mind-bending properties. Yet combined, "out of hundreds of thousands of observations" across space and throughout history, "astronomers have pieced together an accurate picture of the universe," the narrator, speaking for the many, tells us, evoking the ritual temporality and dispersed spatiality of astronomical work. The scientific process, as it is articulated here, is not so very different from that of a filmmaker, like Conner, using found footage: it is a process of accumulating glimpses, partial perspectives, pieces of a story of the past, and constituting a cohesive vision of some kind—however precarious the universe revealed to us in the process may be. Astronomy tells a history through the mobilization of an unstable archive—not the simple witnessing of a single viewpoint somewhere in the sky—and through constant experimentation to reveal more about the properties of the universe. Experimental film is entangled with that mission doubly, through metaphor as well as practice. As I have already proposed, the work of the experimental filmmaker can supplement that of the scientist, bringing emotional life to abstract subject matter. And just as an astronomer ideally works to find out more about the universe, an experimental filmmaker strives to reveal more about the properties of film, working at the boundaries of the medium to access new aspects of its ontology. *Universe* closes with a familiar allusion to the deep past to which the universe allows access: "When we look this deeply into space, we are looking at a ghostly image of a distant past. For the light by which we see these regions started traveling towards us long before the dawn of life on earth." Notably, the film understands the partiality of any such cosmocinematic gaze: it is not a transparent, solid look at a known past but a collective effort of constant probing that reveals fragments of an unknown. And as the astronomer gazes into the interstellar archives and studies this ghostly past, audiences watch a film that is an archive of its own, documenting not simply an indexical imprint of the night sky but a creative, solemn cinematic reconstitution of the universe in all of its darkness and wonder.

Barnouw's compilation documentary *Hiroshima–Nagasaki, August 1945*, akin to Conner's A MOVIE, revives and reconfigures archival footage, drawing out alternative meanings latent in those images rather than filming new ones. Because the footage it draws on originated in the immediate aftermath of the war, revisited a quarter century later, it provides a point from which to reflect on that earlier period. Like Kracauer's viewer on a distant star reviewing the earthly past, this film provides the exilic, cosmocinematic perspective on reality that can only come into focus at a remove. It gives viewers the chance to travel back in time and see the reality of what transpired, fulfilling Nakai's call for a cinema that could "ignite our historical consciousness" by bringing the present into direct contact with the past.[76]

Hiroshima–Nagasaki, August 1945 makes use of the scientific survey footage that had previously been compiled into the three-hour documentary *The Effects of the Atomic Bomb on Hiroshima and Nagasaki*, but it reorganizes the footage to show human experiences of the bomb and radiation instead of cataloging their effects. For the earlier film, Akira Iwasaki, under supervision of the U.S. Strategic Bombing Survey, had led teams of filmmakers to document the effects of the atomic bomb on city infrastructures, plant life, and human life. Footage had been compiled to emphasize "detailed scientific observation," using "scientific data-gathering" as its "supervisory guiding principle."[77] As a result of its scientific usefulness, the footage was confiscated from Japan and kept for inspection by U.S. scientists studying the atomic bomb, rather than being used to reflect the experiences of people in Japan affected by the bomb, as Iwasaki would have preferred. Barnouw and his team, who had uncovered the footage in the National Archives after its declassification, sought to organize it in a way that would reflect how the bomb had affected human beings, their lives, and their bodies.[78] The filmmakers tried different configurations of the footage before settling on the final version, a "quiet, 16 minute film with a factual, eloquently understated narration."[79] The result is a documentary whose stark difference from the earlier film comprising the same footage reveals just how much editing alters the kind of testimony archival images can provide. Like avant-garde films, *Hiroshima–Nagasaki, August 1945* is deeply experimental and not intended as an objective record. It extends further the postwar efforts of avant-garde filmmakers to rethink the relationship of cinema to scientific observation and revelation, as well as to the concept of a historical archive that is mobile and manipulable rather than simply an accumulation of chronological time.

Countering the data-driven scheme of the three-hour documentary produced for the U.S. Strategic Bomb Survey required a new, creative approach. While Barnouw hoped to construct a film that spoke directly to the effects of the bombings on human beings, the footage he encountered in the archive was primarily of "ruins in grotesque formations."[80] He and his team were at first frustrated with how overwhelmingly impersonal these images were. One can imagine the trouble of having to construct an archival documentary out of images that primarily show ruins. Barnouw's version includes many shots of rubble, which play a paradoxical role of documenting annihilation—of preserving the nothingness left behind by an utterly destructive force. *Hiroshima–Nagasaki, August 1945* relies heavily on sound to summon an emotional dimension that lends meaning to the images of devastation. The narration written and spoken by Ronder allows us to see the rubble as an index of loss rather than simply a vision of nothingness. "In an instant, fifty thousand people died," we are told of the bombing of Nagasaki. While the visual register shows us the spaces of destruction emptied of human life, the audio incorporates a plaintive weave of sirens that seems to suggest the mournful voices we can never hear, for, as the voiceover repeats, "near the center, there was no sound." The combination of eerie, dissonant sirens and Ronder's sobering recounting of the number of lives lost in each location allows us to envision the hollowed-out buildings as once occupied with life. Two other voices are added to this soundscape: first, the distant voice of Kazuko Oshima, whose voice testifies to the horrors of the bomb she witnessed as a young child, and in the film's final moments, the crackly, recorded voice of Oppenheimer recounting with gravitas the moment he first witnessed an atomic detonation. Kazuko's voice reverberates slightly as she speaks of the unspeakable, evoking a sense of both spatial and temporal distance, in accord with the empty sites we are confronted with visually. The grainy quality to Oppenheimer's voice, as if taken from an archived recording, likewise emphasizes the time that it has taken for his powerful testimony to be brought back to life.

Much of the original footage Barnouw incorporates into this documentary was originally filmed by the Nippon Eiga Sha film unit and was recorded out of a sense of "obligation to posterity."[81] Iwasaki and his fellow filmmakers wanted to document the scope of wreckage in order to memorialize it. The responsiveness of Japanese audiences, including survivors, to the use of this footage in *Hiroshima–Nagasaki, August 1945* attests to the film's success in that regard.[82] In short, it was an archival experiment mobilized to affect the future. Iwasaki saw it immediately as "an appeal or warning from man to man for peaceful reflection—to prevent the use of the bomb ever again," and Barnouw himself emphasized that the "footage was meaningful for today and tomorrow rather than for yesterday."[83] The film's foreboding conclusion obviates its future-minded aims: we return to the footage from the very first atomic test, whose visual impact so impressed the scientists who had created it. After a sickening sequence in which we see images of hands and faces whose skin bears the traces of atomic radiation, and hear the sound of sirens mounting in the background, the soundscape and visual frame are pierced by an explosion. We witness the atomic bomb explode three times, from the perspective of each camera that recorded it, as Oppenheimer's crackly voice recounts the experience and how the line from the Bhagavad Gita flashed through his head. As inconceivably enormous as are the clouds of smoke accompanying Oppenheimer's recollection, as unthinkable their capacity for destruction, the narrator then cautions us that in the time since the detonation we are now witnessing, the force of the nuclear arsenal at the time of the documentary's production had become 2,500 times more powerful. This force could indeed be mobilized to destroy the world and any trace of human life on it, except, perhaps, the archives of light in the sky.

In the face of such cataclysmic potential, Deren, in the concluding paragraphs of *An Anagram of Ideas,* spells out the relationship between film and modern cosmology in no uncertain terms. Embracing the theory of relativity as a pertinent, necessary framework for understanding a cosmos shaped not by a distant and almighty creator but by the everyday actions of man, she writes:

> The theory of relativity can no longer be indulgently dismissed as an abstract statement, true or false, of a remote cosmography whose pragmatic action remains, in any case, constant. Since the 17th century the heavens—with God and His will—and the earth—with man and his desires—have rapidly

approached each other. The phenomena which were once the manifestations of a transcendent deity are now the ordinary activities of man. A voice penetrates our midnight privacy over a vast distance—via the radio. The heavens are crowded with swift messengers. It is even possible to bring the world to an end. From the source of power must emanate also the morals and the mercies. And so, readily or not, willing or not, we must come to comprehend, with full responsibility, the world which we have now created.

Having articulated the massive shift in the cosmos brought on by the forces of modernity, including the technologies of the air and the atomic bomb, Deren goes on to call forcefully for artistic, and particularly cinematic, efforts that can counteract the cosmic ruptures of the worst of scientific invention.

> The history of art is the history of man and of his universe and of the moral relationship between them. Whatever the instrument, the artist sought to recreate the abstract, invisible forces and relationships of the cosmos, in the intimate, immediate forms of his art. . . . It is not presumptuous to suggest that cinema, as an art instrument especially capable of recreating relativistic relationships on a plane of intimate experience, is of profound importance. It stands, today, in the great need of the creative contributions of whomsoever respects the fabulous potentialities of its destiny.[84]

Each of the avant-garde filmmakers I have discussed in this chapter strove to seize hold of these "fabulous potentialities" of cinema in their cinematic explorations in an era of relativity and atomic threat. They struggled to represent a reality that was shaped by relativity, both moral and spatiotemporal. Through their engagement with science and its modes of observation, experimental filmmakers found new expressive possibility in cinema that countered and critiqued the godlike creative and destructive force Deren attributes to modern science, destabilizing scientific rationalism as an overarching explanatory paradigm while embracing the imaginative horizons and reconsiderations of reality it offered. The cosmocinematic gaze, through these cinematic practices, became intentionally relativistic, partial, assembled, and incomplete.

EPILOGUE

Witnessing after the End

AS THE COLD WAR ERA of space travel began and cameras were liberated to take cosmic perspectives that were once only the province of the imagination, astronauts on board Apollo 17 looked back at Earth and took the iconic 1972 *Blue Marble* photograph (see Figure 9). The image is simple: a largely blue planet surrounded by darkness. But it had an outsized rhetorical effect. Seeing photographic documentation of the earth in its entirety, many argue, emphasized its singularity, vulnerability, and oneness.[1] The *Blue Marble* photograph linked the distant, backward-looking gaze from above to a budding ecological consciousness—an awareness that the earth was finite both spatially and temporally, as well as under permanent threat from human activity. Discourses that surrounded the *Blue Marble* photograph at the time of its emergence were concerned largely with futurity, with what could be done to protect this vulnerable planet and prevent catastrophe. But such discourses are also imbued with the implication of a past gone awry: the vulnerability of the future exists only because of the ways human beings have acted in the past. The photograph is thus also a kind of testament to what is already slipping away.

Since this moment, a photograph of the earth as a planet has become commonplace in ecological imagery, standing in for the interconnectedness of humankind and the fragility of our planet.[2] Ursula K. Heise writes about the ubiquity of this view, which is associated with a "sense of planet" that transcends connections to individual localities.[3] Yet the *Blue Marble* photograph and others like it are also supremely limited in what they can tell us about the earth and the entanglements of its occupants. Yaakov Jerome Garb critiques the *Blue Marble* photograph for the way it erases human and other natural life, making the planet appear "distant and abandoned" at the expense of any true environmental consciousness.[4] There

Figure 9. The *Blue Marble* photograph taken by astronomers aboard Apollo 17 in 1972. Courtesy of NASA.

is a god trick in the gaze this photograph espouses, in the way it erases differential experience across the globe. We are not all one, after all. Some will be able to reap the benefits of a melting planet up to the last moment, while others already face the deadly consequences of a currently unfolding catastrophe.[5] The view from above here, as throughout history, performs various kinds of erasure along with its documentation.

The simultaneous yearning for and impossibility of fully documenting human history through its light archives is evident in the Black Marble product suite released by NASA in 2012. With its haunting images of Earth from above, Black Marble complements the *Blue Marble* image from decades earlier (see Figure 10).[6] Combining the interweaving temporalities and interplay of light and darkness intrinsic to cosmic cinema, the

Black Marble project embodies a cosmocinematic gaze via advanced satellite-imaging technologies. The project amalgamates data from satellites that record nighttime light in order to visualize human presence on the earth and track "light pollution, illegal fishing, fires, disaster impacts and recovery, and human settlements and associated energy infrastructures."[7] The series of images that appear at the top of the Black Marble website are accompanied by captions that suggest they display migration patterns, follow action in the Russia–Ukraine War, evince the effects of hurricanes and their aftermath, and reveal human energy consumption. The images themselves are stark, showing an earth that is mostly in shadow but that emanates light whose capture claims to serve as an archive of human activity and natural disaster—two entangled sets of light-traces that evoke the impending apocalypse, the increase of the former leading to the escalation of the latter. Yet the resulting archives are not simply the result of a single camera looking down at the earth and passively recording all that occurs, as some theorists or filmmakers I have discussed imagined in their cosmocinematic visions. Rather, they are data sets overlaid on maps to provide the illusion of transparent visual information, while the separate parsing of light to trace these distinct patterns of human and natural occurrences reveals how selective these images really are. Compiled from multiple sensors and constructed into various kinds of visual media, including composite photographs, interactive maps, and time-lapse animations, the Black Marble data manifests one reality of the fragmentary cosmocinematic gaze in today's media environment. This cosmocinematic gaze is manufactured and explicitly technologized. Moreover, the images that display this data signal overall trends, including that of increasing population, energy consumption, and accompanying natural disasters as the end times approach, but there is no illusion that they provide a compelling record of what is human about human history— no culture, no individuals; instead, the gleaming harbingers of apocalyptic wreckage. This cosmocinematic gaze makes clear that there is no all-seeing, all-archiving cosmos: too much remains in shadow or is documented in signals other than light.

It is nevertheless still worth considering the kinds of documentation such astronomical views of the planet have sparked. An increased awareness of the vulnerability of the planet has been accompanied by an archival impulse, as well as an environmental one. As activists push for reforms that could prolong the hospitality of our planet to human life, there has also been a different kind of conservationism, one that seeks to salvage

Figure 10. Map from the "Earth at Night" series, part of NASA's Black Marble project, 2016. Courtesy of NASA.

and make meaning of human pasts. The very idea of what constitutes an archive is in flux as this environmental consciousness shapes our sense of history and time. Jussi Parikka points out that the use of the word *archive* has been changing to refer not just to specific institutional sites of preserved cultural heritage but to "discussions of geology, the earth, its natural history, and hence the scale of the supra-historical."[8] Scholars like Dipesh Chakrabarty address the Anthropocene as a geological era in which human beings are the primary agents of geological change and in which the timescale of global social history and that of geological history are converging, necessitating a converging notion of what constitutes "archives," too.[9] Archive and memory, Parikka writes, are being reframed in "planetary terms" through such scholarship, as well as through documentary films such as *Into Eternity* (dir. Michael Madsen, 2010) and *Nostalgia for the Light* (dir. Patricio Guzmán, 2010) that address enormous scales of time in relation to traces of human life.

This reframing of *archive* is evident in a resurging interest in trying to document everything in the history of the world within a cosmic context.

Popular astronomy texts like Stephen Hawking's 1988 *A Brief History of Time*, as well as Carl Sagan's thirteen-episode series *Cosmos: A Personal Voyage* (PBS, 1980) and the 2014 update with Neil deGrasse Tyson, *Cosmos: A Spacetime Odyssey* (National Geographic), have incarnated this interest in the temporalities of human history and the cosmos. There has been a simultaneous turn toward "Big History" among historians concerned with the coming together of human and geological timescales in the Anthropocene.[10] A group of interdisciplinary scholars formed the International Big History Association in 2010 to "understand the integrated history of the cosmos, Earth, life and humanity."[11] Educators have debated the virtues of reforming high-school history curricula to take this longer view in light of climate change, and some have turned to digital media tools to bring such a large-scale view of history to life. One such project, UC Berkeley's ChronoZoom, developed in 2009 and updated in 2012, uses interactive timelines to "travel backward in history" and "understand the vastness of time."[12]

This turn toward taking stock of planetary time writ large is perhaps best encapsulated by the Big History Project, a multimedia course to be used in classrooms or explored independently, which was spearheaded and funded by Bill Gates. The project seeks to explain the history of everything, from the Big Bang to our human present, connecting all phenomena across time. It uses digital media—timelines with embedded videos, for example—as an update to the cosmocinematic gaze, with the same nostalgia and sense of grandeur and attempts at linearity we see in early cinematic fantasies of looking back through time. Just as the imagined cosmocinematic gaze preceded cinema as a set of technologies, it persists in various forms in related nonfilmic digital media. The timelines of the Big History Project give a user a sense of control; we can easily bound across millennia, glimpsing deep pasts with a quick swipe. A video preview of the course, with Bill Gates's cheery endorsement, lays out the project's aim. As cosmic images move across the screen to the banal pulse of motivational music, a series of intertitles tells us: "We're part of a larger story. One that is still unfolding. To see where it leads, we need to go back to the beginning." Unlike the Black Marble project, which perhaps inadvertently hints at dark futures with its documentation of increased industrialization and disaster, this project clings to the notion of an anthropocentric future. Its dive into a deep, prehuman history serves only as the backdrop for our narrowing in on the accomplishments of humanity. Yet a discerning viewer might hold a mirror up to the narrative this tells, zooming back out into a cosmos that will persist long after our human part of this "larger story" is over. After this introduction, the video begins to pan seamlessly across time, with iconic images and films of history flashing briefly across the screen before sliding rightward out of the frame to make room for the next document of a deeper past, the gaps of time between depicted events increasing drastically, from a few years at the outset to millions of years by the end. Notably, all film footage is played in reverse—just as in Bruce Conner's CROSSROADS, the mushroom cloud at Bikini Atoll miraculously recedes into nothingness. Even as this promotional video, and the project more largely, embrace conventional progressive timelines of history (the course itself proceeds from the Big Bang and goes monodirectionally forward in time), this dive into history mimics some of cinema's temporal playfulness that has directly challenged such conventionality.

Perhaps this hints just the slightest bit at the anxieties at work in any attempt to dig through history at a moment when that history seems to be galloping to a close. The project's fascination with cosmic timescales is symptomatic of a precarious future: when there is not much to look forward to, it is time to look back.[13] As Jennifer Fay writes astutely, "What drives preservation and the creation of the archive is the knowledge and fear of death and an acute sense that the collective culture and its laws must be recorded to persist beyond the event of annihilation."[14] It is as if the threat of finitude necessitates a resuscitation of a kind of history that reassures us of our importance, as well as that of the stories our civilizations have told themselves about progress, victory, and greatness. This is an impulse that resonates with Felix Eberty's cosmocinematic gaze, updated with an array of digital media that allow a user to browse through history at their fingertips. The Big History Project presents us with an archive that draws as much on simulation as any light-imprints of the past: the past here is manufactured to convince us of continuity, both of time and of meaning.

And even as we see this resurgence of understanding history as a march of civilizational progress, laid out on timelines that assure viewers of stability and a transparent access to the past, we also see a reckoning with media archives more generally: there is an overwhelming amount of media content being generated all the time, creating an explosive archive of immediacy with an emphasis on presence. If André Bazin worried about the proliferation of films during the Second World War and the planet's constant shedding of history, he would feel utter consternation at the ubiquity of documentation today. Digital media now present an archive of excess, an archive through which it would be impossible to sift except by selective algorithms whose automatically generated histories would be as selective and biased as any Big History.[15] And these archives face another crisis: that of ephemerality, of inherent loss, of infrastructural instability as we move from one format to the next with increasing speed. Ina Blom elaborates:

> Issues of fragility and ephemerality that come with informational transformation of space perennially haunt digital archives. How safe is cultural memory if it depends less on locked, temperature-controlled vaults than on software updating, compatibility, synchronization, energy flow, and channels of transfer? And how to select what to remember when the exponential growth in the processing power of microchips seems to promise that there will, in principle, be "capacity" for everything?[16]

Digital archives have also precipitated concern about the future of cinematic archives and indeed prompted discussion about the possible end of cinema's intrinsically archival nature, premised on an indexical relationship to its subject made indelible with the chemical imprint of light on filmstock. Not only does a digital image "sunde[r] the contact between world and image," to use Philip Rosen's phrase; it makes possible the very crisis of image as truth that we see unfolding across new media's hellscape of deepfakes, fabricated news, images generated by artificial intelligence, and rampantly replicated misinformation.[17] We might add this ever-fragmenting relationship between a cinematic image and reality to the factors that confound early visions of cinema as a moving record of human history.

A February 28, 2022, *New Yorker* cartoon by Ellis Rosen pokes fun at the crisis of archives in an age of digital media as precarious as they are ubiquitous. Taking a familiar view from above, the cartoon depicts God and an angel perched on a cloud, looking back at the earth. Superimposed over the image of our planet is an error message: "Error. Application cannot start." The hapless angel asks, "Did you remember to back up the last 4.5 billion years?" In this cartoon, the archive becomes postcinematic, and the gaze from above is infused with futility. The cosmocinematic gaze of the past seemed to assure futurity—even just of an archive, a trace— in the face of mortality and apocalypticism. A postmodern attitude in the face of digital archives seems more resigned to having no future, even an archival one. In a time when so much of our visual culture alludes to climate change and the end of the world, the annihilation of the archive of

EPILOGUE · 129

the earth presumed here seems doubly sad: there is no hope of recovery, even of the trace; all is lost. This cartoon flippantly suggests that the technological modernity that has precipitated our earthly apocalypse also forecloses an archival imaginary despite a proliferation of images or fails to give us an imaginative horizon through which to envision an archive beyond our species or planetary demise. The cosmocinematic gaze is rendered inept, as glitchy as anything else, allowing 4.5 billion years to be lost because of a technical error. Archives, like the universe itself, are on the brink. The world could end with no possibility of looking back.

In the face of this cultural frenzy around archiving the past, cinema has continued working through its role in documentary human and planetary histories, at times self-reflexively. The relevance of cosmic cinema in our apocalyptic moment is undeniable. The past decade or so has seen the release of a spate of cosmic films. In large part, these recent films

"Did you remember to back up the last 4.5 billion years?"

Figure 11. *"Did You Remember to Back Up the Last 4.5 Billion Years?"* Ellis Rosen, *New Yorker,* February 28, 2022. Courtesy of Condé Nast.

address a sense of despair at the impending demise of our planet due to climate change and a sense that the "end times," as Slavoj Žižek deems our current era, necessitate either an expansion into outer space, a mobility through time—a salvage temporality, we could call it—or both.[18] A few blockbuster examples hint at the pervasiveness of these themes. *Gravity* (dir. Alfonso Cuarón, 2013) takes a material approach to the artifacts of human civilization. Its adventure through space is triggered by a spacecraft's collision with accumulated debris in the circumterrarium, raising questions of the extent to which outer space, too, has become an archive of human waste. *Interstellar* (dir. Christopher Nolan, 2014), meanwhile, is quite optimistic about humankind's ability to forestall the end of humanity despite catastrophic climate change, mobilizing theories of time travel loosely based on the astrophysical theories of Einstein and the contemporary astrophysicist Kip Thorne, who served as an adviser on the film. Adding to the mix a sentimental reflection on the boundless power of love, *Interstellar* posits the possibility of saving human civilization by finding a new home in another corner of the universe. In a similar vein, the global sensation from China *The Wandering Earth* (dir. Frant Gwo, 2019) imagines a group of people who come together to move the earth after a series of climate disasters has made its current location unsustainable. As in *Interstellar*, the goal is to work around the end of nature, though in this case the earth itself is saved. Both films make loose use of cosmic theories to imagine how such feats might be accomplished within the logics of known astrophysics. Einstein's theories have also remained pertinent prompts for self-reflexive explorations of the medium of film itself; *Arrival* (dir. Denis Villeneuve, 2016) draws on a creative interpretation of Einsteinian relativity, combined with a belief in the power of dream, to plot a narrative in which the past is revised and redeemed in advance.

I now turn my attention to two films that express a resignation to the reality of finitude rather than centering narratives that work around it. These films, *Melancholia* (dir. Lars von Trier, 2011) and *Don't Look Up* (dir. Adam McKay, 2021), both imagine a range of human emotions and reactions in the face of immanent apocalypse brought on by astronomical bodies gone astray. Denial features prominently in each, but the primary characters are in both cases wise to the reality of final destruction and, by extension, so are we as audience. Both films use these characters to explore how meaning can be made even as the end of time looms, with all records of human pasts—our ways of clinging to what has been lost and ensuring continuity in the face of that loss—also under threat. Each film is also guilty of the Western-centric view of apocalypse that characterizes much of the U.S.-based ecological literature and popular attempts to document Big History. In *Don't Look Up,* there at least seems to be an awareness of the utter selfishness of the wealthy, White, U.S.-based elite whose greedy decisions destroy the world, but the rest of the world remains entirely at the periphery of the film. In *Melancholia,* the situation is worse: we are trapped in an enormous country estate in Europe with a cast of only supremely privileged White characters, with no allusion to the existence of a world beyond except at such an astronomical distance that human life feels irrelevant. What is more, in the final moments of the film, the main characters take spiritual refuge from the apocalypse in a self-styled teepee, a move of cultural appropriation that feels especially forceful given the apocalypse that European settlers wrought on the Indigenous cultures to which this icon alludes.[19]

Don't Look Up explores the range of affects that accompany imminent destruction at the hands of cosmic forces, as a comet barrels toward Earth and its citizens must decide collectively whether to avert its course with sophisticated, scientifically calibrated defense mechanisms or to allow it to get as close as possible to mine its wealth of minerals. An obvious allegory for and farcical critique of human responses to climate change, the film satirizes the cleft between left- and right-wing American politics, painting the response to news of this comet as polarized between those who rely on expertise and recognize the direness of the situation, on the one hand, and those who either deny the comet's existence or view it opportunistically as a resource for extraction of valuable minerals, on the other. Those who do recognize the threat move between despair, grief, anger, and resignation.[20] Concerned largely with the present—the film is almost entirely contained within the six-month period from the comet's detection to the moment it collides with Earth—*Don't Look Up* nearly dodges the question of archives, of what matters from the past and what remains after everything is gone.

Indeed, instead of imbuing media with a backward-looking, archival cosmocinematic gaze, the film thematizes the omnipresence of digital media and the obsession of that media with the present at the expense of any engagement with either history or an evidence-based acknowledgment of what the future holds. We watch as news reportage proliferates without saying anything and as social media posts redigest the same nonreportage in increasingly inane and misinformative fragments. The frame often fills with these media tidbits, their nonsense a deluge of "vulgar revisions and reprints," to use Walter Benjamin's description of a universe characterized by eternal return, with no hope of progress.[21] This unwieldy archive of everything is as far from cinematic dreams of archiving history as we can get, speaking to a splintering of media formats as well as the impossibility of a unified or unifying look at human history. It is all a mess of an inescapable present tense, a constant shedding of the skin of the world, to return to Bazin's image. The chaotic media archive is complemented with images that bookend the film of the grotesque archive of material goods floating in space above the earth, blasted into orbit by the comet that destroys human life itself. This material archive is as bleak as that of contemporary media, a sign of a species whose production and consumption were out of control, its greed precipitating an end that may otherwise have been forestalled. Fay writes evocatively that "the archive grows in proportion with (perhaps in excess of) the forces of its destruction." The wild proliferation of material waste is both the face of the Anthropocene's apocalyptic destructiveness and "the ultimate human archive inscribed into and onto the planet"—and around it, we might add.[22]

The film at first seems to conclude with an image of orbiting waste, suggesting that human life on earth is over, with these artifacts the only traces that remain. Yet there is a resistance to such finality: even as the film insists on the reality of the impending doom, it includes two segments, embedded during and at the end of the credits, that carry us past a definite end. After the initial credit sequence, we see a select group of the rich and powerful, who rescued themselves the moment they saw that their mission to exploit and explode the comet was a failure, land on a new idyllic planet. They step out, thrilled not only to have survived but to have arrived in a lush, Edenic environment, only to be decimated by an alien species within seconds. Here the film seems to suggest that any escape hatch from apocalypse—the idea that one might escape, embodied in prepper culture—can only be temporary; even those with the most wealth and power must eventually succumb.[23] But yet another afterward after the final roll of credits reveals that the film cannot quite let go of the idea of an ongoing human presence. Here, we see the U.S. president's pathetic, oafish chief of staff (Jonah Hill) dig himself out of a pile of rubble, clutching the president's designer handbag. All along he has been party to greedy and exploitative responses to the news of the asteroid, but now he is left behind on his own. When he looks around and calls out without response, he whips out his smartphone to record and share a selfie video of "the last man on Earth." As the camera pans and we track away from the earth, it seems clear his fate is sealed—a survivor not for long, given his general ineptitude and the inhospitableness of his surroundings. But the very fact that the film includes this extra scene, complete with self-documentation, shows an impulse to witness, to see the rubble that testifies to the existence of our species even at its destruction. The film cannot resist the allure of a posthuman cosmocinematic gaze, giving us a look at the archive of humanity that tells of our presence beyond this apocalypse. *Don't Look Up*, like the conniving characters it presents us with, tries every loophole to avoid an end—of the film and of the world. It thus oscillates between an attitude of resignation to the combination of natural threat and human stupidity, on the one hand, and a sentimental unwillingness to let go of human pasts, on the other.

The narrative of familial reconciliation at the heart of the film underscores this sentimentality and its accompanying desire to return comfortably and uncritically to the past. Svetlana Boym terms this impulse "restorative nostalgia," a form of nostalgia that fails to recognize its own idealization of an impossible past. In *Don't Look Up*, Dr. Randall Mindy (Leonardo DiCaprio) is an astronomer whose research group discovers the comet and who, as he skyrockets to fame, loses track of his priorities, cheating on his wife and turning his back on scientific integrity in favor of power and privilege. In the end, he is called back to the truth, and his wife welcomes him home to celebrate the apocalypse with some nice, home-cooked food, plentiful wine, and polite conversation about what everyone is thankful for. There is a profound amnesia manifest here, a sense that simply restoring what was and taking shelter in the security of the past provides an emotional fortification, at least, against impending demise. But it also feels dishonest. This rosy image of familial pastness is undermined by the horror of what humanity actually leaves behind, the trash heaved into outer space that marks our culture of overconsumption. The beautiful archive of human memory is premised on amnesia, and the material archive that remains is utterly depressing.

Taking a similarly cosmic approach to allegorizing the apocalypse of climate change, *Melancholia* addresses the question of the end of the world by staging the earth's collision with a larger planet, ending all of human civilization.[24] It asks, what has the meaning of human life been if it will only disappear without a trace? What will we have mattered in the absence of any archive? Like *Don't Look Up*, the film takes place in the months leading up to the end of the world, though this time consensus in the scientific community is that the planet will not, in fact, collide with the earth. Our melancholic heroine Justine (Kirsten Dunst) knows otherwise. She observes the rogue planet (aptly named Melancholia) before her amateur astronomer of a brother-in-law and seems to be psychologically synced with its melancholic voyage. The story begins with Justine's wedding—conventionally, an event that concludes a film, with promise for the futurity and reproductivity of the characters—which does not go as planned. She ends up in a field having sex with a man who is not her husband and spots, for the first time, an oddly bright planet in the sky. The remainder of the film follows Justine's psychological deterioration and the planet's approach. "Life is only on Earth," she tells her sister Claire (Charlotte Gainsbourg), "and not for long." Around her, people continue with routines and the pretense that all is fine: their human temporalities ignore the larger timescale that engulfs them and renders all that meaningless. Justine, unable to function within the daily grind, instead basks in the light of the menacing planet and resists the niceties of human interaction. And yet, despite her inability to function in daily life, she is able to collect herself at the end and lend a sense of protection to those around her: while everyone else falls apart, she builds a fortification in which she, her sister, and her nephew hold hands, as if the power of their coming together, however transiently, can stave off the absoluteness of annihilation. It is a moment not unlike the final family moments in *Don't Look Up*: a dysfunctional family of privileged people who do not even really like each other band together and forget those dislikes in order to assure us that something about their love, expressed in that moment, is potent and enduring even in the face of apocalyptic forces.

But the film's opening, like the multiple endings of *Don't Look Up*, stages something else. Finitude is acknowledged from the beginning, when we witness the annihilation of the earth to which the diegesis of the film builds up. The film brings together cosmic and human temporalities in its surreal opening sequence, which stands apart from the rest of the film. The first shot, of Justine in close-up opening her eyes in slow motion, invites us into her psychological state, whose temporality rejects the routines of the everyday. To the intense, doleful but lush score of Wagner's *Tristan und Isolde*, the sequence alternates between wordless, surreal images of Justine and her family members moving in slow motion through distorted natural environments and a cosmic perspective that slowly reveals a planetary dance of death, concluding with the obliteration of Earth as it collides with a much larger planet. In one shot, we see Justine in her wedding dress, attempting to march forward as a tangle of vines tugs her back. In another, we see her sister struggling to carry her son across a golf course, sinking deeply into mud with each impossibly slow step. Nature pulls; time pulls; there is no escape. Everything has the quality of a nightmare in which all agency is lost: the body cannot do what one wills it to, because other forces work too strongly and inexplicably against it. It is both mesmerizing and excruciating to watch. The music tugs, too, and we feel as stuck as the characters, glued to the images but exhausted by the way they force us into an alternate temporality. This temporality reminds us of the coming together of geological time and human time so central to how Chakrabarty describes the Anthropocene. The union is supremely unnerving.

The sequence, which lasts just over eight minutes, ends in blackness. There is no ambiguity: this is a complete loss. Even before the story begins, we know the end to this and all other possible stories. But then, of course, the narrative portion of the film begins. What does it mean to stage the entire story of the film after this end?[25] There is a pervasive sense of inevitability as we watch—we know exactly what will happen, despite some characters' denial. But this decision also lends the film a privileged archival gaze that does not end in the face of apocalypse. This film, and "film" more abstractly, still exists in the place and time beyond the ultimate end. It moves beyond any possible human, mortal gaze, temporally and spatially, suggesting an alignment with some kind of cosmocinematic witness that does indeed render human life still meaningful, in some small way, even after it is gone.

Cosmocinematic Witness

These popular films speak to widespread anxiety around world-ending and accompanying concerns around human legacy and the transience of contemporary media. Their engagements with the cosmos deal peripherally with cinema's role in preserving that legacy and its relationship to temporalities of apocalypse and postapocalypse. But throughout this book I have probed how this relationship is expressed through fiction, experimental, and, perhaps most importantly, documentary forms. If fiction film is relevant to this book because it has freed filmmakers to manipulate cinematic time at will, documentary in some ways manifests the cosmocinematic gaze whether or not it even deals with cosmic themes, because it transports viewers through archives (or creates archival material of its own) and thus provides a metaphorical cosmic voyage imagined by Eberty, Élie Faure, Siegfried Kracauer, and various filmmakers.

One documentary film, in particular, brings together many of the threads that I have sought to weave throughout this book, cementing a sense of the cosmocinematic gaze as a form of witness. While *Melancholia* and *Don't Look Up* obliquely hint at the value of such a witness, *Nostalgia for the Light* explores the idea more explicitly and dodges the imperialism and god trick of which the cosmocinematic gaze from above (and backward through time) is so often guilty. *Nostalgia for the Light*, a documentary film that explores the layers of history and prehistory preserved in the earth and sky of the Atacama Desert in Chile, functions as a powerful and sustained reflection on cinema's responsibility to the past and its unique ability to recall, reframe, and redeem that past in the face of near total loss. With its direct engagement with how astronomers conceive of cosmic and historical time, and its implicit interrogation of how documentary film relates to and mediates these temporal strata, the film presents us with an eloquent demonstration of the ways astronomy and cinema intersect and diverge in their excavations of history both recent and primordial from a postapocalyptic vantage point. In many ways, *Nostalgia for the Light* thus provides a culmination of the cosmocinematic discourses and gazes at work in the films and theories discussed in the previous chapters.

In *Nostalgia for the Light*, Guzmán brings together cosmic and cinematic time, exposing the need for both documentary evidence based in material reality and an imagination that escapes the bounds of a painful history that can never be wholly salvaged. Both cinema and astronomy, in the film, become media for witnessing a past that has been forcefully erased and for accessing the imaginative horizons that allow those whose relatives have disappeared to find a connection with the past that does not depend on tangible fragments. The film begins with a slow segment of nearly three minutes in which a telescope's gears are set in motion, its lens cap flips open, and the roof that protects it parts its doors to expose it to the light of the sky. The visual similarities between the whirring wheels and lenses of the telescope and those of a film camera are striking, lending a sense that the telescope somehow provides the point of view of the film to follow. We view the film through its lens—that is, as if it is a silent witness of history aligned with the gaze of a documentary cinematographer. We later learn that this telescope heralded a new era of Chile being a central node in international astronomy and that Guzmán himself encountered it as a child, opening his mind to the reflections that shape this film. Both film and astronomy promise to expose new worlds, but the resonance here turns inward and backward, interrogating human history. One astronomer tells us that "the past is the astronomer's main tool—we manipulate the past." This could just as well be said of the process of filmmaking, as Guzmán illustrates through his construction of a documentary out of multiple kinds of footage encompassing different historical moments.

The Atacama Desert is a setting with particularly strong ties to deep pasts, both astronomical and archaeological: the lack of atmospheric interference caused by humidity makes the conditions ideal for astronomical observation and the lack of moisture in the ground preserves the remnants of past human life. It is a desolate setting, and the documentary presents it as a postapocalyptic landscape. The first fifteen minutes of the film show only empty spaces, devoid of life. Even in the observatory and homes in which one might expect human figures to pass through, the camera focuses on old objects—a chair, a radio, an oven—that mark the trace of prior human activity but underscore the eerie absence of anyone now. As scintillating stardust whirls across the frame and these spaces fade to black, relegated to a nostalgia-tinged past, Guzmán's voice tells an apocalyptic story: one day the "peaceful life" that transpired in these spaces "came to a close." A "revolutionary tide . . . woke us from our slumber," disrupting the present-mindedness of the past with what he calls a "time of hope"—a temporality that recalls the rupture of Benjamin's *Jetztzeit*—that quickly gave way to oppression and violence. The film then turns to scenes of the desert, its starkly barren landscape emphasized by the voiceover that calls it a "condemned land" in which not even birds can live. It is, however, hospitable to the telescopes that become our "window to the cosmos," taking us on a "celestial mystery" that invites us to look at the stars above in order to imagine their reciprocal gaze at these spaces from which life seems to have been largely eradicated.

The documentary follows a number of people whose lives are devoted to finding traces of or studying the past, including survivors of the Augusto Pinochet regime, under which thousands of people were killed and many more displaced. On the one hand, the film focuses on a group of women who comb the desert for physical remains of those who were killed. On the other, it shows extensive interviews with a team of astronomers working at the desert's renowned international observatories. While the astronomers use the machines of the observatory to understand a deeper past, they articulate their work in relation to the work of excavating the past of the military dictatorship. Guzmán weaves together these two approaches to probing the past, one that seeks the material traces of the dead who exist only in the past and the other that imagines the dead as part of a cosmos infused with the possibility of temporal mobility.

Importantly, *Nostalgia for the Light* emphasizes the vitality of the past—the way it comes to life for the present and anticipates the future, rather than receding and dying. As one astronomer at the observatory asserts, in fact, "the present doesn't exist," at least not in any perceptible form. Everything we see, hear, or feel has already become part of the past by the time we perceive it, "because the signal takes time to arrive." Astronomy magnifies this relationship to time because of the immense gulfs of space over which light from stars and galaxies must travel to reach our eyes or the instruments of detection we devise. Thus, the astronomer identifies the crux of the ontological bond between film and astronomy that so consistently fascinated early film theorists. Both the night sky and cinema allow us to access a past that has otherwise escaped our grasp. Through both, the past becomes reanimated to our perception, like the signals that reach us from a much less distant past, such as light bouncing off the page on which these words are written. In the story that Guzmán tells in *Nostalgia for the Light,* this reanimation is crucial for uncovering a past that has been suppressed and for providing closure and redemption for those who have struggled to unearth the truth of what happened to those who disappeared. A historian states that those who have lost loved ones are "morally obliged to preserve [their] memory." "We cannot forget our dead," he continues. "The courts of justice must do their work . . . but we absolutely must not forget a tragedy like this." The work of history, archaeology, astronomy, and filmmaking alike is to ensure traces of the past are not erased or obscured. Guzmán's film, in bringing various voices and endeavors together, illustrates the vital importance of cinema as articulated by Benjamin and Kracauer: its potential to stage an encounter with the victims of history.

The material search undertaken by the women in this film provides the most obvious example of historical excavation of the Pinochet regime's victims. But Guzmán deftly convinces us of the sustained role astronomy plays in confronting and transcending the horror of a past whose traces have been forcefully fragmented and eradicated, preventing a satisfying reconstructive effort through archaeological digging or embodied testimony alone. Astronomy allows the past to be made meaningful even in the absence of such material evidence. Astronomers cannot witness the earthly past, as in Faure's and Kracauer's imagined cosmocinematic flights back through history. One woman, having searched for the bones of her brother for decades, laments the limitations of astronomical tools, summoning a yearning for a cosmocinematic witness: "I wish the telescopes could see through the earth so we could find them. I would give thanks to the stars for helping us find them." She adds, "I'm just dreaming." But these dreams, too, hold power. Rather than reviving the past in its entirety, astronomers and filmmakers use technology and creativity to piece together what they can and leave much open to the imagination. The night sky, in this film, becomes a space where the dead can be imagined, both immaterially and materially, even if their earthly traces are not recuperable. After all, the calcium in our bones and that in the stardust of the Big Bang are one and the same, one astronomer muses. Similarly, *Nostalgia for the Light*, which draws on only fragments of archival footage and accesses history primarily through conversations with these women and astronomers instead of relying on a conventional, linear historical narrative, requires of us a certain leap of faith that the past matters and can speak to us in the absence of substantial material evidence.

Film and astronomy share much in common in this film. The project of the astronomer is not the abstract scientific endeavor that Kracauer decried in his *Theory of Film*.[26] Instead, as the astronomers depicted here train their equipment on the heavens, they also provide a way for the people who search for their loved ones to connect their experiences, and those of the dead, with a larger, cosmic sphere. Much as Sir Arthur Eddington's confirmation of relativistic theory through the carefully mechanized process of photographing the eclipse became the fodder for a larger set of temporal experiences, here the process of recording astronomical phenomena is clearly linked to the ways people understand their own perceptions of time and memory. In its probing of the past via the collective endeavors of the astronomers and the searching women, the film unites the vital preservative function of cinema with the medium's capacity for transcendence. It brings into focus a cinematic cosmos that does not shy away from documenting the fractured cosmos of human history, while embracing the possibility of a universe connected across space and time.

How, ultimately, do the archives of light associated with cinema and those of the cosmos come together to witness loss? The indexical quality associated with film, its ability to archive light from the past, is one of the more obvious parallels with the night sky, and one that is repeated across texts by Eberty, Faure, and Kracauer, as well as, implicitly, in films from *The Einstein Theory of Relativity* to *Universe* to *Nostalgia for the Light*. But that is only one aspect of film's power to transport across the cosmos and across time, and one that has been called into question by the digital age, when the photographic image can so easily be doctored and its indexes so readily compromised. Rather than try to make a claim above all for the ongoing indexical power of films in the digital era, however powerful that index still is, I want to point to the cosmocinematic gaze as a set of positionalities that allows for such voyages into the depths of the unknown, whether the dark recesses of the universe or the shadows of hidden histories, in documentary, fictional narrative, avant-garde film practices, and related media from photography to digital timelines alike. Historically, filmmakers have long been concerned with how the moment captured on film can be mobilized—how the past can reenter the present, activate the future, resonate across gulfs of space and time. Cosmic temporalities are an apt model for construing cinematic time because in addition to promising indexical traces of light, like cinema it too embraces resonances, recurrences, and detours that bring new facets of the past to light.

The dreams of a cosmocinematic witness in *Nostalgia for the Light* remain just that—dreams. And this is true beyond this film, too; we can look up and see the light of the past, but our own light, cast outward, creates an incomplete cosmocinematic archive of our existence. And yet there is still tremendous desire to use image-based media to take this position of witness from above. The imagined cosmocinematic archives evoked in *Nostalgia for the Light,* in cinema and cinematic theory across their histories, and even in the composite images of the Black Marble project, are imbued with enormous power as they promise partial testimony to what has passed. For what we do have, in whatever signals emanate outward, in whatever imprints of light remain in the terrestrial archives of a cinematic media that dream and document and compile the world over and over, is an ever-unstable, ever-fragmentary, wondrous and horrifying glimpse of this planet and those who have lived on it. If there is any reassurance to be had in these archives, it comes less from the idea that they might be seen by some faraway, future viewer and more from the notion that some flickering record, at least, persists beyond us, beyond the detritus of our excessive material existence—a record that in its incompleteness testifies to darkness and loss as well as light and presence of our species for some time on some planet somewhere in the great universe.

ACKNOWLEDGMENTS

MY DEEPEST THANKS go to the generous and brilliant professors in the Film and Media Studies Department at UC Santa Barbara who guided this project from the beginning. Bhaskar Sarkar has continually asked just the right questions, and prodded me with just the right readings and films, to get me to think more expansively and theoretically. Lisa Parks was an incredible mentor, taking me to new places geographically and methodologically. Janet Walker was the first person to make me feel that I belonged in graduate school, and her seminar on the spatial turn planted the initial seeds of my interest in how media and the cosmos might be explored in tandem. Peter Bloom helped this project take flight as he guided my writing of the initial prospectus and helped my ideas find form. Stimulating conversations with Naoki Yamamoto and Bishnupriya Ghosh have greatly informed the theoretical aspects of this work. Other UCSB faculty were supportive at various stages and helped me grow intellectually in ways I could not have predicted: Cristina Venegas, Anna Everett, Anna Brusutti, and Patrice Petro. And I owe the world to Charles Wolfe, who helped me develop this project out of a whiff of an idea that emerged during his seminar on film theory. His dedication to this project sustained me and enriched it at every step. It is truly no exaggeration to say that without his patient counsel and insight, this work would not have been possible.

This manuscript and the dissertation it emerged from were written in large part alongside many friends and colleagues, at cafés and kitchen tables and in classrooms and the TA office: Bianka Ballina, Bhargavi Narayanan, Katie Jan, Naomi DeCelles, Maria Corrigan, Jett Allen, Stephan Boman, Rachel Fabian, David Gray, Juan Llamas-Rodriguez, Rahul Mukherjee, Alston D'Silva, Lindsay Palmer, John Vanderhoef, and

Lisa Han. Their scholarship has shaped mine and their friendship has been invaluable. I owe special thanks to Naomi, who generously showed me her book proposal and advised me throughout the process of publishing this book.

I have reaped the benefits of mentors, colleagues, and students at other institutions as well. Colin Milburn served on my dissertation committee and provided enthusiastic and enlightening feedback even though he knew me only through Zoom. And my colleagues at Mount Holyoke—Robin Blaetz, Eleanor Townsley, Bianka Ballina, Elliot Montague, Karen Remmler, Amy Rodgers, Ajay Sinha, Paul Staiti, Sabra Thorner, and Elizabeth Young—have supported my work in myriad ways. The students of my Media and Scale course at Brown University in 2018 and those in my Envisioning Apocalypse course at Mount Holyoke in 2019 were particularly helpful in sharpening my thinking around central ideas of this book.

My research was aided by many wonderful archivists and private collectors: Sian Prosser at the Royal Astronomical Society; Tony Simcock at the Oxford History of Science Museum; George Aukland, Jeremy Brooker, and Willem Hackmann of the Magic Lantern Society; and Adam Green at the Trinity College Library. My time in the archives was facilitated by the Borchard Fellowship and an Interdisciplinary Humanities Center Fellowship at UC Santa Barbara.

Thank you to Leah Pennywark at the University of Minnesota Press, who has been as perceptive and responsive an editor as anyone could wish for. I am also grateful to Anne Carter for her assistance with the manuscript and Ziggy Snow for copyediting it. The detailed feedback of James Leo Cahill and Oliver Gaycken has strengthened this work tremendously and helped me understand and express my arguments more clearheadedly.

I am forever grateful for the support of my family, nuclear and extended. My parents, Steve Goodwin and Sarah Goodwin, have always encouraged and modeled curiosity and intellectual exploration. My siblings, Eva Goodwin and Stephan Goodwin, are some of the most intelligent and giving people I know, and, serving as my first teacher and first pupil respectively (apologies, Stephan!), they have honed my critical thinking and argumentative skills and given me countless ideas. Jenna Haywood's stalwart belief in me buoyed me at moments when a path forward was not obvious. Neil Hannon, Hannah Jo Smith, Bill McClung, Paul Goodwin, Janet Goodwin, Denise Hingle, Octavia Hingle-Webster, and James Webster have all supported me in various ways throughout this endeavor. And Andrew McClung has been a steadfast partner and ally, allowing me to ramble about new ideas, telling me to stop worrying about the laundry, and, more important, being stubbornly scientific in my world saturated with humanities scholars. Thank you, Andrew, for being thoroughly consistent and optimistic through the highs and lows of this process.

This book is above all for my grandparents, who have compelled me to reckon with memory, archives, and endings, and my marvelous children, Thea and Carl, who connect me to untold pasts and futures and whose own future is, I hope with all my might, more abundant than this book's title suggests.

NOTES

Introduction

1. Thomas Elsaesser identifies the film logo as a crucial component of the phenomenon of cinephilia in "Cinephilia or the Uses of Disenchantment," in *Cinephilia: Movies, Love, and Memory,* ed. Marijke De Valck and Malte Hagener (Amsterdam: Amsterdam University Press, 2005), 29.
2. Scott Curtis, *The Shape of Spectatorship: Art, Science, and Early Cinema in Germany* (New York: Columbia University Press, 2015), 8.
3. Thomas Blount, *Glossographia,* 5th ed., s.v. "cosmology" (London: The Newcomb, 1681), 166, cited in *Oxford English Dictionary,* s.v. "cosmology," accessed March 13, 2023, https://www.oed.com.
4. Denis Cosgrove, *Apollo's Eye: A Cartographic Genealogy of the Earth in the Western Imagination* (Baltimore: Johns Hopkins University Press, 2003). My use of *cosmology* resonates with Cosgrove's description of the discipline of cosmography: a "discourse that brought together celestial and geographic exploration, represented space and scale, and theorized the place of humans within nature" (114).
5. Philip James Edwin, *Principles of Physical Cosmology* (Princeton, N.J.: Princeton University Press, 1993), 3.
6. Zachary Horton, *The Cosmic Zoom: Scale, Knowledge, and Mediation* (Chicago: University of Chicago Press, 2021), 118.
7. Élie Faure, "The Art of Cineplastics," in *French Theory and Criticism, 1907–1939,* ed. and trans. Richard Abel (Princeton, N.J.: Princeton University Press, 1988), 261.
8. Faure, "Art of Cineplastics," 262.
9. Jean Epstein, "The Senses I," in *French Theory and Criticism, 1907–1939,* ed. and trans. Richard Abel (Princeton, N.J.: Princeton University Press, 1988), 243. As an aside, one wonders whether Terrence Malick read this passage before

filming *The Tree of Life* (United States, 2011), which captures precisely this interplay of scales, imbued with a sense of religious fascination.
10. Camille Flammarion, "Le movement de rotation de la terre représenté par le cinematographe," in *Bulletin de la Société Astronomique de France* (January 1898). Translation provided by Sarah Webster Goodwin. I am grateful to my anonymous reviewer for pointing me to this source.
11. See David Aubin, Charlotte Bigg, and Otto Sibum, "Introduction: Observatory Techniques in Nineteenth-Century Science and Society," in *The Heavens on Earth: Observatories and Astronomy in Nineteenth-Century Science and Culture*, ed. David Aubin, Charlotte Bigg, and Otto Sibum, 1–32 (Durham, N.C.: Duke University Press, 2010).
12. Walter Isaacson, *Einstein: His Life and Universe* (New York: Simon and Schuster, 2007), 281–308.
13. Siegfried Kracauer, *Theory of Film: The Redemption of Physical Reality* (New York: Oxford University Press, 1960), 292.
14. See Lorraine Daston and Peter Galison, *Objectivity* (Cambridge, Mass.: MIT Press, 2007).
15. See Jimena Canales, "Photogenic Venus: The 'Cinematographic Turn' and Its Alternatives in Nineteenth-Century France," *History of Science Society* 93 (2002): 585–613. Walter Benjamin also mentions this in *The Arcades Project*. See Walter Benjamin, *The Arcades Project*, trans. Howard Eiland and Kevin McLaughlin (Cambridge, Mass.: Harvard University Press, 2002).
16. Jimena Canales, "Einstein's Films: Reversible," in *The Physicist and the Philosopher: Einstein, Bergson, and the Debate That Changed Our Understanding of Time* (Princeton, N.J.: Princeton University Press, 2015), 283–91.
17. Curtis, *Shape of Spectatorship*, 22.
18. Oliver Gaycken, *Devices of Curiosity: Early Cinema and Popular Science* (New York: Oxford University Press, 2015).
19. Brooke Belisle traces cinema's fascination with registering cosmic scales to precinematic visual forms, including the panorama. See Belisle, "Nature at a Glance: Immersive Maps from Panoramic to Digital," *Early Popular Visual Culture* 13, no. 4 (2015): 313–35.
20. Among the theorists whose work I discuss in my introduction, Walter Benjamin and Siegfried Kracauer consistently reiterate the ways film works as a medium of this modern era. Benjamin famously identifies film as a medium whose mass dissemination is suited to an era devoid of any sense of aura, and Kracauer notes that the medium provides a crucial point of analysis for a mechanized culture that film embodies and represents. See Benjamin, "The Work of Art in the Age of Technological Reproducibility [Third Version]," in *Walter Benjamin: Selected Writings*, vol. 4, *1938–1940*, ed. Michael W. Jennings, Howard Eiland, and Gary Smith, 251–83 (Cambridge, Mass.: Belknap Press of Harvard University Press, 2003); Kracauer, "The Mass Ornament," in *The Mass*

Ornament: Weimar Essays, trans. and ed. Thomas Y. Levin, 75–88 (Cambridge, Mass.: Harvard University Press, 1995).
21. "Modern Astronomy," *Film Fun* 356 (December 1918): 25.
22. Stephen Kern, *The Culture of Time and Space, 1880–1918* (Cambridge, Mass.: Harvard University Press, 1983), 1.
23. See Benjamin Singer, "Sensationalism and the World of Urban Modernity" and "Making Sense of the Modernity Thesis," in *Melodrama and Modernity* (New York: Columbia University Press, 2001), 59–100, 101–30; Tom Gunning, "Modernity and Cinema: A Culture of Shocks and Flows," in *Cinema and Modernity,* ed. Murray Pomerance, 297–315 (New Brunswick, N.J.: Rutgers University Press, 2006); Mary Ann Doane, *The Emergence of Cinematic Time: Modernity, Contingency, the Archive* (Cambridge, Mass.: Harvard University Press, 2002); Philip Rosen, *Change Mummified: Cinema, Historicity, Theory* (Minneapolis: University of Minnesota Press, 2001), 98; Leo Charney and Vanessa R. Schwartz, eds., *Cinema and the Invention of Modern Life* (Berkeley: University of California Press, 1995); Miriam Bratu Hansen, *Cinema and Experience: Siegfried Kracauer, Walter Benjamin, and Theodor W. Adorno* (Berkeley: University of California Press, 2012); Murray Pomerance, ed., *Cinema and Modernity* (New Brunswick, N.J.: Rutgers University Press, 2006); Lynne Kirby, *Parallel Tracks: The Railroad and Silent Cinema* (Durham, N.C.: Duke University Press, 1997).
24. Rosen, *Change Mummified,* 99–101.
25. Doane, *Emergence of Cinematic Time,* 108–39.
26. Matthew Avery Sutton, "Apocalypticism in U.S. History," *Oxford Research Encyclopedias, Religion,* August 31, 2016, https://oxfordre.com/religion/display/10.1093/acrefore/9780199340378.001.0001/acrefore-9780199340378-e-415?print=pdf.
27. Yvan Goll, "The Cinedram," in *The Promise of Cinema: German Film Theory, 1907–1933,* ed. Nicholas Baer, Anton Kaes, and Michael Cowen, 52–54 (1920; Oakland: University of California Press, 2016).
28. Erich Burger, "Pictures-Pictures," in Baer, Kaes, and Cowen, *Promise of Cinema,* 64–65.
29. Vladimir Nabokov, *Speak Memory* (1947; New York: Vintage International, 1989), 19.
30. See Lutz Greisiger, "Apocalypticism, Millenarianism, and Messianism," in *Oxford Handbook of the Abrahamic Religions,* ed. Adam J. Silverstein and Guy G. Stroumsa, 272–95 (Oxford: Oxford University Press, 2015).
31. CenSAMM, *Critical Dictionary of Apocalyptic and Millenarian Movements,* s.v. "Apocalypticism," January 15, 2021, https://www.cdamm.org/articles/apocalypticism.
32. Peter Szendy, *Apocalypse-Cinema: 2012 and Other Ends of the World* (New York: Fordham University Press, 2015), 2.

33. Szendy, *Apocalypse-Cinema*, 134.
34. This has been written about extensively in the context of the *Blue Marble* photograph from 1972, which I discuss in my final chapter.
35. Jennifer Fay, "Cinema and the Anthropocene," interview by Nicholas Baer, *Film Quarterly* 71, no. 4 (2018): 82.
36. Jennifer Fay, *Inhospitable World: Cinema in the Time of the Anthropocene* (New York: Oxford University Press, 2018), 3.
37. Fay, *Inhospitable World*, 1.
38. Rev. 6:13.
39. Sean Redmond and Leon Marvell, introduction to *Endangering Science Fiction Film*, ed. Sean Redmond and Leon Marvell (New York: Routledge, 2016), 2.
40. Leon Marvell, "Section Two Introduction," in Redmond and Marvell, *Endangering Science Fiction Film*, 83; Sean Redmond, "Eye-Tracking the Sublime in Spectacular Science Fiction Film," in Redmond and Marvell, *Endangering Science Fiction Film*, 35.
41. Jimmy Carter, "Voyager Spacecraft, Statement by the President," July 29, 1977, available online at American Presidency Project, curated by John Woolley and Gerhard Peters, accessed August 22, 2023, https://www.presidency.ucsb.edu/documents/voyager-spacecraft-statement-the-president.
42. Carter, "Voyager Spacecraft."
43. Alice Gorman, *Dr Space Junk vs. the Universe: Archaeology and the Future* (Cambridge, Mass.: MIT Press, 2019), 217.
44. Doane, among others, writes of cinema's peculiar temporality; film is both preservative and a reminder of the temporary nature of what it has preserved. See Doane, *Emergence of Cinematic Time*.
45. Cahill also writes about cinema's ghosts in relation to the "ends of cinema" and the catastrophes we face today. See "What Remains, What Returns: Garbage, Ghosts, and Two Ends of Cinema," in *Ends of Cinema*, ed. Richard Grusin and Jocelyn Szczepaniak-Gillece (Minneapolis: University of Minnesota Press, 2020), 86.
46. This is a literal translation of Eberty's original German title, *Die Gestirne und die Weltgeschichte*, but not that of the version published in London in 1846. The latter was entitled *The Stars and the Earth*, which loses quite a bit of the original meaning. Eberty was interested not in Earth as a planet, as the translated title implies, but in the world as a stage for human history that might be viewed from the stars.
47. F. Y. Eberty, *Die Gestirne und die Weltgeschichte* (Breslau, Poland: August Schulz, 1846), 23 (my translation).
48. Eberty, *Die Gestirne und die Weltgeschichte*, 16.
49. André Bazin, "The Ontology of the Photographic Image," in *What Is Cinema*, vol. 1, ed. and trans. Hugh Gray (Berkeley: University of California Press, 1967), 14.

50. Numerous film historians in the last few decades articulate the difference between the cinematic and cinema, both in tracing mechanisms like optical toys that can be seen as precursors to film and in identifying theories that provide insight into film and cinema without directly referencing it, as in the case of Eberty. While a complete list is impossible to provide here, for a sense of the way "the cinematic" has been conceived, see Charney and Schwartz, *Cinema and the Invention of Modern Life*; Leo Charney and Vanessa R. Schwartz, introduction to Charney and Schwartz, *Cinema and the Invention of Modern Life*, 1–14; Jonathan Crary, "Unbinding Vision: Manet and the Attentive Observer in the Late Nineteenth Century," in Charney and Schwartz, *Cinema and the Invention of Modern Life*, 46–71; Vanessa Schwartz, "Cinematic Spectatorship before the Apparatus: The Public Taste for Reality in Fin-de-Siècle Paris," in Charney and Schwartz, *Cinema and the Invention of Modern Life*, 297–319; Thomas LaMarre, *Shadows on the Screen: Tanizaki Jun'ichirō on Cinema and "Oriental" Aesthetics* (Ann Arbor: University of Michigan Press, 2005), esp. 60; Jonathan Crary, *Techniques of the Observer: On Vision and Modernity in the Nineteenth Century* (Cambridge, Mass.: MIT Press, 1992).
51. Karl Clausberg, *Zwischen den Sternen: Lichtbildarchiv: Was Einstein und Uexküll, Benjamin und das Kino der Astronomie des 19. Jahrhunderts verdanken* (Berlin: Akademie Verlag, 2006).
52. Faure, "Art of Cineplastics," 267.
53. Faure, 265. Eberty's ideas had more recently been reiterated in the writing of Camille Flammarion, an astronomer, science-fiction writer, and advocate of popular science whose works circulated widely in early twentieth-century France.
54. Eduardo Cadava emphasizes this relationship between stars and photography in his book *Words of Light*, writing, "Like the photograph which is no longer there, starlight names the trace of a celestial body that has long since vanished." Cadava, *Words of Light: Theses on the Photography of History* (Princeton, N.J.: Princeton University Press, 1997), 30. I should note that the celestial body may in fact still exist, but the light that reaches us is from its past and persists beyond the life of that body.
55. Faure, "Art of Cineplastics," 265.
56. Donna Haraway, "Situated Knowledges: The Science Question in Feminism and the Privilege of Partial Perspective," *Feminist Studies* 14, no. 3 (1988): 581.
57. Simone Browne, *Dark Matters: On the Surveillance of Blackness* (Durham, N.C.: Duke University Press, 2017), 49–50; Paul Virilio, *War and Cinema: The Logics of Perception*, trans. Patrick Camiller (London: Verso, 1989), 88.
58. Denis Cosgrove, *Apollo's Eye: A Cartographic Genealogy of the Earth in the Western Imagination* (Baltimore: Johns Hopkins University Press, 2003).
59. Greg Mitman and Kelley Wilder, introduction to *Documenting the World: Film, Photography, and the Scientific Record* (Chicago: University of Chicago Press, 2016), 1–22.

60. Patrick Ellis, *Aeroscopics: Media of the Bird's-Eye View* (Oakland: University of California Press, 2021), 2.
61. Ellis, *Aeroscopics*, 6, 15.
62. Kracauer, *Theory of Film*, 300.
63. Matt. 5:5.
64. Kracauer, *Theory of Film*, 78.
65. Kracauer, 78.
66. James Leo Cahill, *Zoological Surrealism: The Nonhuman Cinema of Jean Painlevé* (Minneapolis: University of Minnesota Press, 2019), 16, 25.
67. Siegfried Kracauer, *History: The Last Things before the Last,* completed by Paul Oskar Kristeller (Oxford: Oxford University Press, 1969), 5.
68. Volker Breidecker, ed., *Siegfried Kracauer—Erwin Panofsky: Briefwechsel 1941–1966* (Berlin: Akademie Verlag, 1996), 16, cited in Gerd Gemünden and Johannes von Moltke, "Introduction: Kracauer's Legacies," in *Culture in the Anteroom: The Legacies of Siegfried Kracauer,* ed. Gerd Gemünden and Johannes von Moltke (Ann Arbor: University of Michigan Press, 2012), 2.
69. Gerd Gemünden and Johannes von Moltke call attention to Kracauer's continued embrace of an exilic perspective, which they argue becomes a motif throughout his later work and reflects his own position as an exile from Germany. Gemünden and von Moltke, "Introduction," 2.
70. Gertrud Koch, *Siegfried Kracauer: An Introduction,* trans. Jeremy Gaines (Princeton, N.J.: Princeton University Press, 2000), 107–8.
71. Cahill, "What Remains, What Returns," 90.
72. Walter Benjamin, "Theses on the Philosophy of History," in *Illuminations,* ed. Hannah Arendt, trans. Harry Zohn (1940; New York: Schocken Books, 1968), 256.
73. Benjamin, "Theses on the Philosophy of History."
74. See Benjamin, "Theses on the Philosophy of History."
75. For more on the way messianism figures in Benjamin's thought, see Hansen, *Cinema and Experience.* To Benjamin, any sense of predestination makes us servants of the future, foreclosing the present as a time of possibility and securing the fate of the past as dead.
76. Benjamin, "On the Theory of Knowledge, Theory of Progress," in *Arcades Project,* 462.
77. Slavoj Žižek, "Living in the End Times," *Polygraph* 22 (2010): 263.

1. Lights All Askew

1. Jean Eisenstadt, *The Curious History of Relativity: How Einstein's Theory of Gravity was Lost and Found Again* (Princeton, N.J.: Princeton University Press, 2006), 63.
2. Frank Dyson to John Sykes, March 27, 1914, Box 8, File 91, Royal Greenwich Observatory Archive, London.

3. Jimena Canales, "Photogenic Venus: The 'Cinematographic Turn' and Its Alternatives in Nineteenth-Century France," *History of Science Society* 93 (2002): 585–618.
4. Sir Arthur Eddington, "The Stars and Their Movements," Lecture, Perth, Australia, 1915, Eddington Archive, Box C, File 1, Wren Library, Cambridge, U.K.
5. "Jedenfalls gibt es kein anderes Mittel, irgend einem Menschen die Relativitätstheorie anschaulicher zu machen, als das Mittel Film." The critic goes on to say that this film in particular makes use of all of film's devices to explain the theory ("und was ein Film in dieser Richtung überhaupt geben kann, gibt dieser Film"). U. T. Nollendorfplatz, "Die Grundlagen der Einsteinschen Relativitätstheorie," *Filmkurier*, April 4, 1922. Courtesy of Herbert Birett, librarian and curator of the online archive for German silent film materials *Kinematographie* (https://kinematographie.de).
6. Albert Einstein, *Relativity: The Special and the General Theory*, trans. Robert W. Lawson (1915; New York: Crown Publishers, 1961), 135.
7. Einstein, *Relativity*, 26.
8. Sommerfeld cited in Paul Foreman, "Weimar Culture, Causality, and Quantum Theory," *Historical Studies in the Physical Sciences* 3 (1971): 99.
9. Einstein comments, it is "particularly ironical that many people believe that in the theory of relativity one may find support for the anti-rationalistic tendency of our day." Einstein, *Vossische Zeitung*, July 10, 1921, cited in Foreman, "Weimar Culture, Causality, and Quantum Theory," 99.
10. Katy Price, *Loving Faster Than Light: Romance and Readers in Einstein's Universe* (Chicago: University of Chicago Press, 2012), 41. The concurrence of relativistic theory with changing global, cultural, and technological formations outlined above is not a mere coincidence. Karen Barad emphasizes this in *Meeting the Universe Halfway*, arguing that Einstein's theories were developed in part because "clock coordination was an important problem of great practical significance," not just an abstract theoretical enterprise. She writes, "Social, technological, and scientific practices that included the entangled apparatuses of colonial conquest, democracy, world citizenship, antianarchism, trains, telegraphs, clocks, and other electromechanical devices composed of wires and gears all played a role in the production of a special theory of relativity." See Karen Barad, *Meeting the Universe Halfway: Quantum Physics and the Entanglement of Matter and Meaning* (Durham, N.C.: Duke University Press, 2007), 54–55.
11. "The Dimensionist Manifesto," Paris, 1936, accessed March 23, 2023, https://www.amherst.edu/system/files/media/DM%2520Translation%2520library%2520case.pdf. For more on this artistic movement, see Vanja Malloy, ed., *Dimensionism: Modern Art in the Age of Einstein* (Cambridge, Mass.: MIT Press, 2018).
12. Annette Michelson, "The Wings of Hypothesis: On Montage and the Theory of the Interval," in *Montage and Modern Life*, ed. Matthew Teitelbaum (Cambridge, Mass.: MIT Press, 1992), 65.

13. Sergei Eisenstein, "Through Theater to Cinema," in *Film Form: Essays in Film Theory*, ed. and trans. Jay Leyda (New York: Harcourt, 1949), 5.
14. Eisenstein, "The Filmic Fourth Dimension," in *Film Form*, 69.
15. Eisenstein, "Methods of Montage," in *Film Form*, 73–83, esp. 81.
16. "Nebulae, Five Quintillion Miles Away, Are Found to Be Spiral Groupings of Stars," *New York Times*, January 31, 1927.
17. W. J. Luyten, "Deeper into Infinity Astronomy Peers," *New York Times*, March 27, 1927, 8.
18. Luyten, "Deeper into Infinity," 21.
19. See, for example, Amir Razavi, "Polar Scare: Incredible Photo of Polar Bear Lazing on Iceberg Highlights Climate Change & Wins Prize at Photography Awards," *Sun*, October 12, 2021, https://www.the-sun.com/news/3843845/climate-change-golden-turtle-polar-bear-iceberg/.
20. *Encyclopedia Britannica Online*, s.v. "Quantum Mechanics," by Gordon Leslie Squires, February 24, 2017, www.britannica.com/science/quantum-mechanics-physics.
21. Einstein, "On the Present State of the Problem of Specific Heats," November 3, 1911, cited in Walter Isaacson, *Einstein: His Life and Universe* (New York: Simon and Schuster, 2007), 169.
22. For more on how quantum theory entered a cultural vernacular, see Robert P. Crease and Alfred Scharff Goldgaber, *The Quantum Moment: How Planck, Bohr, Einstein, and Heisenberg Taught Us to Love Uncertainty* (New York: Norton, 2014); Juan Miguel Marin, "'Mysticism' in Quantum Mechanics: The Forgotten Controversy," *European Journal of Physics* 30, no. 4 (2009): 807–23; Jennifer Burwell, *Quantum Language and the Migration of Scientific Concepts* (Cambridge, Mass.: MIT Press, 2018).
23. Tom Gunning, among other scholars, writes about the "complex history by which photographs were granted evidentiary status," particularly in legal discourses. Photographs were not accepted wholesale as transparent, objective evidence, whether for scientific or legal purposes—their mechanical relationship to the unfolding of events in time had to be ideologically negotiated as well. Gunning, "What's the Point of an Index?," in *Still Moving: Between Cinema and Photography*, ed. Karen Beckman and Jean Ma (Durham, N.C.: Duke University Press, 2008), 29. Moreover, the validity of photographic evidence of astronomical phenomena could only be established through the consensus of scientific institutions—the "circuits of power" that determine what is or is not "proper" science. See Tom Gunning, "Tracing the Individual Body: Photography, Detectives, and Early Cinema," in *Cinema and the Invention of Modern Life* (Berkeley: University of California Press, 1995). As Jimena Canales chronicles, the scientific establishment tended to view photography, particularly in its projected forms, as cheapening science through entertainment—and when viewing films that were passed as having science

educational value, one can understand why. Canales, "Photogenic Venus," 603.
24. Previous expeditions to confirm the theory had encountered quite a few hurdles, with one contingent of the 1914 expedition headed by Father Aloysius Cortie stranded in Russia, its equipment detained until the end of the First World War. Minutes of the Solar Eclipse Committee, November 10, 1917, Box 54, MS 2, Royal Astronomical Society Archive, London.
25. See, notably, Matthew Stanley, "An Expedition to Heal the Wounds of War: The 1919 Eclipse and Eddington as a Quaker Adventurer," *Isis* 95, no. 1 (2003): 57–89.
26. Ernest Rutherford, quoted in S. Chandrasekhar, "Of Some Famous Men: Verifying the Theory of Relativity," *Bulletin of the Atomic Scientists* (June 1975): 17.
27. A. Ruth Fry, *A Quaker Adventure* (London: Nisbet, 1926), 355, cited in Stanley, "An Expedition to Heal the Wounds of War." Even the trans-European aspect of this seemingly politically transcendent moment was ephemeral, with Germany disavowing Einstein's theory as England began to accept it. A recent *New York Times* article succinctly explains the tangle of politics around Einstein's theory, including the ways it was disavowed by Nazi Germany because Einstein was Jewish. David Kaiser, "How Politics Shaped General Relativity," *New York Times*, November 6, 2015.
28. F. W. Dyson, A. S. Eddington, and C. Davidson, "A Determination of the Deflection of Light by the Sun's Gravitational Field," *Philosophical Transactions of the Royal Society of London*, Series A, vol. 220 (1920), 313. Slavery was officially abolished in 1875 but continued unofficially into the twentieth century. *Encyclopedia Britannica Online*, s.v. "Sao Tome and Principe," by Gerhard Siebert, accessed February 2, 2016, http://www.britannica.com/place/Sao-Tome-and-Principe#toc278739. This history resurfaced in 2009 events to commemorate Eddington's expedition, which brought out tensions around Portugal's lasting influence on the island, as well as the marginalization of local people descended from enslaved people. See Gisa Weszkalnys, "Príncipe Eclipsed: Commemorating the Confirmation of Einstein's Theory of General Relativity," *Anthropology Today* 25, no. 5 (2009): 8–12.
29. Alex Soojung-Kim Pang, *Empire and the Sun: Victorian Solar Eclipse Expeditions* (Stanford, Calif.: Stanford University Press, 2002), 121–43.
30. Donna Haraway, "Situated Knowledges: The Science Question in Feminism and the Privilege of Partial Perspective," *Feminist Studies* 14, no. 3 (1988): 581. For more on scientific expeditions and anthropological photography, see Gregg Mitman, "A Journey without Maps: Film, Expeditionary Science, and the Growth of Development," in *Documenting the World*, ed. Gregg Mitman and Kelley Wilder (Chicago: University of Chicago Press, 2016), 124–49.
31. For example, on his way to Brazil in 1912, Eddington wrote that in Saint Vincent, "we were surrounded by boats. . . . These were all occupied by n—;

the little n—boys were very amusing. I tried to photograph them" (Eddington to Sarah Eddington, September 11, 1912, Box A2, File 3, Wren Library, Cambridge, U.K.). Eddington's journal and letters never delve into the histories of the places to which he travels, and he never writes of conversations with anyone other than fellow Europeans, even though he spends ample time describing visual features of his destinations.

32. See, for example, Gerald Horne, *The Apocalypse of Settler Colonialism: The Roots of Slavery, White Supremacy, and Capitalism in Seventeenth-Century North America and the Caribbean* (New York: NYU Press, 2018).

33. Jessica Hurley and Dan Sinkyin, "Apocalypse: Introduction," *ASAP Journal* 3, no. 3 (September 2018): 451–66.

34. Miscellaneous correspondence in Box 7, Solar Eclipse Records, Royal Greenwich Observatory Archives, Cambridge University Library. The program of observations for the May 16, 1901, expedition to Mauritius, for example, involved the following: general corona photographs, which would require a four-inch Dallmeyer coronagraph set up with a twelve-inch coelostat; photographs of spectra and flash of corona, which could be taken with a two-inch prismatic camera rigged with a twelve-inch coelostat; short-exposure photographs of coronal extensions taken with a four-inch Dallmeyer Rapid Rectilinear lens in combination with a sixteen-inch coelostat; photo-heliographs taken with a sixteen-inch coelostat "during totality of the prominences and inner corona." Walter Maunder to Herbert Turner, August 30, 1901, Box 7, File 201, Royal Greenwich Observatory Archives, University of Cambridge. Each coelostat, a rotating mirror that allows cameras to remain trained on the sun even as it arcs slowly across the sky, had to be specially calibrated for the Southern Hemisphere. Frank Dyson to Dr. Common, February 14, 1901, Box 7, File 201, Royal Greenwich Observatory Archives, University of Cambridge.

35. Eddington to Sarah Eddington, October 13, 1912, File A 218, Eddington Archive, Wren Library, Cambridge, U.K.

36. Eddington to Sarah Eddington, June 21, 1919, Box A4, File 9, Eddington Archive, Wren Library, Cambridge, U.K.

37. Arthur Eddington, "The Stars and Their Movements," lecture, Perth, Australia, 1915, Box C, File 1, Eddington Archive, Wren Library, Cambridge, U.K.

38. "Einstein Expedition to Cable Results," *Film Daily*, September 26, 1922, 2.

39. Charles R. Acland and Haidee Wasson, eds., *Useful Cinema* (Durham, N.C.: Duke University Press, 2011). Acland and Wasson in part respond to Vinzenz Hediger and Patrick Vonderau, *Films That Work: Industrial Film and the Productivity of Media* (Amsterdam: Amsterdam University Press, 2009).

40. Acland and Wasson, *Useful Cinema*, 2.

41. See Eric Smoodin, "'What a Power for Education!': The Cinema and Sites of Learning in the 1930s," in Acland and Wasson, *Useful Cinema*, 17–33; Alison

Griffiths, "'A Moving Picture of the Heavens': The Planetarium Space Show as Useful," in Acland and Wasson, *Useful Cinema*, 230–61; Oliver Gaycken, *Devices of Curiosity: Early Cinema and Popular Science* (New York: Oxford University Press, 2015); Devin Orgeron, Marsha Orgeron, and Dan Streible, eds., *Learning with the Lights Off: Educational Film in the United States* (Oxford: Oxford University Press, 2002).

42. See Mark Butterworth, "Astronomical Lantern Slides," *Magic Lantern Gazette* 19, no. 2 (2007): 3–11.
43. Stewart Tryster and Stefan Drössler, "Wer war Hanns Walter Kornblum?," notes accompanying *Wunder der Schöpfung*, directed by Hanns Walter Kornblum (1925; Munich, Germany: Edition Filmmuseum, 2009), DVD.
44. Scott Curtis, *The Shape of Spectatorship: Art, Science, and Early Cinema in Germany* (New York: Columbia University Press, 2015), 149.
45. See Orgeron, Orgeron, and Streible, "A History of Learning with the Lights Off," in *Learning with the Lights Off*, 16.
46. Publicity materials, 1925, included on Kornblum, *Wunder der Schöpfung*.
47. William Randolph Hearst, cited in "Hearst's Tribute to the Pictures," *Motography* 6, no. 6 (1911): 257.
48. Ford W. Eaton, "The Schoolhouse of the Future," *Motography* 8, no. 2 (1912): 56. Columbus again surfaces here as a reference point for the excitement of visual travel through outer space.
49. Harvard University president Charles William Eliot voiced similar enthusiasm over what he called "education through the eye," the use of film in teaching, which he imagined would have transformative effects. See "Miscellaneous Notes," *Visual Education* 1, no. 4 (1920): 45. Additionally, the entire publication of *The Educational Screen*, founded in 1922 to grapple with "the new influence in education" and addressed broadly to a "thinking American public," is testament to a wider sense of film's educational value and impact. As the editors write in their opening issue, "The screen educates—for better or for worse—wherever it hangs." *Educational Screen* 1, no. 1 (1922): 7.
50. Zachary Horton, *The Cosmic Zoom: Scale, Knowledge, and Mediation* (Chicago: University of Chicago Press, 2021), 3.
51. *The Einstein Theory of Relativity* ran under multiple titles, including *The Einstein Theory of Relativity* and *Einstein's Theory of Relativity*. Much of the footage was taken from the longer German film *Die Grundlagen der Einsteinschen Relativitätstheorie,* the U.S. distribution rights for which were purchased by Edwin M. Fadman for Equity Films and subsequently transferred to Premier Productions and then Red Seal Pictures ("Equity Gets Einstein Film," *Film Daily,* September 13, 1922, 2). The German film was much abridged and re-edited, and Max Fleischer was enlisted to create animations that would make it more palatable for entertainment. The film had long theatrical runs throughout the United States, but articles in the *Moving Picture World* evince the

difficulty of marketing a film that was neither pure entertainment nor simply educational. One particularly innovative theater manager, E. B. Roberts of Austin, Texas, was celebrated for his attractive display with the film titles hanging on golden star cutouts. An article joked, "He put most of the solar system in his lobby" ("Einstein Theory Helps a Feature," *Moving Picture World*, July 21, 1923, 223). After its theatrical run, it continued to be shown sporadically at special events and entered the Kodascope Library of Motion Pictures, which distributed it for educational viewing into the 1940s. An *Educational Screen* listing for the film deemed it "Excellent for Physics classes of High Schools and Colleges" ("Reference List of Films Previously Reviewed," *Educational Screen*, June 1924, 250). While I will not discuss it here, Fritz Lang's *Woman in the Moon* (Germany, 1929) provides an interesting link between these two sets of films, incorporating footage and pedagogical elements—astronomical photographs from Mount Wilson Observatory and charts of trajectories, for example—that bear striking resemblance to the modes of address in the science-education films I reference, but within a fantastic narrative of space travel that echoes Georges Méliès's earlier work.

52. "Einstein Film Given Broadway Run," *Motion Picture News*, March 17, 1923, 1,304.

53. "Two Hundred Understand Einstein, It Is Said," *New York Times*, January 26, 1930. The article does not mention which film the association screened, but it does make plain the disdain of scientists for such a crude popularization of a theory only those with a sophisticated university education might be equipped to understand. The subhead expresses a sense of defensiveness around the theory: "Crowd at Film Explaining [Einstein's] Theory Called No Index of Popular Knowledge." The film in question is presumably the Fleischer adaptation of Kornblum's film.

54. See, for example, Einstein to Elsa Einstein, January 7, 1921, in *The Collected Papers of Albert Einstein*, vol. 12, no. 11, ed. Diana K. Buchwald, Ze'ev Rosenkranz, Tilman Sauer, József Illy, and Virginia Iris Holmes (Princeton, N.J.: Princeton University Press, 2009), 31; "Professor Einstein und der Einsteinfilm," *Berliner Tageblatt*, June 2, 1922, evening edition. For a more complete discussion of this film's reception in the German scientific community, see Milena Wazeck, "The 1922 Einstein Film: Cinematic Innovation and Public Controversy," *Physics in Perspective* (June 2010): 163–79.

55. In the original, "Dass im Laufe der Herstellung des zur Anwendung gekommene Tricktechnik erst entwickelt und vervollkommnet worden ist." Translation my own. Nollendorfplatz, "Die Grundlagen der Einsteinschen Relativitätstheorie."

56. *Berliner Börsen-Zeitung*, September 16, 1925, trans. by and cited in Stewart Tryster and Ronny Loewy, "The Kornblum Puzzle," notes accompanying Kornblum, *Wunder der Schöpfung*.

57. The charts that compare sizes and trace orbital paths of planets draw directly on the visual motifs of magic-lantern slides that circulated widely in the late nineteenth and early twentieth centuries. A set by Carpenter and Westley in 1838 in particular provides a visual template for these shots. For an overview of the history of astronomical lantern-slide lectures, see Butterworth, "Astronomical Lantern Slides." I had the opportunity to view Mark Butterworth's extensive collection of astronomical slides thanks to the generous hospitality of Willem Hackmann, a retired Oxford historian and avid collector of lantern slides and scientific instruments.
58. See Sean Redmond and Leon Marvell, eds., *Endangering Science Fiction Film* (New York: Routledge, 2016).
59. Tom Gunning, "Shooting into Outer Space," in *Fantastic Voyages of the Cinematic Imagination,* ed. Matthew Solomon (Albany: State University of New York Press, 2011), 102–4.
60. "*Wunder der Schöpfung*: Ein Film in sieben Akten," program notes (Berlin: Universum Film Verleih, 1925).
61. Jean Epstein, "The Senses I," in *French Theory and Criticism, 1907–1939,* ed. and trans. Richard Abel (Princeton, N.J.: Princeton University Press, 1988), 244.
62. Program for *The Einstein Theory of Relativity* (*Die Grundlagen der Einsteinschen Relativitätstheorie,* Berlin, 1922). This document is part of a collection by German silent-film historian Herbert Birett, who digitized a large number of archival materials on German films up to 1945 and made them available on his website, https://kinematographie.de. The translation is my own.
63. This film seems to have left no trace in any film journals or newspapers of the period, making it difficult to pinpoint its exact dates. It was discovered by Skip Elsheimer, an avid educational-film collector who has contributed to the Prelinger Archives thousands of archival films that he finds at estate sales, auctions, and flea markets. Elsheimer catalogs this film as a product of the 1920s, which seems very likely given its strikingly similar content and style to the other films I reference here. Hoey Lawlor also made another film for Service Films called *A Trip to the Moon,* which blends sci-fi-style visions of future space travel with some astronomical facts.
64. M. Briefer, "Student Psychology and Motion Pictures in Education," *Transactions of the Society of Motion Picture Engineers* (1925): 17.
65. "Einstein Theory," *Variety* 69 (February 1, 1923), 41.
66. Dorothy E. Cook, "Romance of the Skies," *Educational Film Catalog* (New York: H. W. Wilson Company, 1939), 99.
67. Jean Epstein, "To a Second Reality, a Second Reason," trans. Sarah Keller, in *Jean Epstein: Critical Essays and New Translations,* ed. Sarah Keller and Jason N. Paul (Amsterdam: Amsterdam University Press, 2012), 323.
68. See, for example, Pang, *Empire and the Sun,* 49–50, which describes British astronomers' assumptions about local beliefs during an expedition to India.

69. "*Wunder der Schöpfung*: Ein Film in sieben Akten."
70. All intertitles I cite from this film are translated from the original German. All translations are my own, except those from the Bible, which quote the English Standard Version.
71. Karl Clausberg, *Zwischen den Sternen: Lichtbildarchiv: Was Einstein und Uexküll, Benjamin und das Kino der Astronomie des 19. Jahrhunderts verdanken* (Berlin: Akademie Verlag, 2006), 7.
72. "Kein Wesen kann zu Nichts zerfallen! / Das Ewige regt sich fort in allen. / Am Sein erhalte Dich beglückt! / Das Sein ist ewig, denn Gesetze / Bewahren die lebend'gen Schätze, / Aus welchen sich das All geschmückt." Johann Wolfgang von Goethe, "Vermächtnis," in *Goethe-Lexikon* (1829; Stuttgart, Germany: Kröner, 1998), 1,112, my translation.
73. This notion of cinematic time resembles what Mary Ann Doane discusses in *The Emergence of Cinematic Time: Modernity, Contingency, the Archive* (Cambridge, Mass.: Harvard University Press, 2002).
74. Early twentieth-century statistics and the law of temporal irreversibility are a focus of Doane's explanation of the temporalities of modernity into which cinema emerged.
75. Walter Benjamin, "Theses on the Philosophy of History," in *Illuminations*, ed. Hannah Arendt, trans. Harry Zohn (1940; New York: Schocken Books, 1968), 256.

2. New Constellations

1. André Bazin, "On Why We Fight: History, Documentation, and the Newsreel" (1946), in *The Documentary Film Reader*, ed. Jonathan Kahana (New York: Oxford University Press, 2016), 348–49.
2. Rey Chow, *The Age of the World Target: Self-Referentiality in War, Theory, and Comparative Work* (Durham, N.C.: Duke University Press, 2006), 26–33.
3. Walter Benjamin, "To the Planetarium," in *One-Way Street* (New York: Penguin, 2001), 59.
4. See Richard J. Overy, *The Air War* (1980; Lincoln: University of Nebraska Press, 2005).
5. Adriaan Blaauw, *History of the IAU: The Birth and First Half Century of the International Astronomical Union* (Dordrecht, Netherlands: Kluwer Academic Publishers, 1994), 116. The International Astronomical Union (IAU) consisted initially of members from Allied nations of the First World War, and within three years of its establishment it also included a number of other nations that had assisted the Allies, including Brazil, South Africa, New Zealand, Poland, Portugal, Romania, Serbia, and some neutral states. The IAU was thus at once strikingly international and subject to the most rigid political divisions of the day; it was global in an age of an undeniably fractured globe. The organization was

designed to make astronomy more resilient in the face of war, allowing scientists to forge networks across borders and instantiate a kind of scientific diplomacy that would bind the communities of member nations more closely.

6. Blaauw, *History of the IAU*, 129–50. In Germany, moreover, many scientific disciplines were thrown into turmoil with the exile and emigration of Jewish scientists. By the early 1930s, Jews—including, most famously, Einstein— were banned from positions at German universities. Adolf Hitler responded to an appeal by Max Planck to retain Einstein at the Prussian Academy: "Our national policies will not be revoked or modified, even for scientists. If the dismissal of Jewish scientists means the annihilation of contemporary German science, then we shall do without science for a few years!" Quoted in Walter Isaacson, *Einstein: His Life and Universe* (New York: Simon and Schuster, 2007), 407–8.

7. I am grateful for archivists at the British Film Institute, Imperial War Museum, and Royal Air Force Museum film archives for their assistance in allowing me to see over thirty films from these film units during a research trip in April 2016. While my analysis in this chapter lingers on more broadly available films, the wide array of films I was able to see during that trip allowed me to locate the major productions I analyze within the context of an astounding volume of documentary film production in wartime Britain. The themes and images I discuss in a limited number of films here resonate and recur across dozens of films about aerial warfare to which my reference, for reasons of length and repetition, is only cursory.

8. See Paul Virilio, *War and Cinema: The Logistics of Perception* (New York: Verso, 1989); Caren Kaplan, *Aerial Aftermaths: Wartime from Above* (Durham, N.C.: Duke University Press, 2017); Chow, *Age of the World Target*; Lisa Parks, *Rethinking Media Coverage: Vertical Mediation and the War on Terror* (New York: Routledge, 2018); Peter Sloterdijk, *Terror from the Air,* trans. Amy Patton (Los Angeles: Semiotext(e), 2009).

9. Paula Amad, "From God's-Eye to Camera-Eye: Aerial Photography and Modernity's Post-Humanist and Neo-humanist Visions of the World," *History of Photography* 36, no. 1 (February 2012): 85.

10. Patrick Ellis, *Aeroscopics: Media of the Bird's-Eye View* (Oakland: University of California Press, 2021), 2.

11. It is worth noting a parallel with Japan, another island nation with imperial influences and ambitions, which produced a great number of films about aerial warfare. See Markus Nornes, *Japanese Documentary Film: The Meiji Era through Hiroshima* (Minneapolis: University of Minnesota Press, 2003); Michael Baskett, *The Attractive Empire: Transnational Film Culture in Imperial Japan* (Honolulu: University of Hawai'i Press, 2008).

12. Jack C. Ellis, *John Grierson: Life, Contributions, Influence* (Carbondale: Southern Illinois University Press, 2000), 85.

13. Though its documentary film movement as such did not begin until the late 1920s, Britain already had a history of actuality filmmaking prior to then, largely devoted to exposing or exploring natural and technological phenomena. In the first years of the twentieth century, Charles Urban produced a popular series of loosely scientific films called *The Unseen World*. *The Cheese Mites* (Britain, 1903), a minute-long film in which a man accidentally sees his cheese, teeming with mites, under microscopic magnification, may be the most well-known. Like the films I discussed in the previous chapter, the films of the *Unseen World* series combined scientific ambitions with imaginative impulses. Despite their tenuous claims to scientific validity, the films were frequently shown in educational contexts. Two decades later, British Instructional Films made another popular series of natural science films, *Secrets of Nature* (1922–1933), which also revealed microcosmic biological worlds. These films were more complex, adopting editing techniques from Soviet filmmaking, and influenced Britain's expanding documentary scene as it began to solidify into institutionalized creative units with international resonance and acclaim. Timothy Boon, *Films of Fact: A History of Science in Documentary Films and Television* (New York: Wallflower, 2008); Paul Swann, *The British Documentary Film Movement, 1926–1946* (Cambridge: Cambridge University Press, 1989), 14–17.

14. Under Grierson's influence, the EMB strongly advocated for education film in Britain, becoming the most extensive distributor of film to British schools. Swann, *British Documentary Film Movement*, 38. The documentarists' pedagogical mission continued as the film unit found a new home with the GPO, which Grierson saw as a "unifying and integrative" filmmaking effort that could serve to inform people of all ages and from all social classes, providing "education for a democratic society." While the GPO Film Unit reached out to theatrical audiences as well, schoolchildren and other nontheatrical audiences continued to be Grierson's primary target. Jeffrey Richards, "John Grierson and the Lost World of the GPO Film Unit," in *The Projection of Britain: A History of the GPO Film Unit*, ed. Scott Anthony and James G. Mansell (London: BFI, 2011).

15. John Grierson, "The Documentary Idea," in *Grierson on Documentary*, ed. Forsyth Hardy (New York: Praeger, 1971), 249.

16. Cited in Elizabeth Sussex, "Cavalcanti in England," *Sight and Sound* (1975): 205–11, republished in Anthony and Mansell, *Projection of Britain*, 52.

17. Examples from the interwar period include *Contact* (dir. Paul Rotha, 1933), *The Future's in the Air* (dir. Alexander Shaw, 1937), *Air Outpost* (dir. Paul Rotha, 1937), *Wings over Empire* (dir. Paul Fletcher and Stuart Legg, 1939). Notably, aviation was also a popular topic for film in Hollywood during the years Grierson resided in the United States; see, for example, *Wings* (dir. William A. Wellman, 1927).

18. Lisa Parks, *Rethinking Media Coverage: Vertical Mediation and the War on Terror* (New York: Routledge, 2018), 6.
19. Parks, *Rethinking Media Coverage*, 15.
20. See James Hay, "The Invention of Air Space, Outer Space, and Cyberspace," in *Down to Earth: Satellite Technologies, Industries, and Cultures*, ed. Lisa Parks and James Schwoch, 19–41 (New Brunswick, N.J.: Rutgers University Press, 2012).
21. *Aircraft Cine Cameras (Gunnery) and Ancillary Equipment* (1940), 2, RAF X001–6406 AP 1749 v. 1, Royal Air Force Museum, London.
22. The manual goes on to explain that assessment of the film would be made by playing it back to the pilot and analyzing the location of the target relative to the frame. It furthermore describes how to set up a model aircraft between the projector and the screen in order to cast a shadow that allows the viewer to track the angles of attack relative to the target aircraft, adding an interactive element to the viewing of the film (*Aircraft Cine Cameras*, 5). Paul Virilio traces the link between guns and cameras back further in *The Vision Machine*, trans. Julie Rose (Bloomington: Indiana University Press, 1994).
23. Kaplan, *Aerial Aftermaths*, 4–5.
24. Kaplan, 5.
25. Charles Wolfe, "Mapping *Why We Fight*: Frank Capra and the US Army Orientation Film in World War II," *American Film: Selected Readings, Origins to 1960*, ed. Cynthia Lucia, Roy Grundman, and Art Simon, 326–40 (Malden, Mass.: Wiley Blackwell, 2016), 331.
26. Wolfe, "Mapping *Why We Fight*," 31–32.
27. This division is one of the themes of *We Live in Two Worlds*, Cavalcanti's 1937 documentary for the GPO that illustrates the increasing interconnectedness of the globe and concomitant persistence of national boundaries, evoking a sense of cosmic (dis)order in a world on the brink of war.
28. Publicity Committee Progress Report no. 27, March 31, 1939, cited in S. P. Mackenzie, *British War Films* (London: Hambledon and London, 2001), 23.
29. André Bazin, "The Ontology of the Photographic Image," in *What Is Cinema?*, vol. 1, ed. and trans. Hugh Gray (Berkeley: University of California Press, 1967), 14.
30. "Aerial Photography: Value in War," *Aerial Photography: Air Publication* 838 (September 1921): 21.
31. Kaja Silverman, "What Is a Camera?, or History in the Field of Vision," *Discourse* 15, no. 3 (1993): 25.
32. "Aerial Photography," 21.
33. Harry Watt, in interview with Elizabeth Sussex, in Sussex, *The Rise and Fall of British Documentary: The Story of the Film Movement Founded by John Grierson* (Berkeley: University of California Press, 1976), 130.

34. In addition to being used as a recruitment film to instill future members of the RAF with a sense of pride and bravery, the film was a great theatrical success.
35. Aubrey Flanagan, "Squadron Leader," *Motion Picture Herald*, November 28, 1942, 1,030; Aubrey Flanagan, "In British Studios," *Motion Picture Herald*, December 5, 1942, 38.
36. At the time of the film's release, the central piece of the score, the "Warsaw Concerto," was released by RCA. See "Suicide Squadron," *Showmen's Trade Review*, April 25, 1942, 24.
37. Bernard Holland, "The Solo Concerto as a Paradigm of Social Struggle," *New York Times*, December 21, 1986. Debates about its quality were rampant, indicating just how central the score was to the film's story and reputation. The *New York Times* obituary for Addinsell mentions some of his other film scores but devotes nearly half of the text to this concerto, noting that "it puzzled some listeners as much as it delighted others" and could be taken as either a parody of Rachmaninoff's work or a failed attempt at a serious concerto. See "Richard Addinsell, Writer of Scores in Hollywood; Did Warsaw Concerto!," *New York Times*, November 17, 1977.
38. Historian Arthur I. Miller explains, "Einstein believed much the same of physics, that beyond observations and theory lay the music of the spheres—which, he wrote, revealed a 'pre-established harmony' exhibiting stunning symmetries. The laws of nature, such as those of relativity theory, were waiting to be plucked out of the cosmos by someone with a sympathetic ear" (Arthur I. Miller, "A Genius Finds Inspiration in the Music of Another," *New York Times*, January 31, 2006). Walter Isaacson argues that Einstein's love of music did not provide an escape from the problems raised in astronomy and physics but was wholly compatible with Einstein's engagement with such problems. Music was connected "to the harmony underlying the universe. . . . He was awed, both in music and physics, by the beauty of harmonies" (Isaacson, *Einstein*, 37). Eddington seems to have perceived this link as well, comparing the cosmos and music metaphorically in his writing. In his efforts to extend Einstein's relativity into a larger fundamental theory, he writes that we may "look on the universe as a symphony played on seven primitive constants as music played on the seven notes of a scale." Sir Arthur Eddington, *New Pathways in Science* (Cambridge: Cambridge University Press, 1935), 277. More recently, NASA scientists discovered that black holes actually emit musical pitches. Not only that, "these sound waves may be the key in figuring out how galaxy clusters, the largest structures in the Universe, grow." See "Black Hole Sound Waves," Science @ NASA, September 9, 2003, https://science.nasa.gov/science-news/science-at-nasa/2003/09sep_blackholesounds.
39. Isaacson, *Einstein*, 37–38.
40. See my introduction for more on these theorists and their cosmological visions.

41. Michael Powell, *A Life in Movies* (New York: Knopf, 1987), 533; David S. Hill, Stuart B. Kamenetsky, and Sandra E. Trehub, "Relations among Text, Mode, and Medium: Historical and Empirical Perspectives," *Musical Perception: An Interdisciplinary Journal* 4, no. 1 (1996): 3–21.
42. Powell, *Life in Movies*, 541.
43. Zachary Horton, *The Cosmic Zoom: Scale, Knowledge, and Mediation* (Chicago: University of Chicago Press, 2021), 118.
44. Edward Casey, *The Fate of Place: A Philosophical History* (Berkeley: University of California Press, 1998), 342.
45. "The Lord Reveals His Cosmic Form," in the Bhagavad Gita, available at "The Bhagavad-Gita," Nazarean Way, accessed March 20, 2023, https://www.thenazareneway.com/gita_chapter_11.htm; Gunhild Pörksen, *Paracelsus: Philosophie der grossen und der kleinen Welt, aus der Astronomia Magna* (Basel, Switzerland: Schwabe, 2008); Immanuel Kant, "Analytic of the Sublime," in *Critique of Judgment*, trans. J. H. Bernard (1790; New York: Hafner Press, 1951).

3. Destroyer of Worlds

1. Bob Serber, James Conant, and J. Robert Oppenheimer, cited in Kai Bird and Martin Sherwin, *American Prometheus: The Triumph and Tragedy of J. Robert Oppenheimer* (New York: Vintage Books, 2005), 307–8.
2. This was famously recounted by Robert Jungk in his memoir of the Manhattan Project and its legacy, *Brighter Than a Thousand Suns: A Personal History of the Atomic Scientists*, trans. James Cleugh (San Diego: Harcourt, 1956), 210.
3. Bird and Sherwin, *American Prometheus*, 309.
4. Bird and Sherwin, 296–99.
5. Bird and Sherwin, 293.
6. Akira Mizuta Lippit, *Atomic Light: Shadow Optics* (Minneapolis: University of Minnesota Press, 2005), 82.
7. Paul Virilio, *War and Cinema: The Logistics of Perception*, trans. Patrick Camiller (New York: Verso, 1989), 81.
8. Jean Epstein, "The Cinema Seen from Etna," in *Jean Epstein: Critical Essays and New Translations*, ed. and trans. Sarah Keller and Jason Paul (1926; Amsterdam: Amsterdam University Press, 2012), 288.
9. Jean Epstein, "To a Second Reality, a Second Reason," trans. Sarah Keller, in Keller and Paul, *Jean Epstein*, 321–27.
10. Nakai Masakazu, "Film Theory and the Crisis in Contemporary Aesthetics," in "Decentering Theory: Reconsidering the History of Japanese Film Theory," ed. Aaron Garow, special issue, *Review of Japanese Culture and Society* 22 (2010): 80.

11. Trond Lundemo, "Nuclear Film Theory: Realism and Montage as Transubstantiation" (conference proceedings, Film Theory in Media History: "Nodes" and "Edges," Shanghai, China, June 4, 2016), 54.
12. Lippit, *Atomic Light*, 4.
13. Lippit, 25.
14. Jennifer Fay, *Inhospitable World: Cinema in the Time of the Anthropocene* (New York: Oxford University Press, 2018), 205.
15. Walter Benjamin, "Theses on the Philosophy of History," in *Illuminations*, ed. Hannah Arendt, trans. Harry Zohn (1940; New York: Schocken Books, 1968), 256.
16. Lundemo, "Nuclear Film Theory," 66.
17. Christine Hauser, "US Nuclear Weapons Tests Come to YouTube," *New York Times*, March 17, 2017.
18. Maya Deren, *An Anagram of Ideas on Art, Form, and Film* (New York: Alicat, 1946), 8–9.
19. Numerous historians discuss this in detail. See, for example, Norman Etherington, "Hot War, Cold War and Decolonization," in *Theories of Imperialism: War, Conquest, and Capital* (New York: Routledge, 1984), 227–61; Paul Kennedy, "Stability and Change in a Bipolar World," in *The Rise and Fall of the Great Powers* (New York: Random House, 1987); B. R. Tomlinson, "The Contraction of England: National Decline and Loss of Empire," *Journal of Imperial and Commonwealth History* 11 (1982): 58–72; William Roger Louis, *Ends of British Imperialism: The Scramble for Empire, Suez, and Decolonization* (London: I. B. Tauris, 2006).
20. Hans Richter, "A History of the Avantgarde," in *Art in Cinema: A Symposium of the Avantgarde Film at the San Francisco Museum of Art*, ed. Frank Stauffacher (San Francisco: San Francisco Museum of Art, 1947).
21. Among other things, the NFB is known for spawning the more documentary style that came to be known as cinema verité.
22. See D. B. Jones, *Movies and Memoranda: An Interpretive History of the National Film Board of Canada* (Ottawa: Canadian Film Institute, 1981).
23. For more on tropes of mainstream science-fiction film in this period, see Patricia Kerslake, *Science Fiction and Empire* (Liverpool: Liverpool University Press, 2010); Vivian Sobchack, *Screening Space: The American Science Fiction Film*, 2nd ed. (New Brunswick, N.J.: Rutgers University Press, 2001); David Seed, *American Science Fiction and the Cold War: Literature and Film* (Edinburgh: Fitzroy Dearborn, 1999).
24. It is important to note that many scientists at the time, including Einstein and even some associated with the Manhattan Project, were frustrated or appalled by this imbrication of military and scientific interests and sought to exercise political influence to ensure the bomb would not be used. Nevertheless, the

detonation of the bomb signaled the subordination of nuclear science to a military cause in which many scientists were wholly complicit.

25. For more on early uses of film and photography in scientific practice and discourses of objectivity, see Hannah Landecker, "Microcinematography and the History of Science and Film," *Isis* 97, no. 1 (March 2006): 121–32; Lorraine Daston and Peter Galison, "Mechanical Objectivity," in *Objectivity* (New York: Zone Books, 2007), 115–90; Jimena Canales, "Photogenic Venus: The 'Cinematographic Turn' and Its Alternatives in Nineteenth-Century France," *Isis* 93, no. 4 (December 2002): 585–613.

26. Oliver Gaycken, *Devices of Curiosity: Early Cinema and Popular Science* (Oxford: Oxford University Press, 2015), 6.

27. Timothy Boon, *Films of Fact: A History of Science in Documentary Films and Television* (London: Wallflower Press, 2008), 37. Rachael Low also develops a sense of the shared institutional and aesthetic histories of documentary and scientific actuality films in *Documentary and Educational Films of the 1930s* (London: George Allen and Unwin, 1979).

28. See Bill Nichols, "Documentary Film and the Modernist Avant-Garde," *Critical Inquiry* 27 (Summer 2001): 580–610; Jonathan Kahana, *The Documentary Film Reader: History, Theory, Criticism* (New York: Oxford University Press, 2016), sect. "Modernisms: State, Left, and Avant-Garde Documentary between the Wars."

29. Joris Ivens, "Reflections on the Avant-Garde Documentary," in Kahana, *Documentary Film Reader*, 28.

30. See especially Mikhail Iampolsky, "Reality at Second Hand," in Kahana, *Documentary Film Reader*, 182–91. Per Conner's consistent preference, I cite titles of his films with all capital letters rather than italics. As Conner explains, "Full Capital Letters . . . are like the signage on walls, monuments, and objects and are like objects in themselves." See Bruce Conner, "Plates, 'etc.': Some Notes to the Reader," in Conner et al., *Bruce Conner*, 13.

31. Amos Vogel, interview by Scott MacDonald, "Cinema 16: Toward a History of the Film Society," *Wide Angle* 19, no. 1 (1997): 28.

32. See William Wees, *Light Moving in Time: Studies in the Visual Aesthetics of Avant-Garde Film* (Berkeley: University of California Press, 1992); P. Adams Sitney, *Visionary Film: The American Avant-Garde, 1943–1978* (Oxford: Oxford University Press, 1974). The French filmmaker Jean Painlevé is frequently considered as both an avant-garde filmmaker and a maker of scientific films, with those two impulses often overlapping. See especially Andy Masaki Bellows, Marina McDougall, and Brigitte Berg, eds., *Science Is Fiction: The Films of Jean Painlevé* (Cambridge, Mass.: MIT Press, 2000).

33. Robert A. Haller, "Galaxy: Avant-Garde Filmmakers Look across Space and Time," catalog for film series, September 4–7, 2001.

34. Haller, "Galaxy."
35. Deren's screenings of her work in Provincetown, Massachusetts, were what gave Amos Vogel the idea to start Cinema 16. See Vogel, "Cinema 16." See also Sarah Keller, *Maya Deren: Incomplete Control* (New York: Columbia University Press, 2014).
36. Maya Deren, "Chamber Films," *Filmwise* 2 (1961): 37–38.
37. It is worth noting that Kracauer was quite excited by Deren's filmmaking, which he saw as externalizing psychological reality "with such vitality that she instills new life into the old patterns." He was taken with her "distortions of time and space" and "artistic time-space relations," which resisted clear interpretations of meaning typical of traditional narrative forms. Siegfried Kracauer, "Filming the Subconscious" (1948), in *Siegfried Kracauer's American Writings: Essays on Film and Popular Culture,* ed. Johannes von Moltke and Kristy Rawson (Berkeley: University of California Press, 2012), 57.
38. Maya Deren, notes on *At Land,* New York, 1944, collected in "Maya Deren: Notes, Essays, Letters," *Film Culture* 39 (1965): 2.
39. Maya Deren, "Choreography for the Camera," in "Maya Deren," *Film Culture,* 3.
40. Deren, *An Anagram of Ideas*. This collection of short essays has received much scholarly attention, including by Annette Michelson, who sees it as a founding document of the avant-garde movement that ripened into the late 1960s. *Anagram of Ideas,* Michelson writes, was part of Deren's consistent "determination to ground innovative practice in theory" and to "provide the solid basis and legitimation of the radically innovative practices" of her film production work. See Annette Michelson, "Poetics and Savage Thought: About *Anagram,*" in *Maya Deren and the American Avant-Garde,* ed. Bill Nichols (Berkeley: University of California Press, 2001), 29.
41. Deren, *Anagram of Ideas,* 8–9.
42. Deren's discussion of the scientist's mounting power as a force of cosmic change in the world resonates with current literature on the Anthropocene, collapsing "age-old humanist distinctions between natural history and human history." See Dipesh Chakrabarty, "The Climate of History: Four Theses," *Critical Inquiry* 35, no. 2 (2009): 201.
43. Deren, *Anagram of Ideas,* 12.
44. Deren, 12–13.
45. Deren, 47.
46. Maya Deren, recorded lecture, Special Collections, Boston University, featured in *In the Mirror of Maya Deren* (dir. Martina Kudlacek, 2003).
47. Maya Deren, "Cinema as an Art Form," in *Essential Deren: Collected Writings on Film,* ed. Bruce Rice McPherson (Kingston, N.Y.: Documentext, 2005), 48.
48. As Sarah Keller traces, *The Very Eye of Night* was in many ways a continuation of Deren's earlier work, in keeping with her interests in formal experimentation

with the temporal and spatial qualities of film while exploring the medium's capacity to summon mythological, ritual registers. See Sarah Keller, "Full Circle," in *Maya Deren: Incomplete Control* (New York: Columbia University Press, 2015), 189–240.
49. Maya Deren, recording of lecture, Special Collections, Boston University, featured in Kudlacek, *In the Mirror of Maya Deren*.
50. Keller, *Maya Deren*, 200.
51. Stan Brakhage, in Kudlacek, *In the Mirror of Maya Deren*.
52. Christine Hauser, "US Nuclear Weapons Tests Come to YouTube," *New York Times,* March 17, 2017.
53. The center of a nuclear explosion reaches sixty to one hundred million degrees Centigrade, roughly one hundred thousand times hotter than the surface of the sun. See Carey Sublette, "Effects of Nuclear Explosions," Nuclear Weapon Archive, May 15, 1997, http://nuclearweaponarchive.org/Nwfaq/Nfaq5.html.
54. W. A. Shurcliff, *Bombs at Bikini: The Official Report of Operation Crossroads* (New York: Wise & Co., 1947), 151–52. Further citations to this work will be in text.
55. Élie Faure, "The Art of Cineplastics," in *French Theory and Criticism, 1907–1939,* ed. and trans. Richard Abel (Princeton, N.J.: Princeton University Press, 1988), 267.
56. Jean Epstein, "The Cinema Seen from Etna," in *Jean Epstein: Critical Essays and New Translations,* ed. and trans. Sarah Keller and Jason Paul (Amsterdam: Amsterdam University Press, 2012), 288.
57. Epstein, "Cinema Seen from Etna," 289.
58. Stuart Conner, Rudolf Frieling, Gary Garrels, and Laura Hoptman, introduction to *Bruce Conner: It's All True* (Berkeley: University of California Press, 2016), 9.
59. Bruce Conner, in interview with Paul Karlstrom and Serge Guilbaut, San Francisco, Calif., March 1972, in Archives of American Art, Smithsonian Institution, Washington, D.C.
60. Conner et al., introduction, 9.
61. Conner, in interview with Paul Cummings, New York, April 16, 1973, Archives of American Art, Smithsonian Institution, Washington, D.C.
62. Conner, interview with Cummings. Even Conner's films that did not draw on archival footage played with cinematic time; BREAKAWAY (1966), for example, reverses at its halfway point.
63. Diedrich Diederichsen, "Psychedelic/Realist: Bruce Conner and Music," in Conner et al., *Bruce Conner,* 347.
64. Jack Ellis, *John Grierson: Life, Contributions, Influence* (Carbondale: Southern Illinois University Press, 2000), 134.

65. John Grierson, "The Documentary Idea," in *Grierson on Documentary*, ed. Forsyth Hardy (New York: Praeger, 1971), 249.
66. Ellis, *John Grierson*, 155–56.
67. Ellis, 172.
68. D. B. Jones, "The Canadian Film Board Unit B," in *New Challenges for Documentary*, ed. Alan Rosenthal and John Corner, 2nd ed. (Manchester: Manchester University Press, 2005), 79.
69. Jim Leach and Jeannette Sloniowski, introduction to *Candid Eyes: Essays on Canadian Documentaries*, ed. Jim Leach and Jeannette Sloniowski (Toronto: University of Toronto Press, 2003), 7.
70. Peter Steven, *Brink of Reality: New Canadian Film and Video* (Toronto: Between the Lines, 1993), 512.
71. Jones, "Canadian Film Board Unit B," 87.
72. Peter Harcourt, cited in Leach and Sloniowski, *Candid Eyes*, 8. Kroitor remarks on the surprising degree of freedom the NFB provided this group of filmmakers: "It's an unbelievable thing that the government of Canada said 'here's some money, go do something in the public interest' and fundamentally kept its hands off. We were allowed to do films that we thought were interesting and we didn't have to think in terms of if this film is a flop then I'm not going to be able to make another." Roman Kroitor, interview by Wyndam Wise, "Roman Kroitor: Master Filmmaker and Technical Wizard," *Take One: Film and Television in Canada* 32 (2001): 20–34.
73. Jones, "Canadian Film Board Unit B," 80.
74. Jones, 80.
75. Kroitor himself was a great lover of music and would sit at the piano "and improvise in [his] own bizarre way." He did not underestimate the power of Rathburn's composition and said that his score of *In the Labyrinth* (1967) was "half the movie." Kroitor, "Roman Kroitor."
76. Nakai, "Film Theory and the Crisis in Contemporary Aesthetics," 82.
77. Erik Barnouw, "The Hiroshima–Nagasaki Footage: A Report," *Historical Journal of Film, Radio, and Television* 2, no. 1 (1982): 91–100.
78. For an explanation of how he learned of and gained access to the footage, see Barnouw, "Hiroshima–Nagasaki Footage," 92–93.
79. Barnouw, 94.
80. Barnouw, 93.
81. Erik Barnouw, "Iwasaki and the Occupied Screen," *Film History* 2, no. 4 (1988): 342.
82. Barnouw, "Hiroshima–Nagasaki Footage," 97.
83. Iwasaki, cited in Barnouw, "Hiroshima–Nagasaki Footage," 97; Barnouw, 98.
84. Deren, *Anagram of Ideas*, 51–52.

Epilogue

1. See Marie Heinrichs, "Navi/Gated/Gaze: Google Earth's Narrative of the Earth and the Privitazation of Gaze," in *Earth and Beyond in Tumultuous Times*, ed. Réka Patrícia Gál and Petra Löffler (Lüneberg, Germany: Meson Press, 2021), 125–52; Homay King, *Virtual Memory: Time-Based Art and the Dream of Digitality* (Durham, N.C.: Duke University Press, 2015), 4; R. S. Deese, "The Artifact of Nature: 'Spaceship Earth' and the Dawn of Global Environmentalism," *Endeavor* 33, no. 2 (2009): 75; Thomas M. Lekan, "Fractal Eaarth: Visualizing the Global Environment in the Anthropocene," *Environmental Humanities* 5 (2014): 174; Benjamin Lazier, "Earthrise, or The Globalization of the World Picture," *American Historical Review* 116, no. 3 (2011): 602–30; Denis Cosgrove, "Contested Global Visions: One-World, Whole-Earth, and the Apollo Space Photographs," *Annals of the Association of American Geographers* 84, no. 2 (1994): 270–94; Robert Poole, *Earthrise: How Man First Saw the Earth* (New Haven, Conn.: Yale University Press, 2008).
2. For a thorough history of planetary visions of Earth in the history of Western representation up to and including the moment the *Blue Marble* photograph entered circulation, see Denis Cosgrove, *Apollo's Eye: A Cartographic Genealogy of the Earth in the Western Imagination* (Baltimore, Md.: Johns Hopkins University Press, 2003); Cosgrove, "Contested Global Visions."
3. Ursula K. Heise, *Sense of Place and Sense of Planet: The Environmental Imagination of the Global* (New York: Oxford University Press, 2008).
4. Yaakov Jerome Garb, "The Use and Misuse of the Whole Earth Image," *Whole Earth Review* (March 1985): 25.
5. See Slavoj Žižek, "Living in the End Times," *Polygraph* 22 (2010): 245; Rob Nixon, *Slow Violence and the Environmentalism of the Poor* (Cambridge, Mass.: Harvard University Press, 2011); for a recent example, Chandni Singh, "Spring Never Came to India This Year," *New York Times*, May 24, 2022, https://www.nytimes.com/2022/05/24/opinion/india-heat-wave-climate-change.html.
6. I am grateful to Quinn Adams, a student in my 2017 course "Media and Scale," for bringing this project to my attention in the context of an enlightening analysis of Eberty's text.
7. "NASA's Black Marble," NASA, accessed March 23, 2023, https://blackmarble.gsfc.nasa.gov/.
8. Jussi Parikka, "Planetary Goodbyes: Post-History and Future Memories of an Ecological Past," in *Memory in Motion: Archives, Technology, and the Social*, ed. Ina Blom, Trond Lundemo, and Eivind Rossaak (Amsterdam: Amsterdam University Press, 2017), 129–52.
9. Dipesh Chakrabarty, "The Climate of History: Four Theses," *Critical Inquiry* 35, no. 2 (2009): 197–222.

10. See Craig Benjamin, Esther Quaedackers, and David Baker, eds., *The Routledge Companion to Big History* (New York: Routledge, 2020).
11. Barry H. Rodrigue, "The Study of All Existence: Big History, Universal Studies, and the Global Conjecture," *International Journal for the Transformation of Consciousness* 3, no. 1 (2017): 15–34.
12. See, for example, Kate Hawkey, "Moving Forward, Looking Back: Historical Perspective, 'Big History,' and the Return of the Longue Durée: Time to Develop Our Scale-Hopping Muscles," *Teaching History* 158 (2015): 40–46; Richard Aldrich, "Education for Survival: An Historical Perspective," *History of Education: Journal of the History of Education Society* 39, no. 1 (2010): 1–14; Roland Saekow and Walter Alvarez, ChronoZoom, accessed April 2022, http://www.chronozoom.com.
13. Notably, the kind of attention to long timescales in projects like this frequently stands in opposition to the kind of historical work that attends to the *longue durée*. When Fernand Braudel argues for scholarly attention to the longue durée in history and the social sciences, he specifically advocates for attention to the parts of history that moved so slowly as to be essentially infrastructural; scholars' overattention to "events" and great happenings have come at the expense of "expanses of slow-moving history" around which everything has gravitated. See Braudel, "History and the Social Sciences: The *Longue Durée*," reprinted in *On History*, trans. Sarah Matthews (Chicago: University of Chicago Press, 1980).
14. Jennifer Fay, *Inhospitable World: Cinema in the Time of the Anthropocene* (New York: Oxford University Press, 2018), 205.
15. See Safia Noble, *Algorithms of Oppression* (New York: New York University Press, 2018).
16. Ina Blom, "Rethinking Social Memory: Archives, Technology, and the Social," in *Memory in Motion: Archives, Technology, and the Social*, ed. Ina Blom, Trond Lundemo, and Eivind Rossaak, 11–39 (Amsterdam: Amsterdam University Press, 2017).
17. Philip Rosen, *Change Mummified: Cinema, Historicity, Theory* (Minneapolis: University of Minnesota Press, 2001), 306.
18. Slavoj Žižek, *Living in the End Times* (London: Verso, 2011).
19. See Jessica Hurley and Dan Sinkyin, "Apocalypse: Introduction," in "Apocalypse," special issue, *ASAP Journal* 3, no. 3 (September 2018): 451–66.
20. Žižek, *Living in the End Times*, 245.
21. Walter Benjamin, "Eternal Return," in *The Arcades Project*, trans. Howard Eiland and Kevin McLaughlin (Cambridge, Mass.: Harvard University Press, 2002), 115.
22. Fay, *Inhospitable World*, 205.
23. See, for example, Evan Osnos, "Doomsday Prep for the Super-Rich," *New Yorker*, January 22, 2017, https://www.newyorker.com/magazine/2017/01/30/doomsday-prep-for-the-super-rich.

24. For more on how *Melancholia* allegorizes climate change, see Tim Matts and Aifan Tynan, "The Melancholy of Extinction," in *Media Culture Journal* 15, no. 3 (2012): https://doi.org/10.5204/mcj.491.
25. For an at-length discussion of *Melancholia* as paradigmatic apocalyptic cinema, see Peter Szendy, *Apocalypse-Cinema: 2012 and Other Ends of the World* (New York: Fordham University Press, 2015).
26. Siegfried Kracauer, *Theory of Film: The Redemption of Physical Reality* (New York: Oxford University Press, 1960), 292.

INDEX

Page numbers in italics refer to figures.

absence, 116, 138; interplay between presence and, 18, 77, 91, 116
acceleration, 11, 32, 33
Acland, Charles R., 41
Addinsell, Richard, 80, 164n37
aerial gaze, 13, 15, 22–23, 38, 71, 123–24, 129. *See also* Second World War, aerial cinema
Air Outpost (Rotha, 1937), 162n17
Amad, Paula, 68
American Cinematographer cover, 3–4, 5, 12–13, 58
Anger, Kenneth, 101
animated films/animation, 7, 8, 31, 57, 98, 114, 125. See also *Einstein Theory of Relativity, The* (animated by Fleischer, 1923)
Anthropocene, the, 13, 126, 127, 133, 136, 168n42
apocalypse, 9, 25; anxiety over, 34–35, 40, 44, 51, 52, 58, 66, 79, 136; archives of, 66, 74; astronomical, 131–32; cinema and, 10–17, 38, 130, 132, 133; cosmocinematic gaze linked to, 23, 125, 134; destruction associated with, 17–18, 87, 97; for Indigenous populations, 38, 62, 63, 132; temporalities of, 26–27, 135; of warfare, 91. *See also* Book of Revelation
apocalyptic view, 13
archival gaze, 136
archives: of apocalypse, 66, 74; cinematic, 1, 17–27, 68–69, 108, 111, 118, 129, 132–33; cosmic, 15–16; cosmocinematic, 63, 78–79, 141; destruction associated with, 11, 66, 71, 96; digital, 128–30; historical, 119, 126–27, 133; of humanity, 134; reframing concept of, 126–27; of warfare, 73–74, 90–91, 161n7. *See also* history: preserving; light: archives of
Arrival (Villeneuve, 2016), 131
Astronomer's Dream, The (*La Lune à un mètre*, Méliès), 8
astronomy, 15, 18, 99, 117; archives of, 66, 74; cosmocinematic, 68, 139–40; expeditions for, 31–39, 41, 44; film's affinities with, 6–9, 11–12, 39–46, 59, 109–10, 137, 140; in Great Britain, 29, 35, 159n68; photography and, 6–9, 20, 31, 38–39, 40, 58–59, 109–10, 154–55n23; twentieth-century

· 175

developments, 34, 98–99; warfare and, 67, 71. *See also* cosmology; International Astronomical Union (IAU); telescopes; universe
astronomy, new, 29–63; and archives of light, 58–63; on film, 39–46; fragmenting and containing the universe, 46–58; visual cultures and, 31–39
astronomy-education films, 43–58, 76, 98, 113; interwar, 72, 85, 162n17; silent-era, 28–30, 115
astronomy films, 85, 159n63; relativity and, 29–63. *See also* astronomy: film's affinities with; cosmology
astrophysics, 3, 33, 99; experimentation with space and time, 20, 71; film and photography used for, 59, 109–10. *See also* metaphysics; physics; quantum physics; relativity: Einstein's theories of
astrophysics-education films: silent-era, 28–30
astrophysics films, 6–9, 44, 49–50, 61, 131
Atacama Desert (Chile), 138
At Land (Deren), 103
atomic bombs: destructiveness of, 94–97; force of explosions, 67, 109, 111, 169n53; imagery of, 93–94, 102, 109–10, 112. *See also* radioactivity/radiation
atomic bombs, cinema of, 93–121; American avant-garde and, 15, 99–102, 104; documentary experiments, 113–21; Maya Deren's vision for a new cinema, 102–6; test films, 93, 97, 100, 106–13; visibility of destruction *vs.* invisibility of radiation, 95–96
Atom Strikes, The! (U.S. Army Signal Corps, 1945), 106, 112

avant-garde films, 98, 168n40; atomic bomb, 15, 99–102, 104; documentaries, 100–101, 106–7, 141; science, 107, 167n32. *See also* experimental films
aviation films: interwar, 162n17

Barad, Karen, 153n10
Barnouw, Erik. See *Hiroshima-Nagasaki, August 1945* (Barnouw, 1970)
Bazin, André: on archives, 71, 83, 90, 128, 133; on cinema, 77; on cosmo-cinematic gaze, 65–66
Belisle, Brooke, 148n19
Belson, Jordan, 101, 110
Benjamin, Walter: Angel of History image, 25, 66, 96; on cinema, 139–40, 148–49n20; constellations conceived by, 26–27, 75, 78, 86, 102; Eberty referenced by, 20–21; *Jetztzeit* concept, 26, 86, 138; on messianicity, 25–26; view of the universe, 87, 133
Bhagavad Gita, 88, 93, 120
Big History Project, 127, 128, 129, 132. *See also* history
bird's-eye view, 22
Birett, Herbert, 159n62
Black Marble project, 124–25, *126*, 127, 141
Blom, Ina, 129
Blount, Thomas, 4
Blue Marble (photograph), 123–24, *124*
bomber's gaze, 71
Book of Revelation, 13–14, 89. *See also* apocalypse
Boon, Timothy, 100
Boym, Svetlana, 134
Brakhage, Stan, 101, 106
Braudel, Fernand, 172n13
Brazil: Eddington's expedition to, 39

176 · INDEX

Brief History of Time, A (book, Hawking, 1988), 127
British Instructional Films, 100, 162n13
Browne, Simone, 22
Burger, Erich, 11
Bute, Mary Ellen, 98

Cadava, Eduardo, 151n54
Cahill, James Leo, 18, 24, 25, 150n45
camera gun, 68, 73, 94
camera obscura, 89
cameras: aerial, 74, 77–78, 90; gaze of, 36, 52; high-speed, 108–9; interplay of universe and, 54, 88; lenses of, 3–4, 137. *See also* cinema; filmmakers/filmmaking; films; photographs/photography
Canales, Jimena, 7, 154–55n23
Cargo from Jamaica (Wright, 1933), 69
Carter, Jimmy, 16
Casey, Edward S., 88
Cavalcanti, Alberto, 70, 98, 114
Cayenne, French Guiana: Eddington's expedition to, 36–37, *37*
celestial view, 23. *See also* drones
Chakrabarty, Dipesh, 126, 136
Charney, Leo, 10
Cheese Mites, The (Urban, 1903), 162n13
Chow, Rey, 66, 68
chronophotography, 7, 58–59. *See also* photographs/photography
ChronoZoom (UC Berkeley), 127
cinema, 22, 121, 139, 150n45, 151n50; Deren's vision for, 102–6; history of, 1, 41; imagery of, 108, 129; imaginary of, 20, 116; political role of, 69–70, 72, 98; preservation role, 19, 21, 66, 136, 140; reality of, 6, 22, 23, 31, 45, 65, 129, 168n7; rethinking, 94–95; temporalities of, 7–8, 10–12, 25, 47, 59, 75, 104, 128; useful, 15, 31, 41. *See also* archives: cinematic; cosmic cinema; cosmocinematic gaze; films; Second World War, aerial cinema
Cinema 16, 97, 101, 102, 106, 110, 168n35
cinematography: slow-motion, 93, 104–5, 107, 135; time-lapse, 19, 30, 44, 57, 125
circumterrarium, 16, 72–73, 131
civilization, human, 21, 25, 84, 128, 131, 134. *See also* human life
Clausberg, Karl, 20, 57
climate change, 13, 127, 129, 131–32, 134. *See also* environmentalism
Cohl, Émile, 9
Coming of Columbus, The (Selig, 1912), 43
compilation films, 101, 110, 118–19
Conner, Bruce, 97, 110, 117, 167n30. *See also* COSMC RAY (Conner, 1961); CROSSROADS (Conner, 1976); MOVIE, A (Conner)
conquering gaze, 22, 75, 78, 86, 102. *See also* god trick; satellites; surveillance
constellations, 66, 95; Benjamin's concept of, 26–27, 75, 78, 86, 102. *See also* galaxies; stars; universe
Contact (Zemeckis, 1997), 17
Cortie, Father Aloysius: 1914 expedition, 155n24
Cosgrove, Denis, 4, 22, 147n4
cosmic cinema, 1–11, 14, 18, 42, 113, 140; apocalyptic, 38, 51, 130–31; temporalities in, 124–25. *See also* cosmocinematic gaze
cosmic gaze, 37–38, 75–78, 86–87, 123
COSMIC RAY (Conner, 1961), 111
cosmocinematic gaze, 25, 43, 52, 89–90, 117–18, 121, 134; apocalypse

INDEX · 177

linked to, 23, 125, 134; by astronomers and film theorists, 45–46; Bazin referring to, 65–66, 72; cinematic archives and, 17–27, 68–69, 108, 132–33; disembodied, 12–13, 95, 109, 115; embodied, 76, 87; imaginary of, 14, 59, 91; moving through spatiotemporal registers, 15–16, 57, 59–61, 129, 130; new ways of manifesting, 102, 104–5; omniscient and omnipotent qualities of, 58, 59; reality of, 68, 69, 74, 87, 118, 125, 129; reconfiguring, 47, 111; technology of, 116, 125, 127; in wartime films, 71, 73, 74, 78; as witness, 67–68, 136–41
cosmography, 120, 147n4
cosmology, 89, 120, 147n4; religious, 56, 57, 97; scientific, 4, 54, 102, 113. *See also* astronomy
cosmos, 85–89; atomic bomb harnessing power of, 93–94; in *Dangerous Moonlight*, 82–83; imagery of, 101–2, 115; imaginary of, 9, 17, 91, 136, 139–40; movement through, 105, 139; music compared to, 81, 164n38; Newtonian model of, 32, 49–50, 56, 58; photographs of, 29–31; precariousness of, 9, 45, 85, 100, 117, 128, 130; science of, 4, 54, 101–2, 113; spatiotemporalities of, 40, 72, 75; wooed down to earth, 66, 87. *See also* cosmic cinema; heavens; temporalities, universe
Cosmos: A Personal Voyage (TV series, Sagan, 1980), 127
Cosmos: A Spacetime Odyssey (TV series, Tyson, 2014), 127
creation, 42, 58, 93, 104. See also *Our Heavenly Bodies* (*Wunder der Schöpfung*, Kornblum, 1925)
Creative Film Foundation, 102

Crockwell, Douglass, 98
CROSSROADS (Conner, 1976), 110–11, 128
Curtis, Scott, 3, 7, 42

Dangerous Moonlight (Hurst, 1941), 72, 79, 80–83, 84, 89, 91, 164n36
Davis, Jim, 101
Deren, Maya, 107, 112; *An Anagram of Ideas on Art, Form, and Film*, 103–5, 110, 120–21, 168n40, 168n42; filmmaking of, 97, 98, 102–6, 168n35, 168n37. See also *Very Eye of Night, The* (Deren, 1958)
Derrida, Jacques, 96
Diederichsen, Diedrich, 111
dimensionism, 33
Disney Studies. *See* DreamWorks Pictures
Doane, Mary Ann, 10
documentaries, 45, 98, 136–41; apocalyptic, 15; avant-garde films' relationship to, 100–101, 106–7, 141; educational, 162n14; experimental, 113–21; fiction films intermingling with, 47, 70, 71, 73, 76, 90, 91; from Great Britain, 163n27; wartime, 15, 65–91, 94, 112. *See also* education films; science films
Don't Look Up (McKay, 2021), 17, 131–34, 135, 137
DreamWorks Pictures: logo, 2
drones, 23, 72, 94
Duchamp, Marcel, 33
Dyson, Frank, 30

Eames, Charles and Ray, 101
earth, 24, 34, 50, 63, 68, 83, 123; astronomical view of, 6, 31, 125–26; documenting photographically, 123–25, *124, 126*, 127, 141; end of, 13, 14, 34, 87; explosion of, *51*; future of, 14, 91;

178 · INDEX

images of, 6, 19; light emitted by, 18, *60*, 65; precariousness of, 13, 42, 50, 75; stars witnessing the past of, 21–22, 52. *See also* circumterrarium; civilization, human; human life; world

Eaton, Ford W., 43

Eberty, Felix, 151n50, 151n53; archives of light described by, 23, 59, 65, 140; cosmocinematic gaze imagined by, 22, 25, 27, 31, 59, 74, 104, 128; cosmology of, 89, 91, 136; *The Stars and the Earth,* 150n46; on the universe, 18–21

eclipse expeditions, 29–31, 35–41, *37*, 62, 77, 86–87, 140, 155n28, 155–56n31. *See also* Eddington, Sir Arthur

Eddington, Sir Arthur, 69, 164n28, 164n38; confirmation of Einstein's theories of relativity, 29–30, 31–41, 63, 140; eclipse expeditions/photographs, 29–31, 35–41, *37*, 62, 77, 86–87, 140, 155n28, 155–56n31; recognizing power of film and photography, 31, 109–10

education films, 41–43, 71, 85, 157n49; cosmic models of, 49–51; Great Britain, 162n13, 162n14; silent-era, 28–30, 115. *See also* astronomy-education films; astrophysics-education films; British Instructional Films; documentaries; Film Unit B; science-education films

Effects of the Atomic Bomb on Hiroshima and Nagasaki, The (U.S. Strategic Bombing Survey, 1945), 95–96, 118

Eigenzeit, Einstein's theory of, 32, 46

Einstein, Albert, 19, 20, 33, 102, 161n6, 166–67n24; love of music, 82, 162n38; recognizing power of film and photography, 109–10. *See also* relativity: Einsteins's theories of

Einstein Theory of Relativity, The (animated by Fleischer, 1923), 40, 43–49, 55, 59–63, 70, 157–58n51, 158n53; advertisements, *47, 48*; light emitted from earth to outer space, *60,* 65; projectile in, 60–61, 71

Einstein Theory of Relativity, The (*Die Grundlagen der Einsteinschen Relativitätstheorie,* Kornblum, 1922), 40–41, 43, 44–45, 54, 140, 157–58n51

Eisenstein, Sergei, 33–34, 81

Eliot, Charles William, 157n49

Ellis, Patrick, 22, 68

Elsaesser, Thomas, 147n1

Elsheimer, Skip, 159n63

Empire Marketing Board (EMB), 69–70, 162n14

Emshwiller, Ed, 101

environmentalism, 34, 123, 125–26. *See also* climate change

Epstein, Jean, 56, 81; on cinema, 94–95, 97, 103, 107–8; film as cosmic medium, 6, 42

Europe, 6, 62, 81; Einstein's theories in, 32–33, 35, 40, 155n27; filmmaking in, 20, 29–30, 44, 98. *See also* Great Britain

experimental films, 8, 45, 98, 121, 168–69n48; on atomic bomb's destructive capacity, 97, 113, 119–20. *See also* avant-garde films; science films

Fadman, Edwin M., 40–41

fantasy, 8, 22, 23, 66, 90; cinematic, 7, 88, 127; reality *vs.,* 71, 79, 87, 88; of space travel, 15, 31, 59–61

Farocki, Harun. See *Images of the World and the Inscription of War* (Farocki, 1989)

Faure, Élie: archives of light described by, 59, 140; on cinema, 4, 6, 21–25, 42, 107–8; cosmic imaginaries, 91, 136; cosmocinematic gaze imagined by, 22–23, 31, 74, 104
Fay, Jennifer, 13, 96, 128, 133
feature films, 28, 51, 70
fiction films, 8, 23, 47, 136, 141; aerial perspective in, 74, 79; documentary intermingling with, 47, 70, 71, 73, 76, 90, 91. *See also* science-fiction films
filmmakers/filmmaking, 15, 34, 138; future, 21–22; in Great Britain, 66–70, 98, 161n7, 162n13, 162n14, 163n27; in Japan, 95, 118, 120, 161n11; live-action, 8, 45, 52; representing cosmic subject matter, 1, 3–4, 8; in United States, 29–30, 55, 79–80, 97–98, 102, 104. *See also* cinema; cinematography; *and individual filmmakers*
films, 20, 22, 89, 110, 120, 159n62; apocalyptic, 12, 17–18; astronomy's affinities with, 6–9, 11–12, 39–46, 59, 109–10, 137, 140; creative capacity of, 116–17; Eddington's use of, 31, 109–10; history of, 9, 30, 41, 42; indexical quality of, 20, 71, 106, 118, 129, 140–41; as medium of modern era, 20, 33, 121, 148–49n20; the past in, 61–62; redemption potential, 23, 24, 26, 71, 97, 139; silent-era, 7–8, 28–30, 42, 115; spatiotemporal qualities in, 37, 107, 168–69n48; studio logos, 2, *2*, 3, 147n1; time in, 15, 33, 43, 61–62, 79, 141. *See also* cinema; *and individual film genres and titles*
film theorists/theory: cinema's promise of immortality, 1, 66; on cosmic attributes of cinema, 4, 9, 18, 20; on cosmocinematic gaze, 23, 45–46, 74; early twentieth-century, 10–11. *See also* Bazin, André; Benjamin, Walter; Eisensten, Sergei; Epstein, Jean; Faure, Élie; Goll, Yvon; Kracauer, Siegfried; Masakazu, Nakai
Film Unit B, 98, 114
First World War, 29, 32, 35, 54, 66
Fischinger, Oskar, 101
Flammarion, Camille, 6, 151n53
Fleischer, Max. *See Einstein Theory of Relativity, The* (animated by Fleischer, 1923)
fragmentation, 15, 83, 101; of space, 9, 46, 113; of time, 9, 46, 112–13; of the universe, 46–58, 63, 74
future, 4, 29, 35, 38, 123, 139; past preserved for, 11–12, 17, 20, 26–27, 47, 60, 62; posthuman, 15–16
Future's in the Air, The (Shaw, 1937), 162n17

galaxies, 2, 4, 31, 34, 44, 57, 98, 139. *See also* constellations; stars; universe
Galaxy (avant-garde film series), 101
Garb, Yaakov Jerome, 123
Gates, Bill, 127
Gaumont Film Company: logo, 2
Gaycken, Oliver, 7, 41, 100
gaze(s). *See* aerial gaze; bomber's gaze; cameras: gaze of; conquering gaze; cosmic gaze; cosmocinematic gaze; heavens: gazing at; hierarchical gaze; masculine gaze; military gaze; objective gaze; omniscient gaze; violent gaze; White gaze
Gemünden, Gerd, 152n69
General Post Office Film Unit (GPO), 70, 162n14, 163n27
geopolitics, 35, 73, 97–98. *See also* politics; transnationalism
Gingrich, Newt, 14
God's-eye view, 22, 58
god trick, 22, 36, 38, 68, 105, 124

Goethe, Johann Wolfgang von: poem by, 58
Goll, Yvan, 10–11
Gorman, Alice, 16
gravity, 29, 32, 50–52, *51*, 61, 90, 105
Gravity (Cuarón, 2013), 17, 131
Great Britain: astronomy in, 29, 35, 159n68; filmmaking in, 66–71, 98, 114, 161n7. *See also* British Instructional Films; Empire Marketing Board (EMB); General Post Office Film Unit (GPO); Royal Air Force (RAF); Royal Air Force Museum; Second World War, aerial cinema
Grierson, John, 69–70, 98, 100, 113–14, 162n14, 162n17
Griffiths, Alison
Gunning, Tom, 10, 154–55n23
Guzmán, Patricio. See *Nostalgia for the Light* (Guzmán, 2010)

Haller, Robert A., 101–2
Hansen, Miriam Bratu, 10
Haraway, Donna. *See* god trick
Harcourt, Peter, 114
Hay, James, 72
Hearst, William Randolph, 42–43
heavens, 85–86, 120–21; gazing at, 12–13, 21–22, 140; lights of, 59, 66–67; perceptions of, 73, 89. *See also* astronomy; constellations; cosmos; galaxies; moon; stars; sun; universe
Heise, Ursula K., 123
hierarchical gaze, 36–38
Hiroshima, Japan: atomic bomb dropped on, 95, 96, 102, 104, 106
Hiroshima–Nagasaki, August 1945 (Barnouw, 1970), 95, 96, 118–20
history, 63, 83, 112, 137, 150n46, 172n13; archiving, 119, 126–27, 133; of cinema, 1, 9; end of, 15, 17, 21; extraterritorial perspective, 24–25; human, 138, 140; preserving, 18–19, 21, 22–23, 24, 59, 60. *See also* Benjamin, Walter: Angel of History image; Big History Project
Horton, Zachary, 4, 43, 88
Hubble, Edwin, 6, 34, 90–91, 98, 102
human life: documenting, 15–17, 22, 61; end of, 11, 13, 18, 131, 133, 136; history of, 138, 140; place in universe, 3, 12, 13. *See also* civilization, human

imagery: aerial, 74; Angel of History, 9, 25, 66; of atomic bomb, 93–94, 102, 109–10, 112; cinematic, 20, 108, 116, 129; cosmic, 101–2, 115; of earth, 6, 19; ecological, 123; of outer space, 14, 19; satellite, 20, 25; scientific, 99, 105; of violence, 90, 94
Images of the World and the Inscription of War (Farocki, 1989), 94, 163n22
imaginaries: cosmic, 9, 17, 91, 136, 139–40; cosmocinematic, 14, 59, 91; global, 9, 69, 74; scientific, 44
imperialism: global networks of, 36; god trick and, 68, 137; Indigenous cultures devastated by, 38; Japanese, 161n11; new forms of, 98–99; violence of, 22; Western, 9
Imperial War Museums (London): wartime archives, 73–74, 161n7
International Astronomical Union (IAU), 67, 98, 160–61n5
International Big History Association, 127
Interstellar (Nolan, 2014), 131
In the Labyrinth: musical score, 170n75
Into Eternity (Madsen, 2010), 126
Introducing the Dial (Legg, 1934), 70

INDEX · 181

irrationality, 8, 55; rationalism intermingling with, 38, 79, 85, 88, 90, 91
Isaacson, Walter, 164n38
Ivens, Joris, 101
Iwasaki, Akira, 95, 118, 120

Jackson, Stanley, 114
Janssen, Pierre, 7, 30–31
Japan: astronomy in, 7; filmmaking in, 95, 118, 120, 161n11. *See also* Hiroshima, Japan: atomic bomb dropped on; Nagasaki, Japan: atomic bomb dropped on
Jetztzeit: Benjamin's concept of, 26, 86, 138
Jones, D. B., 115

Kandinsky, Wassily, 33
Kant, Immanuel, 88
Kaplan, Caren, 68, 74
Keller, Sarah, 105, 168–69n48
Kern, Stephen, 10
Kirby, Lynne, 10
Koch, Gertrud, 24
Kornblum, Hanns Walter. See *Einstein Theory of Relativity, The* (*Die Grundlagen der Einsteinschen Relativitätstheorie*, Kornblum, 1922); *Our Heavenly Bodies* (*Wunder der Schöpfung*, Kornblum, 1925)
Kracauer, Siegfried, 59, 118, 152n69; on cinema, 7, 97, 139, 148–49n23, 168n37; cosmic imaginary, 91, 136, 139–40; *Theory of Film*, 20–21, 23–25, 140
Kroitor, Roman, 97, 101, 170n72, 170n75. See also *Universe* (Kroitor and Low, 1961)

light, 25, 35, 83; archives of, 18, 19, 20–21, 23–24, 58–63, 65, 120, 124, 140; atomic and subatomic scales, 35, 94, 96; from earth, 18, *60*; movement through space and time, 9, 24, 61–62; from the past, 27, 151n54; speed of, 3, 18–19, 20, 29, 59–61, 116; from the sun, 18, 81, 112
Lippit, Akira Mizuta, 94, 96
Locomotives (Jennings, 1934), 70
logos. *See* films: studio logos
Low, Colin, 97, 101. See also *Universe* (Kroitor and Low, 1961)
Lundemo, Trond, 96, 97
Luyten, W. J., 34

MacDonald, Scott, 101
magic-lantern shows, 39–40, 41–42, 159n57
Malick, Terrence, 147–48n9
Markopoulos, Gregory J., 101
Mars, 15, 115
Martian, The (Scott, 2015), 14–15
Marvell, Leon, 14
Masakazu, Nakai, 95, 118
masculine gaze, 22
Matter of Life and Death, A (Powell and Pressburger, 1946), 72, 79, 83–91
Maunder, Edward Walter, 39
Mauritius expedition, 156n34
media, 4, 15, 16, 23, 129; digital, 132–33, 141. *See also* cinema; films; magic-lantern shows; newsreels; photographs/photography
Melancholia (von Trier, 2011), 131–32, 134–36, 137
Méliès, Georges: filmmaking by, 9, 15, 157–58n51
Menken, Marie, 98, 101
messianicity, 25–26
metaphysics, 4. *See also* astrophysics; quantum physics; relativity, Einstein's theories of
Michelson, Annette, 33, 168n40
military gaze, 13

Milky Way, The (Lawlor, 1920s), 43–44, 55–56, 61, 159n63
Miller, Arthur I., 164n38
mobility, 69, 72; of magic-lantern shows, 41–42; spatiotemporal, 45–46, 50, 59–60, 90, 104, 139, 168n37; of time, 15, 45–47, 63, 93, 139
"Modern Astronomy" (poem), 9
modernity, 24, 160n74; film's role in, 20, 33, 121, 148–49n20; imperial, 29, 38; technological, 47, 49, 68, 70, 79, 87, 130
Moholy-Nagy, László, 33
moon, 6, 18, 46, 50, 83. See also *Dangerous Moonlight* (Hurst, 1941); *Spanish Clair de Lune (Clair de lune espagnole*, Cohl, 1909); *Trip to the Moon, A (Le voyage dans la lune*, Méliès, 1902)
Morrison, Bill, 101
MOVIE, A (Conner), 101, 111–13, 118
music, movie: cosmos compared to, 81, 164n38; in *Dangerous Moonlight*, 80–83; in *A Matter of Life and Death*, 83, 86, 87. See also scores, movie
Musk, Elon, 14

Nabokov, Vladimir: *Speak, Memory*, 11–12
Nagasaki, Japan: atomic bomb dropped on, 95, 96, 102, 104, 106. See also *Hiroshima-Nagasaki, August 1945* (Barnouw, 1970)
Nancy, Jean-Luc, 88
National Film Board of Canada (NFB), 98, 113–14, 170n72
nationalism. *See* transnationalism
nature, 71, 94, 129, 131, 147n4; changing, 33, 104; films of, 7, 108, 150n44, 162n13; laws of, 58, 164n38; temporalities of, 9, 136; unruliness of, 30, 35, 39
newsreels: Second World War, 32, 65, 73, 112
Newton, Sir Isaac: model of the cosmos, 32, 49–50, 56, 58
New Yorker cartoon (Ellis Rosen), 129, *130*
Nichols, Bill, 100–101
Nietzsche, Friedrich, 102
Night Mail (Watt and Wright, 1936), 70
nonhuman gaze, 24
nostalgia, 127, 134
Nostalgia for the Light (Guzmán, 2010), 126, 137–41
nuclear bombs. *See* atomic bombs; atomic bombs, cinema of; Hiroshima, Japan: atomic bomb dropped on; Nagasaki, Japan: atomic bomb dropped on

objective gaze, 3
omnipotent view, 3
omniscient gaze, 66, 70, 76, 89, 95, 115
Oppenheimer, J. Robert: reaction to atomic bomb detonation, 93–94, 104, 108, 111, 119, 120
Orgeron, Devin and Marsha, 41
Oshima, Kazuko, 119
Our Heavenly Bodies (Wunder der Schöpfung, Kornblum, 1925), 42, 43, 46, 49–52, 57–58, 61–62; scenes from, *51, 53*
outer space, 16, 57, 65, 73, 131, 134; images of, 14, 19. *See also* space; space travel

Painlevé, Jean, 167n32
panoramas, 23, 148n19
Paracelsus, 88
Paramount Studios: logo, 2
Parikka, Jussi, 126

INDEX · 183

Parks, Lisa, 68, 72
past, the: bringing into the present, 19, 25–27, 59, 61, 138–39; cinematic and cosmic representations of, 4, 9, 18, 21, 129, 137–38; light from, 27, 151n4; preserving, 3, 11–12, 15, 17–18, 20, 26–27, 47, 59–63, 130; uncovering, 23, 125–28
photographs/photography, 8, 26, 94, 109, 141, 151n54; aerial, 73, 77; documenting earth, 123–25, *124, 126,* 127, 141; Eddington's use of, 30, 31, 35–39; Kracauer's essay on, 24–25; radiation not visible on, 95–96; scientific, 6–7, 30, 100, 110. *See also* chronophotography; Eddington, Sir Arthur: eclipse expeditions/photographs
physics, 32, 35. *See also* astrophysics; metaphysics; quantum physics; relativity: Einstein's theories of
Pines of Rome (tone poem, Respighi, 1924), 111
Pinochet, Augusto, 138–40
Planck, Max, 35, 161n6
planets, 50, 52, 97; movement of, 6, 40, 167; relationship between, 22, 105–6; science-fiction films depicting, 14–15. *See also* earth; Mars; solar system; Venus
politics, 38, 155n27; American, 100, 132; cinema's role in, 69–70, 72, 98. *See also* geopolitics; transnationalism
Pomerance, Murray, 10
Pormale, Monika, 101
precariousness, 73, 129; of cinema, 17–18; of the cosmos, 9, 45, 85, 100, 117, 128, 130; of earth, 13, 28, 42, 50, 75. *See also* experimental films
presence: interplay between absence and, 18, 77, 91, 116

present, the: bringing the past into, 19, 25–27, 59, 61, 138–39; media obsession with, 132–33
Price, Katy, 32
Principe (island): Eddington's expedition to, 35–36, 39, 41, 77
propaganda films, 80, 84, 94, 96. *See also* documentaries; Second World War, aerial cinema

quantum physics, 35. *See also* astrophysics; metaphysics; physics; relativity: Einstein's theories of

Rachmaninoff, Sergei, 80
radioactivity/radiation, 34, 95–96, 109, 118, 120. *See also* atomic bombs
Raleigh, Sir Walter: poem, 88
Ramu Films: logo, 2
Rathburn, Eldon, 116, 170n75
rationalism, 100, 102; irrational intermingling with, 38, 79, 85, 88, 90, 91; scientific, 38, 54, 55–56, 91, 121
reality, 35, 96, 121; of atomic bomb, 111, 112; cinematic, 22, 23, 31, 45, 65, 129, 168n37; cosmocinematic, 68, 69, 74, 87, 118, 125, 129; documenting, 70, 99, 137; experiential, 66–67; exposing, 100, 104; fantasy *vs.*, 71, 79, 87, 88; of final destruction, 125, 133; of war, 77–78, 91
redemption: film's potential for, 23, 24, 26, 71, 97, 139
Redmond, Sean, 14
relativity, 8, 105, 164n38; and astronomy films, 29–63; constant speed required, 60–61; Deren on, 120–21; Eddington's confirmation of, 29–30, 31–41, 63, 140; Einstein's theories of, 6–7, 90–91, 153n9, 153n10, 155n27; films addressing, 15, 40–55,

76, 131; morals attached to, 62–63; temporalities of, 54–55, 59, 97, 102
religion, 56–57, 97, 148–49n20
RKO Radio Pictures Inc.: logo, 2
Romance of the Skies (Bray Studios, 1925), 44, 56–57
Ronder, Paul, 96, 118–20
Rosen, Philip, 10, 129
Royal Air Force (RAF): films about, 75–80, 164n34
Royal Air Force Museum: wartime archives, 73–74, 161n7
Rutherford, Ernest, 35

satellites, 16–17, 22, 31, 72, 99; imaging by, 20, 125
Schwartz, Vanessa R., 10
science, 52, 55–57, 107; innovations in, 103–4; of the universe, 4, 54, 101, 113. *See also* astronomy; astrophysics; cosmology, scientific; relativity: Einstein's theories of; technoscience
science-education films, 7, 15, 41–42, 44, 47, 154–55n23, 157–58n51
science-fiction films, 14–15, 69, 73, 99
science films, 3, 6–7, 40; avant-garde, 107, 167n32; early, 100–101, 113; from Great Britain, 69, 70–71, 114, 162n13. *See also* atomic bombs, cinema of; experimental films
scores, movie: *Dangerous Moonlight*, 80, 164n36, 164n37; *In the Labyrinth*, 170n75; *A Matter of Life and Death*, 85; *Melancholia*, 135; A MOVIE, 112; *Target for Tonight*, 78; *Universe*, 116. *See also* music, movie
Second World War, aerial cinema, 65–91; cosmocinematic time in, 78–91; from Great Britain, 67–89, 161n7; from Japan, 161n11; Royal Air Force in, 72, 75–80, 164n34. *See also* aerial gaze; documentaries; wartime

Secrets of Nature (series, British Instructional Films), 162n13
Shanghai Studios: logo, 2
Shurcliff, William, 108–9, 110, 112
Silverman, Kaja, 77
simultaneity, 10, 32
Singer, Benjamin, 10
Sitney, P. Adams, 101
Sloterdijk, Peter, 68
Smoodin, Eric, 41
solar system, 31, 57, 85, 115, 157–58n51. *See also* moon; planets; sun
Sommerfeld, Arnold, 32
Song of Ceylon (Wright, 1934), 69
space, 4, 47, 83, 101, 164n38; astronomical study of, 44, 115; cinematic view of, 18, 33, 43, 89; cosmic, 8, 30, 40, 42, 54; fragmentation of, 9, 46, 113; instability in, 63, 83; manipulating, 90, 95, 103; movement of light through, 9, 60; rational, 8, 71, 91; rethinking, 10–11, 49; time in, 19, 21. *See also* circumterrarium; mobility: spatiotemporal; outer space; relativity: Einstein's theories of; spatiotemporalities
space travel, 3, 15, 20, 23, 30–31, 55, 59–62, 123, 139, 157–58n51, 159n63
Spanish Clair de Lune (*Clair de lune espagnole*, Cohl, 1909), 8
spatialities, 7–8, 54, 117
spatiotemporalities: of the cosmos, 40, 72, 75; of film, 37, 107, 168–69n48; mobile, 45–46, 50, 59–60, 90, 104, 139, 168n37; of the universe, 20, 31–32, 89, 103, 105, 140–41. *See also* relativity: Einstein's theories of
stars, 40, 52, 57, 151n54; cinema's connection to, 3–4, 9, 13–14; in *Dangerous Moonlight*, 80, 81, 82; witnessing Earth's past, 21–22, 138. *See also* constellations; galaxies; universe

Stimson, Henry L., 94
Streible, Dan, 41
sun, 40, 46; distance from Earth, 19, 55, 115–16; light from, 18, 81, 112; longevity of, 34, 52; planets moving across, 7, 50. *See also* moon; solar system; universe
surveillance, 22, 66, 67–68, 72, 83. *See also* drones
survivalism, 14–15, 69
Szendy, Peter, 12

Target for Tonight (Watt, 1941), 72, 76–78, 83, 164n34
technologies, 47, 49, 99, 127; aeronautic, 71, 121; cosmocinematic, 116, 125, 127; film, 6–7, 65, 73; military, 67, 90, 94; modern, 47, 49, 68, 70, 79, 87, 130; of surveillance, 22, 66, 67–68. *See also* camera gun; cameras; science; telescopes
technoscience, 9, 47, 68, 110. *See also* science
telescopes, 3, 8, 37, 137, 138. *See also* astronomy
temporalities, 75, 88, 97, 102, 117, 160n74; apocalyptic, 26–27, 136; cosmic, 30, 54–55, 59, 62, 63, 79, 127, 135, 141; mobile, 15, 90; of relativity, 54–55, 59, 97, 102. *See also* cinema: temporalities of; spatiotemporalities; time
Thorne, Kip, 131
time, 4, 49, 57, 62, 79, 101; in astronomy, 15, 44; connecting people across, 115; cosmic, 8, 30, 40, 42, 54, 57–58, 137; cosmocinematic, 18, 78–91; disjunctions of, 82, 83; experience of, 55, 83; in films, 15, 33, 43, 61–62, 79, 141; fragmentation of, 9, 46, 112–13; manipulating, 59, 90, 95, 103, 136; mobility of, 15, 45–47, 63, 93, 139; movement through, 9, 24, 131; rational, 8, 71, 91; in relation to human life, 126–27; rethinking, 10–11; in space, 19, 21; theory of relativity's understanding of, 29, 31–32. *See also* cinematography, time-lapse; spatiotemporalities; temporalities
time travel, 3, 18, 20, 23, 61–62, 66, 113, 131
transnationalism, 72, 79, 99, 114. *See also* geopolitics; politics
Tree of Life, The (Malick, 2011), 147–48n9
Trinity atomic bomb test, 93, 106, 107. *See also* atomic bombs, cinema of: test films
Trip to the Moon, A (*Le voyage dans la lune*, Méliès, 1902), 8, 52
20th Century Studios, Inc: logo, 2

United States: apocalypticism in, 10; astronomy-education films, 29–30, 55; astronomy studies, 6–7; avant-garde films, 97–98, 99–102, 104; *Dangerous Moonlight's* popularity in, 79–80; Einstein's theories in, 32, 40; experimental films, 102; Japan's surrender to, 86; Vietnam War, 100
Universal Studios: logo, 2, *2*, 3
universe, 33, 58, 61, 103, 113, 130; Benjamin's description of, 87, 133; cinema's potential to expose, 13, 43, 45; cosmic scale of, 84–85; Eberty's description of, 18–21; expanse of, 6, 34; filming, 3–4, 76; fragmenting and containing, 46–58, 63, 74; gaze of, 18–19; humans' place in, 3, 12, 13; in *A Matter of Life and Death*, 87–88, 91; science of, 4, 54, 101, 113; spatiotemporalities of, 20, 31–32, 89, 103,

105, 140–41. *See also* cosmos; galaxies; moon; planets; solar system; stars; sun
Universe (Kroitor and Low, 1961), 113–18, 140
Unseen World, The (series, Urban), 162n13
Urban, Charles, 100, 162n13

Vasulka, Steina, 101
Venus: Janssen's photographs of its 1874 transit, 30–31
Very Eye of Night, The (Deren, 1958), 105–6, 111, 168–69n48
view(s). *See* apocalyptic view; bird's-eye view; celestial view; God's-eye view; omnipotent view
violence, 22, 25, 72, 112; archives of, 66, 83; cinematic narratives of, 70–71; images of, 90, 94; of surveillance, 66, 68. *See also* atomic bombs; warfare
violent gaze, 83
Virilio, Paul, 22, 68, 94, 163n22
Vogel, Amos, 101, 168n35
von Moltke, Johannes: exilic perspective embraced by, 152n69
Voyager mission, 15–16, 17

WALL-E (Stanton, 2008), 17
Walt Disney Studios: logo, 2
Wandering Earth, The (Gwo, 2019), 131
warfare: aerial, 22, 72–74, 78–79, 91, 161n11; archives of, 74, 90–91; chaos of, 86, 91; nuclear, 96–97; realities of, 9, 83. *See also* atomic bombs; First World War; Hiroshima, Japan: atomic bomb dropped on; Nagasaki, Japan: atomic bomb dropped on; Second World War, aerial cinema in
wartime films, 15, 90–91, 94, 114; cosmocinematic gaze in, 71, 73, 74, 78; documentaries, 15, 65–91, 94, 112. *See also* atomic bombs, cinema of; Second World War, aerial cinema; *Why We Fight* (series, Capra, 1942–1945)
Wasson, Haidee, 41
Watt, Harry. *See Night Mail* (Watt and Wright, 1936); *Target for Tonight* (Watt, 1941)
Wees, William C., 101
We Live in Two Worlds (Cavalcanti, 1937), 163n27
Welsby, Chris, 101
White gaze, 22
Whitney, James and John, 98, 101
Why We Fight (series, Capra, 1942–1945), 65, 74–75
Windmill in Barbados (Wright, 1933), 69
Wings (Wellman, 1927), 162n17
Wings over Empire (Fletcher and Legg, 1939), 162n17
Wolfe, Charles, 74–75
Woman in the Moon (Lang, 1929), 157–58n51
world: cinema's attempts to document, 22, 103, 163n27; end of, 15, 18, 134–35; viewing, 3–4. *See also* civilization, human; earth; human life

Žižek, Slavoj, 26–27, 131

HANNAH GOODWIN is assistant professor of film and media studies at Mount Holyoke College.

Printed in the USA
CPSIA information can be obtained
at www.ICGtesting.com
CBHW081208240924
14823CB00002B/5